Alacrity

2018

Alacrity

PUBLIC RELATIONS, POLITICS & JOURNALISM IN WEST VIRGINIA

Dear Dawn,
I hope you enjoy
the read!

Charlie Ryan

Personal Recollections of Charlie Ryan
Founder of Charles Ryan Associates
Featuring Photography by Emil Varney of WSAZ-TV

Back cover photograph by Peter Ovens

ISBN-13: 9781541000209
ISBN-10: 154100020X

In memory of Dean Lewis

Dedicated to Becky Ryan, Harry Peck and the men and women of Charles Ryan Associates, Past & Present

alacrity   a'lakrade

noun

brisk and cheerful readiness: he accepted
the invitation with alacrity

—New Oxford American Dictionary

Foreword

_____ᕳ

By Jack Canfield

RACONTEUR AND ENTREPRENEUR.
Compulsively inventive businessman and spontaneously hilarious writer.

A reporter of history and one who made history.

A kid from Keyser, West Virginia, who quietly observed and learned, and then pursued his dream.

From disc jockey to confidant of governors and *Fortune 100* CEOs, he shaped messages and built one of the country's top advertising and public relations firms.

In this book, his fourth, Charles Ryan steps back from his novels (*Dead Men's Clubs, The Pullman Hilton*) and his reportorial compendium (*My Life with Charles Fraser*) to take on his journey of an exceptional career—how it humbly began, where it led, and the historic events and people who accompanied him along his way.

To those in West Virginia, "This is Charles Ryan reporting," was one of the most trusted phrases in broadcast journalism.

To those in public relations and advertising, Charles Ryan Associates was the standard-bearer, earning respect—and in many cases—envy—as it blossomed from the mind of a 34-year-old with a desk and an idea, into a multi-million dollar firm.

Those from West Virginia interested in politics and governors will view this as witty treasure.

Those who need inspiration to find their goal will see this as a gift—a manual of inspiration and how to accomplish, not just dream of, your goals.

I've known Charlie since Keyser High School. In the interest of full disclosure, I'm mentioned a couple of times. Our careers paralleled in the same towns. Charlie did ask me to fact-check his draft. My suggestions were few. I made none regarding anywhere my name was mentioned. The only things we disagree on are commas and semi-colons (Paul Atkins, our J school mentor, where are you now that we need you?).

So here you have it—a "kick back and pick-it-up-where-you-left off" book.

There's a guide and a history here.

But, more importantly, there is alacrity—a lot of alacrity—as only Charlie would have it.

—Jack Canfield, Charleston, WV, November, 2017

Contents

CHAPTER 1

We Arrive

~&

THERE WERE 12 SHIPS OF Irish that sailed into Philadelphia's harbor on September 22, 1745. Aboard one of them was Timothy Ryan, my great, great, great grandfather. Timothy made the crossing from Dublin, Ireland to Philadelphia, bound and assigned as an indentured servant before James Hamilton, Mayor of Philadelphia.

For Timothy, landing in The City of Brotherly Love, the epicenter of commerce for indentured servants from the Emerald Isle, was indeed fortunate. Philadelphia, unlike Charleston, South Carolina or New York City, had, in its commerce with Ireland, initiated orderly government regulation of indentured servants, providing stability to the trade and preventing abuse. Such was not the case in other ports receiving immigrants.

On October 5, 13 days after Timothy's arrival on American soil, John McCormick of Philadelphia paid Robert Wakely 14 pounds, 10 shillings for Timothy, who then was indentured to McCormick for four years—from September 22, 1745 through September 22, 1749. On the fourth anniversary of his first sight of America, Timothy became a free man. He left Philadelphia soon thereafter, bound for western Virginia.

Timothy fathered my great, great grandfather, Joseph Ryan, in 1775 in Virginia, later West Virginia. It was one year before colonists declared war on Great Britain. There followed the birth of my great grandfather, Benjamin Franklin Ryan, Sr., in 1820 in Monongalia County, West Virginia.

My great grandfather's given name of Benjamin Franklin attests to Timothy Ryan's disembarking in Philadelphia. Franklin was born to poverty and his beginnings and name must have appealed to a family that remembered Timothy as an indentured servant. From that point forward the name "Benjamin Franklin" began to appear in Ryan family history.

During the Civil War my great grandfather served as a Quartermaster in the Tenth Pennsylvania's Company D, also known as "The Jefferson Light Guard". Company D was commanded by Captain James T. Kirk (*Star Trek*, take a bow). Benjamin was mustered into the Union Army on August 12, 1861. His discharge date is unknown. He went into the iron and lumber business in Monongalia County after the war and then became keeper of the county alms house (the poor house). He also was a hotelkeeper of the National Hotel in Morgantown, and then became a farmer. His first wife, Isabelle, died shortly after their fifth child was born in 1861.

Great Grandfather married again on December 17, 1863. His second wife was Nancy Frances Braddee, my great grandmother. Nancy Frances' predecessors produced our family's only (so far as I know) outlaw. His name was John F. Braddee.

The *History of Uniontown, Pennsylvania* recounts that, in the 1880s, John Braddee worked in Tennessee for a physician as a hostler (a person employed to look after horses). Seeing there was money to be made in medicine, he declared himself to be a doctor.

He avoided accredited physicians and became quite popular—"to the extent that the streets were thronged for squares with the vehicles of his patrons". They were seeking his proprietary medicines: *Elroy, Cancer Salve, Cordial Balm of Health, Tincture of Health, Gravel Elixir,* and *Black Drops.*

That's not all—he was a stage robber; in 1840, the 29-year old Braddee was convicted of stealing large sums of money from the United States mail aboard a stagecoach that left Wheeling en-route to Uniontown. He was imprisoned for ten years. While in prison Braddee learned to read.

Deciding to attempt release by feigning illness, Braddee picked his gums with an awl and died in prison in 1846 of laryngeal phthisis. His obituary said he was never known to injure a patient by a wrong or overdose of medicine.

The third child of Nancy Braddee and Benjamin Franklin Ryan was my grandfather, Benjamin Franklin, Jr., born March 24, 1867, in Morgantown. He married Frances Marion Donaldson, and they had two children: my father William

Donaldson Ryan, in 1898, in Cumberland, Maryland and my aunt, Mary Beatrice Ryan, in 1900, in Loch Lynn, Maryland. Grandfather, a Baltimore & Ohio railroad engineer, died April 17, 1962. He was 92.

My dad went to work at sixteen years of age for the Baltimore & Ohio Railroad in Cumberland and also became a railroad engineer. At one point he was a member of my granddad's crew.

Dad was furloughed by the B&O after several years and moved to Rowlesburg, West Virginia, where he worked in a mechanic's garage repairing automobiles. The B&O recalled him within two years and he would spend the next forty-five years ascending from crewmember to brakeman to fireman, and, finally, engineer.

My dad had two boys and two girls with his first wife, Emma Jane Rathbun. The four were my half-brothers and half-sisters. They were, in order of birth, Anna Margaret, William Donaldson, Jr., Hellice, and Theodore. Tragically, Dad's wife Emma contracted a disease that was, in the 1930s, incurable. She died as a young woman.

Three years after his first wife died, Dad married my mother, Mabel Theastle Miner, on November 10, 1937 in St. George, West Virginia. Mom's birthplace is listed as Licking, Tucker County, West Virginia. Her father's given name was Jackson. Mom always claimed to have some Indian blood and there may be credence in that claim because her mother's given name was *Slewamie*. My dad was 17 years older than my 23-year old

Mom, who was born in 1915. Pictures of my mom at that age show a thin, beautiful young woman with black hair and fetching eyes.

My dad's second marriage produced three children. My sister and I were both born at home in Cumberland, Maryland—she in 1938 and I in 1940. Mary Virginia had arrived after our parents' first-born, Billy, died. My mom always said Billy died at birth as a "blue baby", a syndrome that occurs when newborn babies have heart defects. She named the baby William Donaldson Ryan after my dad. No doubt as a result of having lost her first child, my mother held both my sister and me close to her at all times, physically and mentally,

Mary Virginia and I grew up in Keyser, originally known as Paddy Town, in the eastern panhandle of West Virginia. It was a place of minimum crime and maximum friendship in the picturesque Potomac Valley.

The town was on the valley floor along the Potomac River that separated West Virginia from Maryland.

The flat land contained the business district and the railroad yards of the Baltimore & Ohio Railroad. We were five miles from Luke, Maryland at the beginnings of foothills where West Virginia Pulp and Paper Company was located. The rank smell of the residue from the paper company regularly drifted down river and through Keyser. My mother would sniff the air on those days and say, "Old Luke is washing his feet."

CHAPTER 2

Hellice's Story

As I grew older I learned more about Dad's first family and my half brothers and sisters. Theirs was a family that had been torn apart by alcoholism. Dad would take a drink and not be able to stop until the liquor or the money ran out. My half-sister Hellice said it was harder for her older sister Anna Margaret than it was for her because Anna was old enough to fully understand the situation. Anna witnessed fights between her parents and knew there was no food in the house because all Dad's wages went to whiskey.

Hellice said, "Anna told me I was lucky I did not remember the fights between Mother and Dad—fights that would begin in the house and move, as loud confrontations, into the front yard—where neighbors would listen to the accusations that Mom and Dad hurled at each other."

Hellice said, "We all had red hair like Dad. My sister and brothers had blue eyes while I had brown eyes. I remember that Mom was very pretty."

Dad's drinking was such that Hellice's maternal grandmother would journey from Florida to Mountain Lake Park,

Maryland each year to bring food, clothes, and money for her grandchildren.

Dad's first wife Emma's cause of death was blastomycosis—a rare fungal infection believed inflicted by an insect bite. The disease caused her to lose a leg, amputated at the Mayo Clinic in Minnesota. Hellice, who was six years old at the time of her mother's death, said it was awful; the disease virtually ate her mother's flesh. Hellice held her ears to drown out the screams.

At her mother's funeral in Oakland, Maryland, Hellice's grandmother took Dad aside and said he was in no condition to raise a family. She said she would take his children and raise them herself, provided he would swear he would never try to contact them and never have anything to do with them. Dad knew she was correct; he could not raise children with his addiction, and he agreed to the bargain.

Hellice said, "After Mother's death I never thought about the fact I had no mother or father. My life was my life. I didn't look for parental comfort—even when my right eye was badly damaged when I was eight years old when a boy stuck a bamboo cane in it. The cane, the kind kids got at a fair, was under his arm. He turned toward me as I turned toward him and the cane went right into my eye—It popped right out of the socket. Years later I had surgery at the Cleveland Clinic and ended up with partial, but double, vision."

Hellice said Dad did not visit her as she recovered. She said the last thing he wanted was to be confronted in the hospital by her grandmother. "I didn't know it at the time, but Dad was fretting over me—he knew about my accident shortly after it occurred, and he knew I had been taken to a hospital in Cumberland. While he didn't come to the hospital to see me; he kept daily checks on my condition through contact with my Uncle Hick. But he did not visit the hospital because he had made a promise to my grandmother that he would not contact his children."

Dad adhered to that promise even when his youngest child from the first marriage, Teddy—16 at the time and without alerting anyone—got in a car when he was visiting at Mountain Lake Park, Maryland and drove to Keyser. He appeared unannounced on the doorsteps at 174 Maple Avenue and knocked on the door. My dad—who, by that time, had stopped drinking—answered the door and saw a young man standing there. Teddy said he was his son.

Dad welcomed Teddy and they sat in the house and talked for several hours. Teddy had come to stay. But Dad told him he could not. He told him his grandmother, who had raised him, would be devastated. He told Teddy to return to Mountain Lake Park. Teddy did and was questioned as to why he had left without telling anyone what he was going to do. His answer was simple, "I wanted to meet my dad."

CHAPTER 3

Mrs. Elliott Makes A Decision

My SISTER AND I WERE introduced to our half-sister Hellice in Mountain Lake Park in the early 1950s. Anna's kids were having a summer visit with her mother-in-law, Olga Elliott. Anna called Hellice, who was living and working in Washington, D.C., and said that her kids were at her mother-in-law's home. Hellice decided to join the children at Mountain Lake Park for the weekend. She traveled there by train.

After two days, the visit was coming to an end. Hellice was sitting on Mrs. Elliott's front porch. She was preparing to leave for the train station and her return to Washington.

Hellice said, "All of a sudden this car drives up in front of the house and Mrs. Elliott turns to me and says, 'That's your father. I invited him to take Donna and Pug to visit with him in Keyser.' And Mrs. Elliott sits back in her rocking chair.

"I did not know it, but Mrs. Elliott felt that Dad's children needed to get back to him because Dad had changed his life. Well, I was in shock. I didn't know if I should go in the house, which I felt would be rude, so I just waited to meet him, knowing Mrs. Elliott had set it up. It was like, what in the world has this woman done?

"I watched as Dad got out of the car first, then Mabel, then two cute kids. As I looked at this family I thought, 'Well, there's the missing part of me.' I realized I did not really know the man coming toward me and I felt no animosity toward him. We all were introduced and got to talking and I think the meeting went well. Then I said, 'I've got to get to my train.' And he said, 'Go back to Keyser with us and we can talk, I'll put you on the train there.' We did that and got reunited and I spent time with two cute kids, Mary Virginia and Charlie, and I said to myself, 'Wow, I have a new brother and sister.'

"So, I went back to Washington and called Anna Margaret and said, 'Do you know who your kids have been with?' She answered that they were with Mrs. Elliott in Mountain Lake Park—and she was stunned when I told her they also had been with their granddad. She said, 'What?' and after getting over her shock, asked what I thought of him. I said that he seemed like a perfectly nice guy to me, no horns or anything.

"Anna Margaret laughed and confided to me that she had actually met our dad once. She said she was visiting one time at Mountain Lake Park when her husband Don was overseas and she and Grandma were staying at a boarding house. Dad and Uncle Hick set up the meeting. Grandma asked Anna if she wanted to meet with him and she said yes. So Anna and Dad, with Grandma watching from ten feet away, sat in a corner of the front porch and talked. It was when Anna was pregnant with her first child."

Getting to know my extended family was a blessing and Dad, Mom, Mary Virginia and I owe a great debt of gratitude to Olga Elliott who had the fortitude to bring Hellice and Dad together. Through these actions Mary Virginia and I developed relationships with our sisters Hellice and Anna Margaret and our brother Bill. We were not fortunate enough to know Teddy, who was killed in a car accident in Florida, before our families came together.

CHAPTER 4

Hellice Seals The Deal

"I FOUND MYSELF THINKING A lot about Dad after returning to Washington and I finally called him and told him I was getting married, that I knew no one where I was living, and asked if he would walk me down the aisle and give me away in marriage," Hellice said.

"He readily and calmly agreed, but Mabel said he was shocked and almost hysterical with joy that I had asked him.

"Dad and Mabel and my new brother and sister all came to Arlington and I held Dad's arm as I walked down the aisle toward my soon-to-be husband, Ted Zitkewicz. My brother Bill and his wife Ann showed up for the wedding. It was a total surprise. Bill said they decided at the last minute to come, that he could not let his little sister get married and not be there. Strange how things work out, as he did not know Dad and Mabel would be there. You know, it has all turned out just fine."

The marriage was the beginning of my relationship with Hellice and she became the child from my dad's first marriage to whom my sister, Mary Virginia, and I were closest. Hellice was an exciting development indeed. Who was this woman? What was our new sister really like? Suffice to say, the redheaded Irish girl with the wide smile and freckles captivated us.

CHAPTER 5

Ted Zitkewicz

HELLICE'S HUSBAND TED WAS A dashing young good looker from a first generation Polish family. I liken him now to Kevin Costner—quiet, chiseled face, penetrating eyes—a handsome and nice guy—my mom loved him and Ted came to care greatly for Dad, the father of the bride.

Ted's son-in-law, the Reverend Doug Aey, said in his eulogy for Ted that Ted liked to tell the story of how he and Hellice met during the inauguration of President Eisenhower. Ted was an Army veteran and graduate of the Airborne School at Fort Benning, Georgia (one of his grandsons would follow in his footsteps). Ted said he found himself in Washington during the inauguration, one of hundreds of service men, marching in the Inaugural Parade. He insisted he caught Hellice's eye as he marched by her and her girlfriends as they watched the parade. Parade over, Ted said he returned to the area where he had spotted Hellice and, rather miraculously, found her.

Hellice had a different memory than Ted and said the *real* facts of their meeting were that she and her friends were watching the Inaugural Parade in their Washington boarding house on an early television set that had a postage stamp screen (they had a stack of quarters that were inserted into the TV—one quarter provided a half hour of the broadcast). The women became bored and decided to venture out after the parade was over. Hellice said that was when Ted encountered her and began his pursuit.

Hellice insisted that her version of their encounter was the correct one, but she agreed that Ted, with his superb dry humor, could always create a more interesting tale.

Hellice said Ted began following her, asking if he could accompany her to a movie she and her friends wanted to see. Hellice said, with great sass, "It's a free country, do as you like."

Ted took that as a "yes" and spent the rest of the day with her. He then began corresponding by mail and one day turned up at the home of Hellice's brother Bill, in Gainesville, Florida. Bill's wife, Ann, went to the door and then went to find Hellice. Hellice said Ann said, "There is a really good looking soldier on the front porch, do you know him?" A whirlwind romance began and marriage and four children—Nancy, Diane, John and Steven, followed.

CHAPTER 6

William Donaldson Ryan, Jr.

ON ONE OCCASION DOUG AEY (Hellice and Ted's son-in-law) and I were exchanging stories about Hellice's brother (and my half-brother) Bill, who had been a member of the crew of the Destroyer USS Dale (he was a fireman aboard ship) during World War II. Doug said Bill's marvelous humor was on display one summer day when he and Bill pulled up beside a confused Japanese motorist in Gainesville.

The Japanese driver rolled down his window, stuck his head out toward Bill's open window and said in broken English that he was lost. He asked Bill if he could help him find his way to Jacksonville. Bill readily obliged, saying, "Take this road you are on for the next five miles and turn right. Then go another three miles to an intersection and turn left. Stay on that route for about twenty minutes and it will lead you to the interstate that'll take you to Jacksonville."

The Japanese visitor expressed his heartfelt thanks for the detailed instructions and drove off, whereupon Doug voiced his admiration of Bill for his good deed. Bill responded by saying, "I don't know where he's going, but he ain't going to Jacksonville—remember Pearl Harbor!"

Bill, who served his country with great distinction, took delight in telling humorous stories about himself. He was an able sailor but he insisted to Doug that he was clueless when he first boarded the USS Dale. He said he was going about his duties one day when he saw a huge fish in the water, coming toward the Dale, forming a wide wake. Bill excitedly shouted to the chief mate, "Look at that big fish, he's really moving!" The chief took one look and said to Bill, "That's not a fish, that's a torpedo!" Fortunately, it missed the USS Dale.

Bill, who lived to be 82, always reminded me of our father—both were large men with huge biceps and red, red hair—and they loved to laugh and tell a story. I always looked up to Bill, the man I considered my big brother.

CHAPTER 7

My Dad Takes A Walk

FIFTY YEARS AFTER I FIRST met Hellice I asked her if Dad had ever talked with her in depth about the forced separation from his first wife and children. Hellice said, "It was hard for him to talk about it and I did not ask anything of him because I always felt uneasy with your mother around. But, one summer evening in Florida, while we were sitting on the porch, alone together, he said, 'You know, I just feel I need to tell you, I don't know what your grandmother said…'— and I said, "She never talked about you."

Hellice said Dad replied, "She did not like me at all—but I need to tell you that the separation from my kids was the best thing that ever happened. I had no way of taking care of you and when I married Mabel I was still drinking heavily. I could not seem to stop and on several occasions Mabel threatened to take Mary Virginia and Charlie and leave me."

At one point drinking had interfered with Dad's duties to the point his job was in jeopardy. Mom took matters in her own hands, dressed my sister and me, and boarded the train for Grafton, West Virginia where she went to the B&O

regional offices. There, she pleaded with an official to not fire her husband—to give him one more chance. She clutched her two small children to her side as she made the plea. Her effort—heroic—touched the man who held Dad's fate and his job was saved.

Dad told Hellice, "One day I was talking with my sister Beatrice and she said, 'Bill, if you don't stop drinking and straighten up, you're going to lose your second family like you lost your first family.' Well, Beatrice's words slowly seeped into me and I told myself I had to stop, and I did—and I thought I was going to die. I went to a doctor and he said, 'Bill, you can't just stop drinking suddenly after drinking like you have for years.' He said I needed to slowly back off and I said, 'No, I can't do it that way. I just have to do it now—just quit cold turkey.' And that's what I did. The kids were small and I could not go through that again; I was not going to lose a second family. I quit. I don't do it anymore."

Hellice looked at Dad and said, "That man my grandmother hated? He's not here anymore."

Dad said, "No, I think he took a walk."

I know from both Hellice and Mom that my dad was a man who was *determined* to change his life—and he did just that. I stand in awe of his courage.

With liquor verboten in our home, my dad's work ethic was extraordinary. He was always busy. His workshop was filled with tools for woodworking and he knew how to tear a car engine down and rebuild it. I can smell that garage today—motor oil on the floor and sawdust on his workbench, mixed with a wisp of Old Spice cologne.

CHAPTER 8

Paddy Town

IT WAS SOMEWHAT IRONIC THAT our hometown of Keyser had once been known as Paddy Town because my grandfather was known to one and all as "Paddy"—a popular nickname for one of Irish descent. The nickname was then given to his son, my dad.

When Granddad left the railroad at 65, the mandatory age of retirement for B&O engineers, he thought his work life was over—not so. In his 80s he was called back to service during World War II, when railroad engineers were in short supply.

Our first Maple Avenue home in Keyser seemed big and roomy. Seeing it as an adult I realized it actually was a small home that had been renovated. The front porch had been enclosed and it was there that I have my first memory of my paternal grandfather.

It was Christmas and I was playing on the porch. I looked up at Granddad—white hair, Irish nose and eyes that always seemed to be smiling. My mother was very fond of him and called him "Pop".

Dad and Granddad loved humor and they would laugh long and loud as they and their friend and fellow railroader, Billy Laughey, told Irish jokes and fiddled Irish jigs.

Work as a railroad engineer was demanding. Dad was always on call and the time he spent on the road was considerable. Mother drilled into us how hard Dad worked. She taught us that we should honor and respect him and his work that kept us housed, clothed, and healthy.

My father had a whimsical side; he loved radio and movie entertainment. In 1946 he took my sister and me to a matinee at the Keyser Theatre to see *Song of The South*, Walt Disney's first full-length movie using live actors with animation segments. Uncle Remus, the Tar Baby, Br'er Rabbit, Br'er Fox, Br'er Bear and the wonderful song *Zip-a-Dee-Doo-Dah*—which won an Academy Award. It was an incredible treat for us. At movie's end my father led my sister and me out of the theatre, saying, "I don't know about you two, but I'm dry." The next stop was Romig's Rexall Drug Store and chocolate milkshakes for everyone.

My family often gravitated to Glaze's Ferris wheel and merry-go-round on Armstrong Street in Keyser. The mini-amusement area entertained our pre-TV population. The colorful wheel seemed, to my young eyes, to reach to heaven. I did not enjoy the Ferris wheel rides, feeling as though I were in free fall when the gondola reached the apex of the wheel and began its downward descent. I recalled this at length in my novel *The Pullman Hilton*.

Glaze's Carousel, with its herd of wooden horses, was the treat I loved. Dad would place me on a gaily-carved horse and I would grab the leather strap that led to the horse's bit—stretching to reach the stirrups that were just a bit too long for my short legs.

Thirty years later, in Charleston, West Virginia, I would go out of my way to walk through an area that reminded me of the lot where Mr. Glaze had his Ferris wheel and merry-go-round. The detour always took me back to the summer Mary Virginia and I walked through Glaze's lot, clutching our saved allowance that would eventually be used to buy two toy automobiles.

On Saturdays we would rush in the afternoon to the Keyser Music Hall Theatre where westerns or "cowboy" movies were the fare. Johnnie Mack Brown, Hopalong Cassidy and Tim Holt played the Music Hall while Roy Rogers, Gene Autry, the Cisco Kid, and Lash Larue were staples at the Liberty Theatre. The Liberty was not as well kept as the Music Hall and all us kids called it the "Scratch House".

The father of our classmate, Joyce Thrush, owned the Liberty and that provided a perk. Anyone lucky enough to finagle a seat near Joyce could avoid the Saturday afternoon bouncer. He was a big fellow employed by Mr. Thrush to walk up and down the aisles of the theatre shouting, "Quiet in here!" Oddly enough, his name was Arthur Godfrey.

The bouncer had little success in subduing at least 100 chattering kids. As he walked and shouted he had an angry stare that dissolved into a sweet smile when he spotted Joyce. Tom Harman, Fred Riley, Jim "Munch" Mahood, John "Tank" Allen, Jim Wilcox, Harold Snyder, and I surrounded Joyce and would lean toward Mr. Thrush's attractive daughter and smile back at the bouncer.

Classmate Sharon Wilson and I were soul mates; loving the same comedy shows on black and white TV (The Steve Allen Show was tops, in our estimation), and being pals through high school. Sharon's dad owned Wilson's Shoe Store on Main Street. It was called the Cut-Rate Shoe Store and had an entrance that formed a "Y" with shoes piled along the path into the store. The smell of the leather was wonderful.

Nancy Coffman's grandparents owned Coffman's Dry Goods Store at the corner of Main and Armstrong Streets and Molly Romig's dad owned the Rexall Drug Store on Main. Keyser was typical of the small towns of America in the 40s and 50s and life was good.

CHAPTER 9

Nylon Stockings

WHEN THE CHRISTMAS SEASON CAME to Keyser, it seemed to do so with significant snow. Trudging through the alley behind our house, walking to town with Dad, looking at the sky full of snowflakes, then at the snow beneath our feet, my father would inevitably say, "When you can hear the snow crunch under your feet like that, you know we're gonna' get a big one!"

To my right as we trekked along was a large lot that housed abandoned Pullman railroad cars. I cast an eye toward the silent rolling stock, snow covering all the cars, creating a graveyard of winter white—a theme I would use in writing *The Pullman Hilton*. There were five cars on the lot, but in my novel I would fictionalize the location as having over 212 cars, and I depicted our neighborhood gang as engaging in a Christmas mystery that centered on one of the Pullman cars in which there was a ghostly presence.

As Christmas holidays neared, my sister and I came home from school to find Mom and Dad in our back yard having a fun afternoon in about two feet of snow. My parents had shoveled a circle in the snow and were chasing each other around and around. My sister and I joined our parents and all of us took turns falling in and out of the circle into the snow. It was a day filled with laughter and love.

Christmas Eve finally arrived and I was sitting in our dining room in a rocking chair listening to the radio. Gene Autry was singing *Here Comes Santy Claus, Right Down Santy Claus Lane.* Nearby, Mother's raisin cookies were fresh and cool in jars covered at the top with a cloth in an unheated room. My sister and I sneaked into the room, pulled back the cloth, inhaled the sweet smell, and stole two cookies from the jar, carefully arranging the cloth as we exited. If Mom knew we were making withdrawals without permission, she never let on.

Nylon stockings were hard to come by at the end of World War II; nylon was used in the defense industry and the women who possessed stockings made of the fabric were few indeed. My mother had one prized pair of nylons and that Christmas, after carefully washing her stockings, she placed them to dry on the protective cover of the dining room table. I was playing in the room and as Mom walked from the dining room to the kitchen, I picked up a pair of scissors from atop her sewing machine. I climbed onto a dining room chair and proceeded to cut her nylon stockings into little pieces. It was not done to harm, I did not know what the nylons were—I just thought it was fun to hear the "squish" sound as the scissors laced through the nylon.

My mother walked back into the dining room, saw my artistic effort on the table, and gave out a curdling scream. She yanked me from the table, crying. She turned me over a knee and paddled me—hard. I was surprised and shocked. What had I done that was so bad? When Mom's tears dried she quickly regretted the paddling and sat me down to explain why the nylons were so valuable to her. She hugged me and said it was her fault for leaving the nylons on the table—but I knew it was also my fault. Mom and I relived that moment many times when I became an adult. We loved to tell the story and laughed out loud about the Christmas I sheared her nylon hose.

CHAPTER 10

Lionel & Red Ryder

ONE CHRISTMAS A FAVORITE STOP of mine was Keyser's Western Auto Store on Main Street. I gazed longingly at American Flyer trains and then advanced on to the crème de le' crème, the very top of the pyramid, the train set every kid coveted—Lionel! To aspire to own one of these beauties was like wanting to win the lottery—had I known what a lottery was.

Lying in my bed on Christmas morning I heard a familiar noise (the Western Auto store had that sound), but I did not dare to think it might be a train set. My sister and I ran downstairs on a cue from Mom. We entered the living room and I beheld a train and cars winding around the Christmas tree with Dad lying on the floor, a huge grin on his face. Not only was it a train set, not only was it *not* an American Flyer train set—it was a Lionel, by golly.

Dad had gone for the whole enchilada—engine, tender, boxcar, side dump car, hopper, and caboose. Extras were a tunnel, two "targets", a train station, several buildings, streetlights, switches and a sidetrack. The man was a railroad engineer—he loved the whole setup as much as I. We spent many hours that Christmas day "on the road", as the Lionel went round and round.

Second only to the Lionel was the Red Ryder BB gun received on yet another Christmas. I don't remember Mother telling me I'd shoot my eye out if I had a Red Ryder. I do, however, remember my first and only kill with the smooth metal rifle that glistened in blue shades of shimmering light. My kill was on a winter day when I spied a small sparrow in our backyard near the outdoor kennel where we housed four beagle dogs trained to hunt rabbits. The proximity of hunting animals and the gun in my hand caused the predator to come out in me. I took aim with my Red Ryder and shot the little sparrow dead.

I still remember the shock of seeing the bird stiffen and fall. I picked up the tiny little creature in my hand and began to cry. Why had I done this? I cried and cried. I carried the bird to the back porch and continued to weep. I went inside the house, found a kitchen matches box, put the sparrow in the box and slid the lid closed. I buried the little creature in the back yard near where my BB had felled him. I still regret pulling that trigger.

All my friends had BB guns and on Christmas vacations we would regularly play "war" with them. Mom refused to let me participate. Several times I secretly engaged in the war games with my friends, but I was careful. I knew guns—even BB guns— could hurt in a very painful and permanent way. The sparrow was dead.

Like any boy growing up in rural West Virginia, I eventually learned to be comfortable with firearms. In Christmases to come I would hunt rabbit and squirrel, using my 16-gauge shotgun. I usually did so with my childhood friend Johnny Rogers as he and I visited his parents' farm, gleefully jumping on brush piles, rousting out rabbits that we shot and then skinned.

CHAPTER 11

Munch & Howard

"MUNCH" MAHOOD LIVED NEAR ME on Maple Avenue, two doors away. His given name was Jim, but we called him "Munch." He was offended if we called him "May-hood" and often reminded us that it was "Muh-Hood." He was comfortable, however, with "Munch." Munch and I would remain lifelong friends and I used his nickname for the protagonist in my novel, *Dead Men's Clubs*.

Our sixth grade teacher, Edna Staggers, caught Munch and me in the egregious act of tossing spitballs and ordered us both to the front of the class. She told Munch to bend over and she delivered a roundhouse blow to Munch's rear end. My turn was next. I waited for the blow as I bent forward. Miss Staggers swatted my bottom lightly and ordered us back to our seats. Munch remembered the uneven punishment from that day forward and reminds me of it whenever we are together. "Charlie was Edna Staggers' favorite," he would say. I think he was correct. Miss Staggers was always sweet and kind. Munch, however, may have a different memory.

Classmate Howard Shoemaker lived along the Potomac River in a small ranch house. It was unusual because "ranch houses" were a novelty in Keyser. I often traveled the three or four blocks to play with Howard until I came home from one visit with a bloody nose. Mom demanded to know who, where, what and when. "Howard Shoemaker, Howard's house, Howard's fist and within the hour," I replied.

Mom grabbed me by the hand and off we went to Howard's. Mom knocked on the door and Mrs. Shoemaker answered. Mom pointed to my nose. Mrs. Shoemaker went in search of Howard. Howard arrived at the door as I had, with his mother dragging him.

"Tell us what happened!" my mother demanded. Howard did not speak. I rushed to fill the silence. "I called him a sissy!" I blurted.

Silence.

My mother looked at me and said, "If you said that, you *deserve* a bloody nose." She apologized to Mrs. Shoemaker, and then to Howard, and she led me off the ranch house porch. She repeated, on the walk home, that I deserved the bloody nose. No other punishment was meted out. I, of course, was humiliated.

CHAPTER 12

Growing Up On Maple Avenue

OUR RENTED HOME AT 174 Maple Avenue was a two story house that was located on the upper side of the street. That side of the Avenue featured a three-foot high retaining wall that gave some protection from the excess of the nearby Potomac River during spring floods. It was a beautiful thoroughfare in summer with large maple trees practically covering the street in a canopy as they bent toward each other.

Our egg man regularly came to the front door. He wore a white straw boater hat, had a ruddy red face, and carried his eggs in a woven basket covered with a red and white gingham cloth. He doted on my five-year-old sister, singing to her in a voice with perfect pitch—*Sweet Rosie O'Grady*. It was a Norman Rockwell scene. Fresh milk in glass bottles was placed on the front porch each morning. Our "iceman" delivered ice in large blocks for the icebox and the garbage man, Roy Davy, collected refuse in a wagon drawn by two mules. Mr. Davy used a long whip to maneuver the mules, Sal and Sadie. We could smell the wagon coming several houses away.

"Don't slam the screen door!" Mom would yell from somewhere in the house as the screen door slammed behind us.

Mary Virginia and I opened the kitchen's icebox to retrieve the fresh milk that had been deposited on our doorstep that morning. As I guzzled milk from the bottle, Mom would again scream from somewhere nearby—"Charlie! Don't you dare drink from the bottle!"

"I won't!" I would scream back, removing the bottle from my lips, making sure to wipe the bottle top on my shirt. Mary Virginia would look at me and roll her eyes.

Mom always knew if I was up to no good. She said, over and over, "Always be a good boy, Charlie." When she knew I was not so good, she would dramatically say a switching was due, and with great fanfare, would move from tree to tree, searching for the perfect switch while I watched. Once she found her instrument, she would make me cut the switch from the tree. The search and final selection hurt much more than the swatting to my behind.

Each Sunday I pored over the *Cumberland Sunday Times* comic strips of Dick Tracy, Prince Valiant, and Terry and the Pirates. Elsie and Dutch Sheetz lived two doors from our family and they received by mail on Monday or Tuesday of each week the Sunday *New York Daily News* and its comic strip supplement. The *Daily News* comics were different than those in the Cumberland paper and I walked to the Sheetz house each week to devour the *Daily News* "Funnies".

Less than a quarter-mile from our home was an abandoned pottery with large kilns spacious enough for a family to live in. The Duckworth family did just that, making an abandoned kiln their place of residence. I found myself there on a regular basis in pursuit of comic books they somehow seemed to always have. The Duckworth kids and I traded our comics back and forth. My mother defended my obsession in a knowing way. She knew comic books were the reason I was learning to read at a very early age—educated by *Superman, Batman, Wonder Woman, Green Hornet, Captain America, Archie, Little Lulu* and many others. There was often a musty smell on the comic book pages, a result of being stored in the Duckworth kiln. Yes—even with the smell—I wish I had saved those treasures from *Dell* that now sell for significant dollars.

On nights I cannot fall asleep I often, in my mind, take a tour of our house on Maple Avenue. It relaxes me to think of walking through the wooden frame home amidst a modest but stately group of houses that lined the street. Our place had a large front porch with lattice around the bottom that hid a crawl space. I loved to open the lattice door and crawl under the porch to play.

The three-foot high retaining wall in front of the house had a flat surface on which I ran my toy cars. I could stand straight up and "zoom" the cars down a super highway, complete with indentations that served as exit ramps.

The living room of the home featured a wood-burning fireplace. Walking from the living room a visitor would move through the dining room and then to the "back room" which was closed in the winter to save heat. Double doors opened into the room. In the summer they were left open and the room became our "family room"—although no one had ever heard of or used that term.

To the left of the dining room was the kitchen and the door to the cellar was there. The down staircase led to the cellar door and a landing. The landing took us to the full basement where Mom's washing machine would chug-a-chug cleaning our clothes, which were then dried on a clothesline in the backyard. Turning a corner of the basement we were face to face with a coal bin that was adjacent to a large, hulking, fire-breathing coal burning stove. I had to fire that furnace on winter mornings—a job I hated—second only to cleaning dog poop from the kennel in the backyard.

On the second floor of the house were my sister's bedroom and, next to it, to the right, Mom and Dad's bedroom. My bedroom was at the end of the hall and in my bedroom was the door to the attic. This terrified me when we first moved to the house. What was up there at night? After exploration and finding no ghosts, I regularly climbed the stairs to the attic to play with several toys that the owner had stashed amongst various keepsakes. There I found a large wooden bi-plane with which I logged many hours of flight time.

On September 7, 2013, the day of my 55th high school reunion dinner in Keyser, my wife Becky and I visited Maple Avenue. I was 73. In the back yard was the concrete walk my dad had built. There, sixty-five years later, were the tiny handprints belonging to my sister, Mary Virginia, and me. Etched into the concrete beside our handprints was the date—"1948". Tears came to my eyes.

CHAPTER 13

My Dad's Stories

My parents raised my sister and me with love and with rules. They were not our buddies, they were our *parents* and we knew who ruled the roost. Children want discipline and we received it with fair and equitable dispensation.

Dad attended school only until the eighth grade (as did my mother). His lack of formal education did not, however, stunt his intellect. By sheer determination and force he became a railroad engineer. I have always been very proud to know and say my father held that title.

He worked during that period in history in which railroaders made the transition from steam to diesel engines. He secured his employment in the diesel era by studying many months to pass an exam that required considerable analytical and statistical skills. These were the tools needed for the steam engineer to pass the "air car"—the living laboratory that simulated the workings of a diesel engine and the challenges the steam engineer had to face and conquer in order to transition to diesel engines.

When Dad passed those tests there was a celebration of sorts and the realization that his career would prosper. When he first earned $10,000 in one year's time I became aware of the awesome accomplishment while overhearing my mother and father examining Dad's W2 form. Their conversation was one of wonderment that he had been able to achieve what seemed to them to be a princely sum.

In his mid-70s Dad loved to tell his grandchildren stories from his railroad days and his early teen years in Cumberland where he was thrilled to see Buffalo Bill Cody's Wild West Show. He had some wild days of his own and I'm blessed I have audio recordings of him telling his tales.

Red hair, Irish nose, wide grin and love of humor—here are Bill Ryan's stories, in his own words:

WHISKEY AND THE RAT

There was this brakeman who loved to drink whiskey. I climbed down off a Mallet engine in Deer Park, Maryland and the fellow was standing near a target down the track. "Hey, Bill," he says to me, "come here." I walked down the track and he told me there was whiskey being made nearby by a fellow who was known to have a good still. He said he had been down there the day before.

"Bill," he said, "I knocked on the door of the guy's house and no one answered. I went in the house and down to the basement and there was the still.

"Whiskey was dripping out of the still—drip, drip, drip. I spied a big tin cup nearby and I placed it under the spout of the still and

waited for the cup to fill up. When it did I took a big sip and set the cup down. Right away, a big old rat came out of his hole in the corner of the basement, ran over to the cup, took a big drink and went back in his hole.

"Well, I filled the cup again and I took another big sip. The rat followed up and drank again. I filled the cup up a third time, took a drink and set the cup down. The rat came out of his hole, took another big gulp and went back to his hole in the corner.

"I filled up the cup for the fourth time, took a drink and waited for the rat. The rat stuck his head out of his hole and ambled over to the cup. He drank a great big drink and stumbled back to his hole. Just before he went in the hole he turned around, stood up on his back legs, held out his paws, and yelled, 'Now, bring on your damn Tom Cat!'"

The Whiskey Heist

We stole a whole bunch of whiskey when I went in the railroad shops to work—I was just a kid. We used to go up and down the alleys and find empty bottles of whiskey and take them to saloons—when we went in a saloon we stood up on the rail to see over the bar. We got five cents for each bottle—and back then if you had a nickel you had some real money. The bartenders would fill the bottles with what they called Scul—the rottenest whiskey you could find—and re-sell it for twenty-five cents.

Right at the Cumberland city limits where the railroad yard stopped was a big old hotel and some old eye-talian ran it. The hotel caught on fire and the B&O ran hoses over there and put the fire out. The fire burned the back end of the hotel's saloon and it just ruined that straw wrapped around that eye-talian whiskey. The proprietor cleaned up the bottles and boarded the back end of the saloon up to protect the whiskey.

I was runnin' around with this kid Jimmy, who was not very big and he would do anything you told him. We went down to the hotel and saw that the owner had left cracks this high when he boarded up the saloon. We decided we'd come back at night and see if we could get in between the boards.

We returned that night and I shoved little Jimmy through the crack between the boards and he handed the whiskey out to me. At that time we wore blouses with a drawstring. I tied my drawstring up and I filled my waist full of whiskey—and I had enough for Jimmy to do the same.

We stole the whiskey and went up behind our house and sat down behind the coalhouse. I had never drunk whiskey but both of us drank some and it tasted good! I thought then I was gonna' go down the road—that's what we said when we talked about kids going to reform school.

We drank a lot of that whiskey. It certainly did smell good and tasted good and, by golly, I started going around the ring; I didn't know what it was like to be drunk. I sat there a little bit and I looked at Jimmy and he looked at me. We didn't drink any more and directly—the dang fool couldn't keep his mouth shut—he looked over at me and said, "You know what?" I said, "No, what?" He said, "Now, I've tasted whiskey, and that ain't whiskey."

I said, "What'd we drink?" He said, "We drank bar polish." Oh, my God, I thought then I was gonna' die. I headed for home and I told my mother what I had done—I had drunk bar polish. I was stretched out on the bed and my daddy had just come in off the railroad. Mother went and told him what had happened and he came in and looked at me and said, "Woman, go to bed, they ain't nothin' that's wrong with him—he's drunk!" Daddy said he knew what was wrong with me the minute he looked at me. I got my sleep out and I was all right.

The next day my daddy wanted to know where the whiskey was. I told him where we hid it and he took a sack and went up there and got all of it. I thought he'd keep his mouth shut but he said, " I'm gonna' tell Jimmy's mother and father and I'm gonna' call the cops." Back in that time they had an old wagon with a seat in it and an old horse called "Dig Sam" pullin' it and that's the way they took you to jail. The chief of police came down to the house with his wagon and came in and got me and I thought, "Well, I'm gonna' go down the road to reform school." The chief went up and got Jimmy and both of us knew we were gonna' go to reform school. Eventually the Chief of Police said, "Well, now, I believe if we talk to these boys they'll do better and we won't have to send them to jail."

My daddy and the chief had it all fixed up and they just scared the life out of us. They talked it over and we both got a devil of a whippin'—and that's the last whiskey we ever stole.

SEWER ENTREPRENEURS

South Cumberland back then wasn't a very big part of town and there used to be these outhouses in the backyards and you'd have *to empty them. The city got rid of that and they put this sewer in. Well, Charlie Adams and I were down at the C&O Canal where they had mules to haul coal on canal boats—that's where the sewer emptied—right near a big old tin mill where they made rolled tin. A lot of people worked there.*

Charlie spied what appeared to be theatre tickets in the water—he recognized them because his daddy owned the theatre in South Cumberland. Here were all these theatre tickets, floating in the sewer spill. Charlie noted that the tickets had never been torn in two—that's what they did when you'd enter the theatre. So, we got down there in that old dirty water and gathered those tickets up. Charlie had a bunch and I had a bunch.

You paid five cents to go to the theatre. They had standing pictures—slides—and they'd narrate, explaining the picture. That's what you saw when you went to the theatre back then—still pictures—there wasn't anything else to look at. But, a lot of people went to the theatre and paid five cents to get in. The tickets we fished out of the sewer were wet and dirty, but we sold them for five cents at the door. It didn't take long for Charlie's daddy to figure out his customers were using old tickets that had been floated into the sewer down to the canal. After he found that out he tore the tickets in two before he'd throw them away. We couldn't get sewer tickets any more.

CRAB APPLE BADDIES

There was this traveling picture show where an old man pitched a tent and charged five cents to get in to see the "picture show". Well, just like the theatre downtown, the picture show was just still pictures that were accompanied with music from a Victrola with a big tinhorn. The old man would play the music and talk about each slide.

Little Jimmy and I filled our drawstring blouse waists with big old crab apples that had horns on them, and we went to the tent. The tent was full of benches in a circle facing that old man and his big music horn. Jimmy went to one side of the tent and I went to the other. Directly, Jimmy would toss a crabapple into the horn and—boom— the music was muffled. The old man stopped the music and turned the horn upside down and beat it until he dislodged the apple. Then, he'd start again. I waited a little while and tossed one of my apples into the horn and the music stopped again while the old man shook the horn and got my apple. We did that time and again and the old man couldn't find out who was sabotaging his show—he called the cops. Well, when the cops came little Jimmy and I just opened our drawstrings and let the apples fall out and we sat down. We stopped the show, but no one knew it was us.

JUMPIN' PIT BULLS

Up in Mountain Lake Park old Charlie Wolf had a big pit bull dog at his store. These farmers used to come to town in a middle of a snowstorm—plowin' through snow-clogged fields on bobsleds pulled by horses. The snow might be up over the fences but the farmers came to get their groceries. Those poor old farmers had been out in the elements most of the day and they came in wet. They'd find a chair near the pot-bellied stove and sit down. The chairs were soaked when a farmer would get up and that old pit bull would jump up on a wet vacant chair and settle in. He made his rounds of the chairs there.

This boy Clyde and I saw what was happening and we went and got a coil out of a Model T Ford—the coil would go "bzzzzz" every time a Model T engine would kick off—those Model T's had whatcha' call a "planetary transmission" behind the engine and each one of them fired for each of four cylinders.

Well, Clyde told me to get some wire and hook it to the coil. We then got a six-volt dry cell battery and hooked the whole thing up to that. Then we took a big old copper plate and put it in one of the wet chairs and put a wet cloth cover over it. We hid behind the counter until the dog jumped on the chair. Clyde connected the wire and battery and it went "bzzzz!" and that damn dog jumped, I'll bet, five feet straight up in the air! I'm tellin' you, he looked at those chairs after that and would not get on any of them. If he did light on a chair we'd just yell "bzzzz!" and he'd jump straight up!

CHAPTER 14

Keyser Grade School

—6

MY GRADE SCHOOL YEARS BEGAN in 1947. There were two grade school buildings in Keyser. One was of yellow brick and the other of red brick construction. The two two-story buildings were connected on the second level by an iron catwalk and both yellow and red centers of learning, grades one through six, were ruled over by one principal, S.T. McGee.

Mom took me to my first day of public education because I was frightened of the thought of school. We clambered up concrete stairs at the front of the yellow brick schoolhouse and entered. Wooden floors that shined from years of wear and polish stretched across a large entry area. To the left was what seemed to me a massive staircase that led to the second floor. My first-grade schoolroom was to the immediate right. Mom dragged me to the room and we joined a group of about fifteen kids.

Mrs. Yost was the teacher and she greeted us warmly. After introductions, Mom told me she was leaving and would be back at the end of the school day. I looked up at her and started to cry. The crying became a wail and stream of tears that would not stop. I clung to her skirts and would not let her go, despite Mrs. Yost's assurances that all would be well if I would join the other kids in the room. I refused until Mom whispered in my ear that we were going to board a train and travel to Grafton after school—if I relented. I let her go and formed a stiff upper lip, releasing her skirt.

The rest of the day was a revelation to me. I was part of a reading circle at the front of the room where each of us students was to read a few lines from a first grade reader. I loved the wonder of reading and the ease with which I did it. A few of my counterparts had great difficulty with the assignment and I wondered why; reading was easy for one honed on hundreds of comic books. School was not so bad after all.

The yellow brick building was filled with adventure, learning and play. Recess, which does not exist in today's schools, saw us climbing on monkey bars that would be a trial lawyer's dream today; kids fell to the ground, dusted themselves off, and climbed back on the metal bars. Sixth grade students utilized the basketball courts behind adjacent Keyser High School with their teacher Miss Edna Staggers, playing hard knock basketball with us.

As recess ended and lunchtime began we bought soft drinks, *Nabs* and other assorted sugary things that put decay in our teeth, much to the benefit of our family dentist Dr. Paul Giffin. *Creamsicles* were my special delight along with *Old Nick* candy bars, popularized with the accompanying small comic strip that detailed how *Old Nick* was always arriving in the "Nick of Time" to save the day. Added to that was *Bazooka* bubblegum that we all chewed with relish; again, a Dr. Giffin delight.

CHAPTER 15

Sugar Bowl Days

ROCK AND ROLL MUSIC FILLED our young lives after school hours with a 45rpm record player our parents had purchased for my sister and me. The very first record I remember buying was "Blue Suede Shoes" by Carl Perkins, later made famous by Elvis. Mary Virginia and I bought lots of 45s and the music was always blaring at home. My mom played the organ and my dad and granddad played the violin (or fiddle). I seemed to have no musical ability and squandered the opportunity to study music as we boys made fun of Miss Dorothy Johnson's "Music Appreciation" class (something I regret to this day). I did, however, love to listen on my transistor radio to late night disc jockeys out of Tennessee and Alabama.

In the 7th grade the Sugar Bowl became very important in my life. It was the teenage hangout—located just off the high school campus. The proprietor was Bill Beck, a man with a slight limp and a pencil thin mustache reminiscent of Boston Blackie. The Sugar Bowl featured a soda fountain and a row of booths crammed with bobbysoxers. There each evening the boys and girls of my youth would gather, drinking phosphates and playing "Transfusion" by Nervous Norvous on a jukebox full of the tunes of the day.

At the rear of the establishment stood two pinball machines that were kept in constant action by boys intent on collecting the "payoff" that every joint in town seemed to feature, regardless of the fact that it was illegal. No officer of the law, to my knowledge, cared at all that pinballs were being used to wager—by adolescents. I don't think anyone was harmed.

CHAPTER 16

Keyser High School

I WALKED FROM THE RED brick elementary school across a parking lot to Keyser High School to begin 7th grade. This was the big time in the big building where we would eventually transition to high school and the 9th grade. The school fronted on ten acres of lush grass bifurcated by wide walks and a small esplanade that overlooked the town. The building was stately with beautiful colonnades and a large staircase that led to giant double front doors and side porches that provided students a gathering spot prior to classes.

In 1955 Brown v. Board of Education of Topeka created a national furor when the United States Supreme Court declared state laws establishing separate public schools for black and white students were unconstitutional. Blacks had attended our school early on and full integration of our school and our public swimming pool commenced with little fuss.

I played Junior Varsity basketball at Keyser High School. I was 13 years old and chubby. Coach "Tack" Clark called me "Porky" and would put me in a game when we were behind in the score and he needed someone to fight for the ball.

My job was not to do playmaking or shoot the ball—Tack's instructions to me were to simply assault any foe who had the ball. I loved that. I would foul a player in a full body charge, hold my hand up with a smile on my face to accept the penalty and then grin at Tack, who grinned back, clapping his hands.

In the eighth grade Tack taught West Virginia History and when a classmate could not name the capital of our state Tack pointed to me and said to the stumped student, "Just remember Charles—Charles weighs a ton. Charles—ton."

In today's world I suppose I would be shattered and CNN would do a story on a little guy who was suing his teacher. Thank God we did not think like that back then. In 1953 I was not offended and, in Tacks's defense, I firmly believe he meant no harm. I loved Tack Clark. I have, however, always remembered the reference and I know that throughout high school I always thought of myself as a fat kid. But, Tack was correct—I weighed over 200 pounds in the tenth grade. I would remain heavy until I left home for West Virginia University where I quickly shed 40 pounds in three months' time.

One day Tack came through the classroom door just as I was pegging my pocketknife into the wooden floor. Tack ignored it. He was unaware, however, of the great classroom experience when a fellow student hypnotized me and put a safety pin through the web of my hand between my thumb and index finger—I never felt it. Munch Mahood spread the word, making me a rather famous eighth grader for a short time.

In the 9ᵗʰ grade, Tack and assistant football coach Joe Stani-slawcyk (we called him, at his request, "Mr. Stan") decided to use my weight to the advantage of the "Golden Tornado" and I assumed the position of tackle in junior varsity football. I also played center, a position fraught with repeated tread marks on my chest and face as I would snap the ball in varsity scrim-mage and be literally run over as soon as the quarterback took the ball from me.

My football career lasted only two years. I performed better playing Little League baseball for the Keyser Royal Dairy team. My uniform was all wool and I dripped sweat through two summers. I loved baseball. My hallmark move was an unassisted double play when playing first base. I leaped from the bag (in my mind I jumped ten feet in the air) when a line drive was hit and stabbed the ball with my mitt. As I came down on the bag I tagged out the runner who was trying to return to first when his fellow player did not move off second. I thought, without question, I was destined for the Bigs.

CHAPTER 17

Janitor & Little Merchant

WHEN I WAS 14, I applied for and was hired as an after-school janitor at Shear's Ladies Shop on Main Street in Keyser. I arrived at the store around 4:00 each afternoon and took my orders from Jake Shear. He was one of several Jewish merchants in Keyser and he and his wife were greatly respected.

Mr. Shear seldom had much to say to me except, "Wash the windows and sweep the floors—and clean up my office." Actually, he sort of grunted the order. He wore enormous glasses and occasionally would smile as he walked through the store with a bent-over galloping slouch to greet one of his customers. He had an office over the store that fronted the stockroom. His large desk was covered stem to stern with papers of inventory, billing and correspondence.

Around the desk, on the floor, were pennies, nickels and dimes. Each day when I cleaned the office I would gather the coins he had dropped and carefully place them on the desk. I believed he was testing my honesty and knew exactly how much money was on the floor.

I left the janitor's role to become a member of the ranks of the Little Merchant, as paperboys were called. The paper route was something I coveted with all my might. Joe House, a boy a year older than I, owned it. I had been an apprentice, serving as his helper when he could not cover the route, and therefore had first dibs on buying the business.

As a Little Merchant I would ride my bike down the center of the streets I serviced, tossing the *Cumberland Evening Times* to porches on either side of the thoroughfare. I was proud of being able to do a newspaper fold that gave the paper a tightened mass, enabling it to sail through the air for some distance. I also had pride in my aim and only seldom did one of my papers land on a roof. For some reason, however, I hit Nick Spano's roof on Maple Avenue with regularity. I would circle around and toss one of my "extras" on his porch, leaving the wayward *Cumberland Evening Times* to deteriorate on Mr. Spano's roof. He never complained and occasionally would come out of the house as I rode by, looking up at the rotting papers on his roof, flashing me a large grin.

Owning a paper route, using the coin changer on my belt, accelerated the entrepreneur in me. The *Cumberland Evening Times* Keyser manager was Ross Prysock. Mr. Prysock smoked a pipe and sat at his desk, noting the number of papers each of us delivery boys were given when the truck from Cumberland arrived with the *Evening Times* papers to be distributed in Keyser.

As we waited for the truck we boys would gather next door at Johnson's Meat Market, chugging soft drinks and eating cheese. The cheese was sliced from large blocks Mr. Otis Johnson kept in his meat cabinet. The art of selecting a slice of cheese was to hunker down in front of the meat locker, peer through the glass, and point to the type cheese we wanted. Mr. Johnson would retrieve the block we chose, place it atop the counter, and slice the number of pieces we might select. Then, he would jot down on paper that covered the top of the cabinet the name of the boy who had received the cheese and the running tab number that would be deemed due on the day we collected on our paper route.

The newspaper route *was* a business: Buy the business, acquire inventory with an IOU, sell the inventory, and pay for the inventory and ancillary activities such as cheese and Royal Crown Cola—after which one hoped for a net profit.

I owned the business for two years and my net was roughly $7 each week (give or take a few RC Colas). Alas, for the first six months of my delivery boy years I would take my $7 to the local poolroom just off Main Street and invest it in pinball machines. The establishment "paid off" when one racked up games. This was gambling and illegal. But I was hooked—for six months—when it finally dawned on me I was working my Little Merchant ass off each week, only to lose my $7 in about an hour. I knew that was pretty dumb and the lesson was a lifetime cure of wagering. I never again invested money in gambling, playing not even a football card as the years went by.

CHAPTER 18

McCoole's Men's Store

IN 1956 I SOLD MY paper route to Munch Mahood after I had asked for and was given a job at McCoole's Men's Store in Keyser. There were three men's stores, believe it or not, in a town of less than 7,000 people—Kaplan's, Shapiro's and McCoole's. My mother clerked at McCoole's and she highly recommended me.

I reported to work at McCoole's after school each day. My jobs were to sweep out the store with "dust down" and then tend to the boxes in the box bin. I was once again a janitor during the week; *but,* the new job was a step up in that it carried the bonus that I would be a retail clerk on Saturdays and receive a discount on any clothing I purchased. I was going to be the best-dressed kid in school.

I loved the McCoole's box bin. It was a 10 x 15 area in the rear of the store where all boxes that had been used to ship in merchandise were tossed after their contents were removed. My job was to break up the boxes so that the bin would hold a maximum number of crushed containers. Many days the bin was chock full and I, in an attempt to create more room for additional boxes, would leap into it and jump up and down as though I were on a trampoline. It was great fun for a kid.

I kept the job for several years and I thought I was hot stuff at age 17—clerking on Saturdays, wearing a white shirt and tie during the day, adding a sport jacket at night when the town was abuzz with shoppers. In the clerk's role I loved to sell. My specialties were men's ties, suits and shoes. I could look at any man and determine his suit size and can to this day.

Our suits were the *Style Mart* brand. Top of the line sold for $60. Calvin McCoole and his wife Eleanor heaped praise on me when I sold a *Style Mart*. I was successful enough that, when summer came and school was out, I was asked to work full time, Monday through Saturday.

Calvin McCoole was a lean figure in his sixties who smoked a pipe incessantly. Eleanor was a small little woman who resembled a sparrow. He was Protestant, she was Jewish. They were the first folks I knew who catered to and enjoyed African Americans. The small black population of the town, all of whom lived on "Radical Hill", was always welcome at McCoole's and Mrs. McCoole said the folks on Radical Hill knew more about clothing and fashion than any of the store's white customers. Today, Radical Hill has become the location of the town's biggest homes, occupied mostly by whites.

Calvin, lean, angular face, wiry white hair, hunched over, would walk through the store puffing on his ever present full-bent Billiard pipe, emitting little farts with each step. If he sensed I heard the gurgling sounds from his backside he would glance over his shoulder and say, with a grin, "Speak again, sweet lips, speak again!" Calvin was a funny man.

He loved to take his breaks. Through the summer, as I worked the retail side full-time, David Nuzum, professor of English at Potomac State College, would arrive regularly at 10:30 each weekday morning and he and Calvin would depart for coffee at the Rosemont Restaurant. I was in charge of the store and I relished it.

CHAPTER 19

A Broadcasting Career

OUR HOMETOWN STATION, WKYR, HAD a weekly program called "Teenage Disc Jockey." Each week a guest teenage disc jockey was chosen from postcards sent to the show's host, Kenny Robertson. My card was chosen after I sent dozens of cards and my friend and WKYR employee Gorman Mosser lobbied Kenny for me. After my week on the air Robertson complimented me, saying I was undoubtedly the best teen disc jockey that had hosted the program. I was immediately hooked on radio and began hanging around the station.

In small-town radio, broadcasters would come and go from station to station—WKYR disc jockeys and announcers Wynn Albee, Bud Cole, Leslie Pack and chief engineer Lee Brunner, were soldiers of fortune, coming from afar and landing, for a brief while, at a little station in Keyser, West Virginia.

The itinerate nature of the business left gaps in jobs to be filled and I was standing by when an opening occurred: each Sunday afternoon WKYR showcased a rebroadcast of a morning service taped at one of Keyser's churches. The job I was offered was to pick up a Magnacorder tape recorder and lug it to a church to record the service. The Magnacorder was aptly named—it consisted of two units, each weighing a good sixty pounds. I would set up the recording units in the church, position microphones to capture both the minister and choir, and sit in an adjoining room to the sanctuary, with a large headset on, monitoring the sound levels as the reel-to-reel tape hummed.

When the service concluded, I packed the recorders in my car and drove back to the station. At 2:00 the church service was broadcast in its entirety. This was a big thing back then; church members were pleased to have me arrive and set up my gear. I loved placing the microphones and playing the role of broadcast kid.

I was in the right career, sitting in the perfect pew. It is said Henry Ford recounted that he did not know *how* he knew the workings of a combustion engine, he just *did*. I felt the same about broadcasting. It came to me naturally.

I progressed from recording the Sunday services to "riding the board" on Sunday afternoons. The phrase was used when one simply supplied the manpower at the control board. I sat in the broadcast booth and played the tapes that were to be heard in the afternoon and gave short station breaks: "You're listening to WKYR, serving Keyser, Cumberland, and the Tri State."

Part of the Sunday afternoon work was to meet the radio preachers who paid to broadcast on site in the studios on the Sabbath. I would collect $40 from the minister for a half hour of time. I put the $40 in a cash box that had been entrusted to me by station management, complete with a lock and key. After making the deposit, I would lead the minister and his entourage of musicians and gospel singers to the studio.

Then, I would put the preacher on the air.

I cued the musicians and opened the microphone in the studio. The singers began to sing. After ten seconds I would open my mike and intone in what I hoped was a great broadcast voice, "Good afternoon. Welcome to (here I inserted the name of the program). Here now, is the Reverend (another insert). I then opened the minister's mike, lowered a raised arm and pointed my finger at the preacher, alerting him that he was on the air with the choir in the background singing a familiar gospel tune. The preacher began to speak as the singers quickly concluded their opening number. Ah, I loved production.

One Sunday a minister pulled up to the station door in a huge Cadillac with enormous tail fins. He had two other cars full of his entourage and his own brand new Magnacorders that were superior to those the station owned. He had recorded most of his sermon and music on a home studio and insisted I use *his* recorders to "play back" his recorded music on his program. This involved hauling my Magnacorders off the table behind my announcer's chair and installing his large and heavy machines—only to repeat the procedure in reverse when his program was complete. I did not like to see him arrive, knowing I would have to switch recorders on the back bench, but I dutifully made the change and put him on the air—after he had deposited his cash in my collection box.

The colorful characters and the screamers who crowded through those Sunday afternoons gave me pause when considering their credentials. One minister was, however, from the Methodist church in Westernport, Maryland. I knew this man of God was on the level because of the manner in which he preached and the way his group comported themselves.

One morning, however, the Methodist minister did not show up. I learned later in the week that he had absconded with all the church funds and its secretary. After that I changed my mind about the Sunday afternoon preachers.

CHAPTER 20

The Christian Hour

THE SUMMER OF MY 17TH year, WKYR station management decided to create a new early morning program called *The Christian Hour*. Probably because no one else would get up at that hour, I was selected to run the board for the show. I would arise at 4 a.m. each weekday morning and arrive at the station by 4:30. I unlocked the door, turned on the lights, walked to the 5000-watt transmitter, turned all the dials and flipped all the switches to put the station on the air.

The Reverend H.B. Rittenhouse was a heavy-set, short, balding and jolly fellow. He arrived that first morning, and for two weeks thereafter, cleanly shaved and full of pep. I would welcome him and sign the station on at 5 a.m. with the required FCC verbiage. Then I would play the show's theme music, something from H.B.'s extensive hymnal library.

"Welcome to *The Christian Hour*," I said, into the microphone.

H.B. welcomed the audience, explaining that they were listening to the first broadcast of *The Christian Hour* on 5000-watt WKYR. He noted that the program could be heard throughout the northeastern United States and, with skips on the AM spectrum at that time of the morning, as far away as South America. I never questioned it nor did our audience.

As the weeks went on, H.B. started arriving later and later. When he arrived I would put him on the air and he would shake off his morning weariness and begin to preach. At half past the hour he would tell his audience he would "break" for five minutes for station identification and news headlines from "Our announcer, Charlie Ryan."

He would look at me through the glass separating the studio from the control room, smile benevolently, and say, "While other young men are out all hours of the night sinning and fornicating, our fine young Christian boy Charlie is here in the studio with *The Christian Hour*, helping us bring the word to you! Charlie, take it away!"

I opened my microphone while closing H.B.'s and intoned in solemn tones, "Thank you, Brother Rittenhouse. This is WKYR in Keyser, West Virginia—and now, World Headlines."

I then read the United Press International (UPI) wire service headline news. I frequently saw names I did not know how to pronounce. Eau Claire, Wisconsin was one. I had no idea how to say it, but I had struggled through one year of French; I pronounced it "Clear Water, Wisconsin." Pretty neat save, if I had to say so myself.

One fine morning, H.B. did not show up at all. I did not hesitate. "Good Morning and welcome to *The Christian Hour*. The

Reverend Rittenhouse cannot be with us this morning, but he has asked me to bring you these fine old Christian tunes." At that point I would play hymns by the Chuck Wagon Gang, followed by George Beverly Shea and others.

At the end of the summer, the preacher was AWOL more often than not. I did the same routine, but finally succumbed to sleep that was demanded after a summer of 4 a.m. risings. I would play the Chuck Wagon Gang and, once the 33 1/3 LP began to turn, cleared the bench behind me of the large Magnacorders and lie down, promptly going to sleep.

"Sccc, sccc, sccc," was the sound of the 33 1/3 announcing it was finished—all the songs on the LP had been played, leaving the needle on the turntable arm to idled at the center of the record—done.

I would finally hear the sound, jump from my prone position, open the mike and say, "That was the Chuck Wagon gang. And now, Brother Rittenhouse has asked me to play a wonderful hymn by Tennessee Ernie Ford." I played LP number two, climbed back on the bench, and again fell asleep.

CHAPTER 21

The Boss

STATION MANAGER BILL ROBINSON—KNOWN AS the "Boss"—
and H.B. were buddies and I had a great fondness for both of
them. The Boss rewarded me for my time with the sleepy preacher
by appointing me to host *Rural Route 1270*, the country show,
from 6-7 a.m. and morning drive from 7 until 9 a.m. Duane
Eddy was a rock artist of the time and one morning I introduced
a guitar-laden hit of his by saying, "Now, here's the man with the
big twang, Duane Eddy!" The Boss was not amused.

I also talked the Boss into letting me use the last 15 minutes
of airtime in the summer months to play jazz. I called it the
Jazz Quarter and one evening read from album liners about a
celebrated jazz artist who had started his career in Greenwich
Village. I called it "Green Which Village." Bill Rogers, a celebrated Keyser musician, called me and said, "It's 'Gren-uch'
Village, dummy."

The Boss was my first mentor. He was legally blind, but the
handicap did not deter his spirit. It was his burning desire
to move 5000 watt WKYR from our very small market
(Keyser boasted a population of 7,000) in Mineral County to

Cumberland, in Allegany County, Maryland—the *big* town, but serviced by stations of smaller wattage.

Cumberland, twenty miles away, was home to over 20,000 people. It seemed huge to those of us who manned the mikes at WKYR, and the idea we could enter Cumberland radio and successfully compete with entrenched WTBO ("Why Tubes Burn Out", we called it) and WCUM (with a jingle that said, "Come, Come, Come, Come to Cumberland") was crazy, we thought, but it was a challenge to the entrepreneur in the manager's office and a lesson to me—follow your dream.

Robinson originated one of the very first satellite stations in radio and bet it all. He leased space downtown in the Fort Cumberland Hotel on Baltimore Street and branded WKYR as a powerful 5000 watt voice that simply over powered 1000 watt WTBO and WCUM, serving Cumberland, Keyser and the tri-state (Maryland, West Virginia and Virginia). Sales boomed, and the brand was born.

The Boss would sit at his home in the early morning hours or on Sunday when I was on the mike, and call me to correct my mistakes. The Boss was not content to simply manage. He loved the microphone as much as I. WKYR was a daytime station, signing off at dusk. On a regular basis the Boss would rush in at the close of the day with a new order from the "Half-Price Stores"—a discount chain located throughout the Cumberland market. He and I would work until the early hours of the morning, recording the hard-sell spots that would begin airing the next day.

This legally blind man would read by holding a small magnifying glass that was contained in a circular ring about the size of the top of a Coke can. He would whip the glass out of his pocket and flip the ring open, revealing the magnification pane that he would place against his eye. He then moved the glass across every line, pressing closer to the microphone. Finishing a line, he would quickly move back, allowing me an entry toward the mike where I would shout out the next line. "So, hurry on down to the Half-Price Store! Don't delay, this sale may end today!"

The Boss showed me one could persevere and succeed against all odds. I had a mentor at seventeen—how lucky was I! I did not realize it at the time, but the Boss was moving my basic belief in myself (instilled by my parents) to a whole new level; one that caused me to create goals, have a vision, and know I could succeed if I were totally committed to do so.

CHAPTER 22

A Career In News

AFTER GRADUATING HIGH SCHOOL, I began a full time summer job at WKYR. I hosted the morning drive time (*Rise with Ryan*—some took that as a double entendre*), the afternoon drive time, *Ridin' With Ryan*, and, at 5:00 *The Motorist's Friend*. I would intone at the beginning of *The Motorist's Friend*, with Glenn Miller's *Moonlight Serenade* in the background, "Yes, it's the *Motorist's Friend*—soothing music for you tired businessmen driving home at the end of a day's work."

I acquired tremendous confidence sitting at the control board of a 5000 watt radio station as I turned 18—with no other person on the premises it was mine to make or break, and I reveled in it. Sitting between two turntables, in complete control, was fantastic. I also was grateful when Marty Robbins recorded "El Paso"—it was the first four-minute popular song in radio and disc jockeys all over the country made it a hit because they could take a bathroom break without fear of getting back to the control room with their pants around their knees.

On winter days I called "State Road" offices around the tri-state area and recorded reports on the condition of highways and did interviews. At county fairs I did remotes, broadcasting from barnyards and grandstands. One afternoon I was in the grandstand at the Grant County Fair in Petersburg. I leaned over a young woman who was sitting in the row of seats where I was standing and moved my microphone to her face. I found myself staring at a bare breast as she prepared to breast feed her child. I stuttered and moved on, thankful I was not doing television at the time.

My news career was born at WKYR—my most cherished Keyser news interview was with Teddy Kennedy, stumping for his brother's presidential campaign. The interview was taped at Wolfe's Furniture Store where Teddy was meeting the public. I remember him as a strapping good-looking young guy, not much older than I. He was gracious and laughed a lot—big grin. It would be my pleasure during my broadcast career to interview his brother Bobby and to report live as his brother Jack visited Charleston.

CHAPTER 23

Potomac State College

It was 1958 and I was hopeful of entering college at Potomac State, high on a hill overlooking Keyser. I was one nervous fellow about higher education. I walked hesitantly into the office of Dean K.S. McKee. The Dean, with white hair and handsome features, read my high school record as I nervously glanced about the ornate room that featured a large window looking out over Campus Drive.

He read through some rather erratic grades and, seeing that I was working a 40-hour week, asked me if I planned to cease work as a college student. I assured him that I did not and he frowned. "You'll need to spend your time studying, not working, if you expect to succeed in higher education," he cautioned.

Well, I was stunned. I had worked diligently to achieve my cherished mike-side position and I loved every minute at WKYR. I hesitated and then said, "If I can't work in radio while going to college, I won't go to college."

The Dean frowned and made some notes. He leaned back in the chair and said, "Well, young man, if that's the case, we'll see how it works." He smiled and I was dismissed—but accepted as a college freshman. My radio career continued, and Pot State students would kid me about working at WKYR. The call letters, they said, stood for: "Why Keep Your Radio?"

The first year of college was a struggle and even my favorite subjects were hard. I thought I could breeze through history with Dr. J. Kenna Burke—but I found my written essays (as tests) needed a lot more beef than I could provide, given my scarcity of study. The exception was journalism and speech—two courses I embraced with enthusiasm.

Majoring in journalism, I had the good fortune of being guided by Dr. Elizabeth Atwater. She was a dynamo who made learning fun. She featured a great white mane of hair, a sharp nose, and movements in the classroom that were quick and precise. She laughed. She was poetic. She was fair. She was everything a young student could hope for. We learned—all of us: Jack Canfield, Munch Mahood, Ted Troxell, Judy Burns, and Colleen Davis, to name a few. We learned how to write and how to set hot type at the Keyser *Mineral Daily and News Tribune*, and in "Dr. A's" speech courses we learned how to face an audience and project.

Dr. Atwater allowed Jack Canfield and me to write columns for the school newspaper, the *Pasquino* (of which she was the sponsor, editor and publisher). The name *Pasquino* was taken from the talking statues of Rome—Canfield and I were reminiscent of those statues as our columns appeared on facing pages of the paper—Jack and I staring at one another. I learned that writing a column is different than strict reporting and I was lucky to practice the trade at a very early age—a journalistic gift that served me well through later years of writing columns for newspapers across West Virginia.

The final edition of our sophomore class featured Canfield and Ryan with back-to-back columns on the *same* page where we skewered one another. The layout showed photos of us facing off with dueling pistols, snarls on our faces. Jack and I became lifelong friends—meeting in high school, growing closer in college, and then working for radio and television stations in Morgantown and Charleston as friendly rivals.

The awesome Betty Atwater gave her all and we loved her. She lived to be 101. Those of us who crossed the threshold of her classes will always be indebted to her.

My English and grammar were not the best when I arrived at Potomac State's beautiful campus. I was placed in Bonehead English, taught by Dr. David Nuzum. He was yet another instructor who took his students by the ear and plowed them through delights they did not know existed in the classroom. Dr. Nuzum helped and nurtured all his students, but I have to believe my association with him at McCoole's Men's Store gave me a leg up.

"Inanimate objects do not *sit*, Mr. Ryan!" bellowed the bespectacled and resplendently dressed Dr. Nuzum as he, with flair, assessed papers our class had written. His large cufflinks, bold tie, expensive *Style Mart* suits and sport coats, and his neatly trimmed mustache were elegant. He moved in the classroom like Fred Astaire.

Years later, when I was working for WSAZ-TV in Charleston, Dr. Nuzum and I shared lunch in the elegant Daniel Boone Hotel dining room—it was my first encounter with a finger bowl. I followed the good professor's lead, not knowing what a finger bowl was. From David Nuzum I learned not only English—I came to appreciate style.

My scholastic record at Potomac State was not the best; Dean McKee was correct—I would have had better overall grades if I had spent more time on the books and less in front of the microphone—but I also was correct that my future would benefit greatly from the experiential broadcast years.

I received my Associate of Arts degree at Potomac State in 1960. At that time, two years at Potomac State College of West Virginia University was equivalent to two years at the WVU main campus. I was headed to Morgantown, West Virginia as a full-fledged junior in journalism—and my immediate goal was to find a job to finance my remaining two years in school.

CHAPTER 24

Morgantown

I traveled to Morgantown and went, unannounced, to WCLG, a 1000 watt radio station. The call letters stood for C. Leslie Golliday, a radio entrepreneur who owned a station in Martinsburg, West Virginia near the Washington, D.C. market. Mr. Golliday had sold the station to Bill and Eleanor Freed.

I climbed the stairs of a beautiful vintage building on High Street that once housed a bank but had no elevator. The building had transitioned to a men's store on the street level ("Goldsmith & Sons"—it was referred to by some as "Harry Has 'Em"), a dentist office on the second level, and WCLG on the third floor. I introduced myself to the receptionist and said I was looking for a job as a disc jockey, announcer, or newsman.

Garry Bowers, who would eventually become the owner of the station, was the young program director. I met with him and found I was in luck; the station was looking for a new hire who could be both disc jockey and newscaster. I was given wire copy and led to a studio for my audition, an on-air newscast. These folks had never heard me before and put me on the air, not knowing if I could even read. To this day I am proud that I nailed the newscast. Bill, Eleanor, and Garry were impressed, as was the station news director Jack Johns, and I was hired on the spot.

I drove back to Keyser and packed my gear. The next day Mom and Dad drove me to Morgantown where I rented a room in a house near Willey Street. The bathroom was down the hall and there was no TV or radio. I could really have used an iPod but I would have had to wait forty years.

Mom cried and Dad gave me a hug. They pulled away in the Ford and Mom waved in the mirror. The feeling in the pit of my stomach was huge. I took solace in the fact that I had a job, unpacked my suitcase, organized my room and went to bed.

The next morning I was at the Presto Restaurant eating breakfast at 5:30 sharp—a practice I was faithful to the entire time at WCLG. Lunches were at "Hav-A-Lunch on Walnut Street. We went as a station pack—Jack Johns, Bill Miller, Bowers, Larry Maisel and I.

Station policy was not fond of blacks and black music. Maisel and I could care less and we spun Nat King Cole, Ella Fitzgerald, and a whole array of black artists. Each morning that summer I climbed the three flights of stairs above Harry Has 'Em and opened the doors and the morning mike at WCLG.

Much as I loved WCLG, I really wanted to work across town at 5000 watt WAJR, known statewide for originating the West Virginia University football and basketball games.

WAJR's station manager, Mal Campbell, hired me following a thirty-minute meeting. Ecstatic, I called my parents from a phone booth at the head of High Street, next to the street's iconic frozen custard stand, to tell them with great pride that I was going to work at WAJR. It was a stellar moment in my young career.

Jack Canfield replaced me at WCLG and said years later in his remarks upon being inducted into the West Virginia Broadcaster's Hall of Fame, "Charlie Ryan literally blazed a path for me from the days when we were Keyser High classmates. He worked at WKYR in Keyser and left to go to Morgantown; I got his job at WKYR. He worked at WCLG in Morgantown and left for WAJR; I got his job at WCLG."

Jack and I were the Bobbsey Twins of Keyser—both broadcasters and agency guys. Jack and I began careers as teenage disc jockeys and our lives continually crisscrossed. Jack served with aplomb and distinction in broadcasting, government, politics, public opinion research, public relations and advertising—eventually establishing his own agency in Charleston.

CHAPTER 25

Jack Fleming

I WAS ON BOARD AT WAJR as classes began at WVU. The Evansdale Campus was pretty much farmland when I entered the university and all my courses were on the main campus. WAJR was located on Spruce Street, a ten-minute sprint to Martin Hall where the "J" school was located. It was in a triangle of iconic buildings that featured Woodburn Hall in the middle, Martin Hall to the left, and Chitwood Hall to the right.

There was electricity in the air as kids from all over the state and beyond arrived on campus. I was out in the middle of it with WAJR's mobile vehicle, known as "Black Beauty", broadcasting the arrival, interviewing students and providing "color" of the event. It was heady stuff for a 20 year-old.

WAJR's sports director/salesman, Jack Fleming, was known far and wide as the radio voice of the Mountaineers. Jack was a mentor to me as was the station program director, Jack Tennant. Tennant was the "color man" for Fleming during the WVU broadcasts.

Fleming was an imposing figure, about six feet, two inches tall with a mop of red hair. He was constantly kidding and joking. He succeeded Mal Campbell as general manager when Mal moved to Washington, D.C., joining the station that broadcast the radio segment of the Washington Redskins games, becoming the radio voice of the Redskins.

As Fleming took the WAJR general manager's job and Campbell's career blossomed with the Redskins, Fleming was fighting to retain the broadcast rights to the WVU games. He suffered a terrible loss when WHAR in Clarksburg won the bidding war to originate and broadcast the games. The WHAR sports director was Jay Randolph, son of legendary United States Senator Jennings Randolph.

Jay held the reins of the broadcast for a two-year period and WAJR was then successful in winning back the broadcast, which it held for many, many years thereafter. Jay Randolph moved to St. Louis and became the radio and television voice of the St. Louis Cardinals baseball and football broadcasts.

Both Jack and Jay scored big. Fleming went on to not only broadcast the WVU games but became the radio voice of the Chicago Bulls when Michael Jordan was at his height (no pun intended). Jack also was the radio voice of the Pittsburgh Steelers for more than a decade, broadcasting one of the most famous moments in sports history on December 23, 1972, when, in the last 30 seconds of the AFC Divisional playoff game, Franco Harris reached down and retrieved a Terry Bradshaw pass that had eluded John Fuqua, scoring the winning touchdown against the Oakland Raiders at Three Rivers

Stadium—the feat known forevermore as the *Immaculate Reception*. Jack Fleming was indeed one of sport's premiere broadcasters.

Fleming decided at one point that WAJR would do a 9 p.m. to midnight disc jockey show to attract the WVU campus audience. He chose me to be the anointed DJ and named the show "Charlie's Campus Calling." The basic problem with the call-in show was that WAJR was a child of 40s radio and had not subscribed to any rock and roll record suppliers. Callers were constantly requesting Elvis, The Platters, Bobby Helms and the like. I repeatedly said things such as, "Sorry, we don't have *Be-Bop-A-Lu-A* by Gene Vincent and the Bluecaps, but here, instead, is Perry Como and *Catch A Falling Star*!"

The calls were live, no taped delay, and just before midnight one evening I gave my apology to a caller who wanted a Little Richard hit. "Sorry, but, how about—," was as far as I got. The caller's reply, on air, and very loud, was, "Well, F—K!" Back then the "F" word could cost a station its license to broadcast. When the word was uttered I simply hit the theme music and said goodnight. The next day Fleming instituted a tape delay edict and the show became even more stilted.

One day Jack assigned me to broadcast a remote from the local Studebaker dealership. It was my first remote assignment at WAJR. I played records from the dealer's showroom and in between songs chatted passionately about the new Studebaker and all its features, not knowing Jack was trying frantically to reach me by phone. When I finally took the receiver Fleming shouted, "It's Stood-a-baker, stupid, not Stoody-baker!"

Then there was the Christmas tradition in which Jack played Santa Claus in the annual WAJR Christmas specials, broadcast for 15 minutes each night during the week before Christmas. I was the production guy and Fleming guided his Santa sleigh through rough weather by banging on the walls of the studio and shouting in his Santa voice to his reindeer. It was great fun.

Jack thought I had a big radio voice and gave me wide latitude as a twenty year-old. I was named News Director and anchored newscasts at 6 in the evening; I also wrote a five-minute commentary that I delivered each night called *The News in Review*. Fleming's decision to allow me to learn as I went gave me a tremendous advantage in the world of reporting.

CHAPTER 26

Reportorial Chops

AT 20 YEARS OF AGE in 1960, I was writing and broadcasting WAJR's 6:15 five-minute commentary called The *News In Review*. It featured many of the personalities that came to a University town and I found myself interviewing the iconic Eleanor Roosevelt as she campaigned for Jack Kennedy for President. She did double duty by visiting, during the same trip, Arthurdale in Preston County.

Arthurdale was founded when Mrs. Roosevelt learned that a group of West Virginia miners were to be relocated during the Great Depression in an experimental program to determine if they could have a better life with subsistence farming and small, simple industrial efforts. She lobbied FDR to make the program part of the New Deal and he placed it there in 1933, under the United States Department of the Interior. It was one of Eleanor Roosevelt's chief priorities and her 1960 visit was a reunion and full of remembrances.

I accompanied Mrs. Roosevelt to Arthurdale and did a number of reports for NBC's *Monitor Radio*, the weekend radio news program NBC broadcast nationally on Saturdays and

Sundays. One week later a freelance photographer offered to sell me an 8 X 10 photo of my interview in the Hotel Morgan lobby with the iconic First Lady. I was ecstatic and said I wanted to purchase it.

"How much?" I asked.

"Ten dollars," was the reply.

"Man, I can't afford that—no deal," I shot back.

The photog, to whom I will always be grateful, took me by the arm and said, "Kid, buy the picture, you'll thank me later."

I did. And I fervently thank the photographer.

I covered Jimmy Hoffa at the Hotel Morgan, interviewing him on the roof of the hotel at a party following a day of union organizing, a ballroom speech and a Q&A from the crowd. I was loaded for bear, cornering Hoffa after the event, quizzing him about alleged pension fund loans to organized crime figures and several other charges being made against him as President of the International Teamsters Union.

He was pugnacious as he stood on the canopied roof of the hotel, answering every question I asked about his alleged criminal activities—his finger jabbing toward me, punching the air, at times tattooing my chest, replying to each of my questions, and adding at the end of his statement that he had been indicted many times but he always beat the rap. He emphasized the fact by repeatedly saying, "Hoffa stands here!"

On January 19, 1962, US Labor Secretary Arthur Goldberg, who would later become a United States Supreme Court Justice, came to Morgantown. I interviewed him prior to his addressing a Democratic rally at the Hotel Morgan.

In my coverage, I reported that Goldberg had said to a Democratic rally that ways must be found to bring new kinds of industry to areas stagnating or declining because of market and production changes and that John F. Kennedy sent his warm personal regards:

I reported: *Goldberg told a crowd of over 500 in the ballroom of the Hotel Morgan that it was not strange that seven members of President Kennedy's cabinet have visited West Virginia. "In a very real sense," Goldberg said, "our President was made in West Virginia."*

I interviewed jazz icon Stan Kenton at length and was thrilled to do so. Kenton was especially nice to me and I gushed, *"A New Era in Modern Music proved to be just that last night as Stan Kenton alternately thrilled and astonished a near-capacity crowd at the Field House in West Virginia University's first Cultural Committee presentation of the year. Kenton's 21-piece band produced a driving tempo through the better part of two hours with a mixture of modern innovations and Kentonized standards."*

Kenton told me in my one-on-one with him at intermission that college concerts were more important than playing nightclubs or jazz festivals. He said, "This is where the minds are most susceptible to new things in music."

CHAPTER 27

The Daily Athenaeum

DURING MY TIME AT WEST Virginia University's School of Journalism I entered the world of print, working at the J School's *Daily Athenaeum*. My fellow Keyserite and WVU journalism compatriot, Jack Canfield, also was working at the *Athenaeum* and he and I had a major scoop.

It was January, 1962 and the *"Daily A"* had learned that the University faculty was to meet at 2 p.m. to vote on the successor to Elvis Jacob Stahr, who was leaving the WVU presidency to accept a position as Secretary of the Army in the Kennedy administration. Canfield and I hastened to the auditorium where the faculty was gathering, only to be barred from the meeting; we were to wait outside and would be summoned at the end of the session.

Jack and I fumed as the big double doors were locked and bolted. We were the only two reporters present for a big story in a university town. Glancing around the area we noted another single door about twenty feet from the auditorium doors. We checked it out and found it to be unlocked. We entered a small area leading to a staircase and a door at the top of the stairs.

We opened the door and found ourselves in an overhead projection room. We tiptoed to the openings for movie projectors and, bingo, had a full view and sound of the proceedings below us.

A full half-hour before the meeting concluded Jack and I had phoned the *"Daily A"*, WAJR, WCLG and the Associated Press (Jack was working at WCLG and I at WAJR) to report that Paul Ausborn Miller was the new President of West Virginia University.

The faculty were not pleased but our *Daily A* publisher, the iconic Paul Atkins, was ecstatic. We earned his respect and semester "A's" going away.

Atkins, known by his students as the "Big A", was a small, kinetic little guy who came at you behind large glasses and a small smile that said you were in for it. He spent 33 years guiding the young men and women who entered Martin Hall and the Perley Isaac Reed School of Journalism. Each and every one of them who encountered Atkins, I can assure you, remembers him.

Writing for the *Athenaeum* was a great experience in journalism. Each morning Bob Gornall, Art Corey, Fanny Seiler, Alan Noe, Lee Maynard, Danny Wells, and others with whom I was privileged to learn the print business, would eagerly race to a bulletin board outside Atkins' office to see what his grease pencil had to say about our stories and the day's publication.

The front page of the November 17, 1961 edition of the *Daily Athenaeum* carried two stores written by Charles Ryan. The first was at the top of the page next to the masthead and said: *McConkey Bombards DA In Legislature Meeting.*

My second story on that front page was a feature article on the university's statewide agricultural radio-television information service. Foster Mullenax, the director, was shown at a bank of Magnacorders where audiotapes were duplicated for distribution to radio stations around West Virginia—stations that would air the programs in early morning hours.

The lead for the McConkey story was: *Last night's meeting of the Student Legislature served as a soap box for student body president Sam McConkey as he attacked the Daily Athenaeum with charges of "biased reporting and misquoting".*

My lead for the Mullenax article was: *The voice of Foster Mullenax is known by more West Virginia farmers than any other voice in the United States.*

The "Big A" liked my reporting and scoring both articles on page one was something few *Athenaeum* reporters would do. Atkins gave me an "A" for my semester work.

I treasure Paul Atkins' assessments and gratefully acknowledge his hand in shaping my career. To garner Atkins' approval one had to excel—pleasing the "Big A" was a great accomplishment and my chest will always expand with pride when I read his notes assessing my work. Atkins said that he considered the WVU School of Journalism the best in the United States. How privileged we students were to be there.

CHAPTER 28

Television News

I GRADUATED WITH A BS in Journalism at WVU in 1962 and spent the summer working at WAJR and looking for a job in television. In July of that year I was offered a reporter's position at WCHS-TV, Channel 8, in Charleston—and turned it down.

John Hurd, the WCHS news director, explained that he knew my capability from my work at WAJR and I did not need to journey to Charleston for an interview. I thought about it and decided I should not take a job from a guy I had never seen at a station I had never visited.

No problem for Hurd; he hired Charleston radio personality Ed Rabel (DJ host of *Rabel Rousers*). Ed did a great job at Channel 8 and went on to become its news director. He later moved to New York and CBS where he worked the news desk when Walter Cronkite was anchoring the *CBS Evening News*. He proved his chops and became a "big foot" *CBS* correspondent with a fabulous career at both CBS and NBC where he was the Pentagon correspondent.

A few days after turning down the WCHS-TV offer, I learned of a job opening at WSAZ-TV. The station news director, Bos Johnson, *insisted* I come to Charleston to meet with him and undergo an interview and audition. I sat down with Bos and Charleston News Editor Ken Kurtz and answered the obligatory questions. I was a bit intimidated; this was the big time as far as I was concerned and Bos Johnson was a household name and ultimate professional. Little did I know that Bos and I would be intertwined for the rest of our lives.

We broke for lunch and walked to the Charleston Press Club. I was nervous and ordered the only thing on the menu with which I had great experience—spaghetti. Naturally, I splashed spaghetti sauce all over my three-piece corduroy suit and Bos and Ken pretended not to notice.

After lunch we walked back to Dickinson Street and I prepared for my on-air audition. When the red light went on atop the camera my nervousness vanished and I delivered what I believed to be a top-notch five-minute newscast. I think I am safe in saying Bos was impressed this radio kid could meld into TV delivery with apparent ease. Minutes later I was offered the job and I accepted on the spot. Who wouldn't? The salary was fantastic—$5,000 a year! I broke it down in a letter to my parents: "I'll receive a base pay of $395 a month and should draw from between $420 and $460 a month, according to Johnson. He says it will seldom slip below $420."

I said goodbye to Bos and Ken and promised I would arrive for duty in two weeks. Checking my wallet I found I had about $8 to get back to Morgantown. I went to the Charleston

National Bank and tried to cash a $10 check on my account at the Farmers & Merchants Bank in Morgantown. I was turned away in abrupt fashion.

I then crossed the street to Kanawha Banking & Trust (KB&T) and made my plea: I had been hired at WSAZ-TV and would be back in town in two weeks—honest. The teller took pity on me and called Vic Johnson, a KB&T Vice President. Vic came to the teller's window and listened and walked around the teller area to stand next to me. He looked me up and down and said, in the avuncular way that was his style, "Well, you look to me like you can be trusted," winked, and approved my check. That was 1962—between 1974 and through the late 1980's Charles Ryan Associates ran millions of dollars through Vic Johnson's bank.

When I arrived in Charleston I was thrilled at actually *being* at what I considered the *big time*—the metro area was nearly a half million—a far cry from Keyser and Morgantown. I drove through Charleston listening to WSAZ radio and the exciting voice of Jim Turley. I went to the Charleston YMCA and rented a room, based on the recommendation of WAJR's Jack Tennant, who told me it was a "real nice place and inexpensive." Jack hedged a bit and adjusted his recommendation, saying, "It won't be a bad place to stay, except you have to eat out."

CHAPTER 29

A Damon Runyon City

WSAZ-TV WAS THE LARGEST TELEVISION station in the state and a top 50 station in the nation. Its signal permeated southeastern Ohio, eastern Kentucky and all of central and southern West Virginia. It boasted a state of the art facility in downtown Huntington—huge!

The downtown Charleston studios of WSAZ-TV were located at 310 Dickinson Street above a ladies shop and a drycleaners. The second floor of the building contained about 5,000 square feet of office space and radio studios. At the back of the building, stairs descended to the one television studio the operation featured. A control room was located just off the newsroom.

Across the hall from the TV newsroom were the radio studios of WKAZ radio where disc jockey Jay Jarrell held forth. He was a flamboyant 1960s rocker and forerunner to WKAZ's "Super Duper" Charlie Cooper. Charlie became by far the number one DJ in southern West Virginia when WKAZ moved its studios to the top floor of the Heart

O'Town Hotel. Charlie later established Admix, a production studio that gave me great assistance in my fledgling business years.

Super Duper started Admix on a shoestring, as I had started CRA. Charlie sent me an email while I was writing this book that said, "Do you recall that you once gave me a letter to take to the bank to help me get financing for my business? I believe I wanted to buy $500 worth of equipment, and you wrote a letter promising to do $1,000 worth of business with me. Maybe it was more, I don't remember. The National Bank of Commerce turned me down for the loan. I ended up at Kanawha Valley Bank with a new young personal banker named Phyllis Arnold. That's how I got rolling." Yep, one hand washed the other and Charlie and I established a lifelong friendship.

At 310 Dickinson Street, I reported to Ken Kurtz, the Charleston news editor. Ken, a native of Jane Lew, West Virginia and a Swarthmore graduate, was a brilliant and unique fellow. He was tall and gangly and eschewed a tie with the exception of on-air work. He lived in an apartment in Kanawha City and kept spare tires for his Pontiac station wagon under his kitchen table. He would sweep across the newsroom floor on his roller chair and deposit on my desk stories he had written for the 6 p.m. newscast.

I learned later that I was replacing a fellow who had gone to WSAV-TV in Savannah, Georgia. His name was Ralph Price and he had had a hard time working with Kurtz. I was told he was fired when he had Kurtz down on the newsroom floor, banging his boss' head on the tile.

Once the crew around the station learned a fresh graduate from WVU had been hired to replace the veteran newsman Price, they began to refer to me as "Charlie Lamb"—as in the lamb that was being led to the slaughter. Frances Pinion, a lovable secretary at WSAZ, was not in on the joke. She actually thought my name *was* Charlie Lamb and when I arrived on my first day at the station, she welcomed me, saying, "Hello, Mr. Lamb."

Ken Kurtz knew Charleston like the back of his hand and he knew its denizens of the day and night. Following him, I encountered wonderful capital city characters of the 60s. The city was a Damon Runyon Petri dish—a rip-roaring place with cops and robbers, prostitution and gambling. A Charleston detective ran a prostitution ring at the Daniel Boone Hotel and payoffs to cops on Summers Street were said to be a regular thing. There also were law-abiding citizens who were hardly average in appearance or activity.

Earl Harvey was believed to be a savant. His nickname was "Lightning". He was a small black man who was slightly infirm, walking with a slanted gait. He could instantly do exponential mathematical calculations in his head. I encountered him often as he prowled Virginia Street each afternoon, stopping traffic to sell days old copies of the *Charleston Gazette*. Lightning would carry the papers under one arm and emit a shrill whistle to get cars to stop.

Bernie Wiepper was the Charleston artist whose gallery featured remarkable art portraying denizens of the capital city nightlife. Bernie created the bust of General Chuck Yeager at Yeager Airport in Charleston and sculpted the state Capitol's bronze statue of *Lincoln Walks at Midnight*, perhaps his best-known creation. Bernie dressed all in black and sported a Van Dyke beard. He entertained colorful characters of the capital city that seemed to gather with regularity in his loft in the upper reaches of the Masonic Building on Hale Street. The scene was beatnik and Bernie wore a beret as he held forth.

J. Bender Kuhn was a lawyer who had become an alcoholic and was reduced to panhandling and nights in jail. He was so well-known to Municipal Judge John Charnock (who was a softie for those down and out) that the judge simply sentenced J. Bender to whatever time it took for him to sober up—a night in the drunk tank.

J. Bender regularly accosted attorneys who walked the streets of Charleston, seeking a handout. Each day Kuhn targeted attorney Tom Pendergast. One day Tom became so angry at the daily diversion that he pulled a $100 bill from his pocket and said, "J. Bender, here's $100—don't bother me for a full year!" J. Bender grabbed the bill and kept the bargain. But, time passed, and one day as Tom crossed Capitol Street J. Bender grabbed Tom's arm, saying, "Tom, your year's up!"

CHAPTER 30

Pantyhose & Prostitutes

COLORFUL CHARLESTON ATTORNEY DEAN LEWIS, a name I will mention often in these recollections, once defended a man charged of rape and when the alleged rape victim took the stand he led her through a series of questions. At one point he asked, "What were you wearing at the time of the alleged event?" The lady detailed all she had worn that evening, finishing with the fact that she had worn pantyhose.

"*Pantyhose?*" Dean asked, incredulously. "If you had pantyhose on, how were they removed?"

"Oh, I took them off."

"*You* took them off? Why in the world would *you* take off your pantyhose in a situation such as that?"

"Because he forced me."

"He forced you?"

"Yes, he forced me."

"How did he force you?" Dean asked.

"The lady gave a slight smile as she turned to the defendant and then to the jury, saying, "He said he *haddddd* to have it.""

Dean prevailed—to the delight of a packed courtroom.

Bill Dunn was a homeless person who lived on the streets and beneath the bridges of Charleston. He pushed a grocery store cart filled with his belongings and was known to the community as "Aqualung". Dunn was given the name because of his resemblance to a figure on the cover of a Jethro Tull album called Aqualung. Bill was quickly recognized in his long dirty coat, shopping cart and beard. He would spend his summers in Charleston and migrate to Washington, D.C. for the winter. Asked why, he said Washington was more comfortable in winter, given the large grates that dotted the sidewalks—offering a warm place to bed down.

Aqualung achieved additional notoriety when he was the inspiration for the homeless person in the movie *Down and Out in Beverly Hills*. Actor Nick Nolte, who lived for a time in Charleston (marrying not one, but two Charleston women), studied Dunn and based his movie character on Dunn's persona. One day Aqualung simply disappeared, never to be seen again.

The Hub poolroom on Quarrier Street featured at least 20 pool tables, a full counter for lunch and a series of booths that dotted the far side of the wall. Dominating the pool table area was a giant blackboard where baseball scores were posted and bets were placed—within full sight of the city's police officers who would partake of lunch at the long counter where greasy hamburgers were served.

The WSAZ newsroom was around the corner on Dickinson Street and I, when the news day was slow, would walk to the Hub to see who was having lunch—hoping to find a newsmaker. I would slide onto a stool at the counter beside an attorney, municipal official, or former Mayor D. Boone Dawson, quickly gathering the highlights of the day.

At night I would ride with city detectives as they patrolled the "Back End of Town"—the city's gambling and red light district where Detective Bob Crouse ruled. Weekends I would ride in a Kanawha County Sheriff's sedan as raids were conducted on Mamma Nanny's Boarding House and Edna's Tourist Home. On one occasion a city detective rolled down the window of his cruiser and tossed a lit cherry bomb at a bothersome pit bull. The dog swallowed the treat whole. Thank goodness, the bomb failed to go off, saliva being a damper for the lit fuse.

City Engineer Louie Hark was a tiny little guy with thick glasses and a constant smile. He and his assistant Irene Wright took a liking to me and I gathered gossip in his office that armed me for some interesting meetings with a man I liked and admired, Mayor John Shanklin.

Shanklin loved to pull from his credenza polling results from his last election and proudly show me certain precincts that supported him—precincts where he was said by veteran pols certain to lose. He was an energetic and effective mayor.

CHAPTER 31

Bill Kelley

—ᕦ᠊

CHARLESTON FIRE DEPARTMENT CAPTAIN CLAUDE Saunders could instantly spot a news camera when one was in his vicinity. WSAZ-TV photographer Bill Kelley was shooting a fire one day and was atop an adjacent building to get a great shot. As he rolled film and zoomed in on shooting flames, a ladder slammed onto the side of the blazing building and Claude's head popped up and into the film. Claude loved the media.

Each year Claude selected a "Miss Flame". One summer he placed a hook and ladder truck outside the Stone & Thomas Department Store and invited Mayor Shanklin to join Miss Flame for a photo-op. As our cameras rolled, Claude placed a fire captain's hat on Shanklin and placed him beside Miss Flame. Shanklin grinned, took off his hat, and waved it back and forth in front of Miss Flame's chest, indicating she was red hot.

Claude then raised the fire truck's ladder to the side of the building. Our energetic mayor loved to put on a show so he escorted bikini-clad Miss Flame onto and up the ladder. The mayor followed, right behind Miss Flame's buttocks. I was behind the mayor, my Bell & Howell camera rolling. The upward shot on the 6:00 news showed the Mayor's uplifted face staring straight into Miss Flame's attractive bottom.

Shanklin's predecessor, John Copenhaver, was known as "Jumping John" because of his tendency to make things pop at City Hall—he loved to stage raids on illicit bars downtown. Detectives would burst into the bars, point at certain persons, shouting, "You, you, and you! Up against the wall! The rest of you—out!"

Charleston Police Chief Dallas Bias was a fitness guy with an impressive physique. Each winter he would join the Polar Bear Plunge staged on the banks of the Kanawha River. Bias wore an Indian headdress to draw attention to himself as he shed clothes, revealing his chiseled frame and abs. He once ran for mayor and registered for the race at the City Clerk's office adorned in his chief's headdress—a colorful thing worthy of Sitting Bull. Our cameras could not resist Bias and he garnered prime TV time.

Bias was at one time determined to catch a burglar who was robbing homes in the city's South Hills section. He brought us reporters together and displayed a map, replete with stars that indicated where the burglar had struck. Bias repeatedly referred to the second-story man as "The Phantom". Only, he said "Phanthum" rather than Phantom.

Bill Kelley and I laughed silently as Bias repeated "Phanthum" time and again. The briefings went on for days and the

"Phanthum" was still at large. Each day, at the station, when we began to edit film, I would laugh and say to Bill, "Let's get the 'Phanthum' thing together!" Then I would repeat "Phanthum" every time we mentioned the story in the newsroom. Sure enough, I introduced the story on-air one night by saying, "Chief Dallas Bias said today that the 'Phanthum' is still at large."

Once, Bill and I were at FMC Chemicals in South Charleston during a rather vicious strike and we found ourselves surrounded by threatening workers as Kelley filmed them throwing rocks and accosting guards at the plant site. Realizing Bill had recorded their angry demonstration, they demanded film Bill had shot.

Bill tried a ploy—he opened his camera door, took out yet-to-be exposed film, and handed it over. The striker was on to Bill. He looked at the camera and asked Bill, "Now, which way does the film run in that camera?" Bill grinned, took the exposed film that had recorded the violence out of the camera, and handed it over. Nice try, though. Bill Kelley was the real thing.

Kelley and I were riding one evening with Detective Bob Crouse as Crouse prepared to raid a liquor club. Crouse saw a vehicle race across railroad tracks and up Twilight Drive. He suspected the driver was a person wanted for stealing cigarettes from a warehouse in the area and he gave chase. Bill and I bounced around in the back seat as Crouse flew up the road, taking curves on two wheels, turning on the siren and forcing the fleeing car to the side of the road.

Crouse arrested the driver and ordered Bill out of his seat—placing the fugitive between Bill and me as Bill got back in the car. Bill said later his only thought was that with Kelley and Ryan guarding the guy, escape would not be a problem.

In 1961 Kelley had covered a major flood in Charleston that killed 21 people. Martial law was declared in the area. Bob Crouse had a girlfriend in the Coonskin Park sector of the flood and the detective became jealous that a National Guard Captain who carried a pistol on his hip had assisted his lady friend.

Crouse confronted the National Guard Captain, pulling him bodily from the jeep he and the lady were utilizing and threatened the guardsman. The soldier pulled his .45 and shot between Crouse's legs—the shot missed a sensitive target but Crouse got the message and fled the area. Later, he was reduced to walking a beat as punishment for causing the showdown.

Bias and Crouse sued the *Charleston Gazette* after it had published charges that had been made against both men as speculation emerged about alleged payoffs around town. Crouse was indicted when a federal investigation was launched out of Pittsburgh with future Kanawha County Prosecuting Attorney and Charleston Mayor Mike Roark leading the probe. Crouse was indicted for payoffs, convicted and sentenced to three years in prison.

CHAPTER 32

Kelley & Ryan Give Chase

ONE MUNICIPAL ELECTION DAY BILL Kelley captured on film vote-buying at the city's Chandler School precinct. Bill's film showed a polling official accompanying one voter after another into the polling booth. Bill filmed their entry and panned down to show four feet at the bottom of the booth's curtain as it was swept closed. His film continued to roll when the curtain opened and two people exited the booth.

I was with Bill and I ran the film on the 1:00 p.m. newscast and prepared to run it again at 6:00. However, the rug was pulled out from under us at 5:00 when station management dictated we could not use the story again—the powers that be feared it would place the station in danger of a lawsuit. But, voter fraud it was and the following week both Bill and I were called before a grand jury to show the film and testify to what had occurred. As we waited to testify, we shared a waiting room with the vote buyers.

In that room a man and woman who were the subjects of our film gave us hard looks and we shuddered just a bit. The guy was a well-connected politician and the woman was a sensational looking gal in a yellow dress. I kept whispering to Bill, "Look at the girl in the yellow dress!"—it broke Bill up.

We testified, and both the fellow and the girl were indicted. Later, a judge ruled that there was a flaw in the indictment. He ordered the vote fraud charge reinstated and a new grand jury called. We testified again, but the fix was in. The grand jury dismissed the indictment. Reportedly, one of the grand jurors was a next-door neighbor to the accused fellow. I do not remember if the lady wore the yellow dress in round two. Such was politics in Charleston in the 60s.

Willy Dandy was a local businessman who dabbled in politics. One day he was in Kanawha County Circuit Court facing charges. Bill Kelley and I waited outside the courtroom for Willy and his attorney Chester Lovett. We had a new shoulder-held sound-on-film camera and were prepared to give chase as the duo left the courtroom. They came bounding out past us, and the race was on.

Bill flew across the second floor of the courthouse faster than I. My microphone was jerked from my hand, bouncing on aged tiles. Down the hall and down the steps of the old courthouse we went, the mike bouncing as I repeatedly grabbed for it, catching it briefly, only to lose it time and again as Kelley jerked the camera. It was a circus, and onlookers were laughing out loud as Willy, Chester, Bill and I bobbled along.

We finally caught up with Willy and Chester at the court-house doors where a windbreak between the hall and outer doors forced a backup. A number of visitors and we four court jesters were stuffed like sardines in the windbreak. Obscenities were shouted and pushing ensued as I yelled questions at Willy and Chester, who both ignored me. The doors finally burst open and we all spilled onto the outside steps, film rolling. Bill's final shot was of Willy and Chester hurrying off down Kanawha Boulevard with me in the foreground, solemnly reporting the events of the comical chase.

CHAPTER 33

Mayor John Hutchinson

JOHN HUTCHINSON, A DEMOCRAT, SERVED as Charleston's City Treasurer for four years before being elected Mayor in 1971. I covered his administration from 1971 through August of 1974.

I coined the phrase "Blacktop John" when Hutchinson purchased for the city a cutting- edge street paver that would put down blacktop across the width of a city street in short order, enabling him to pave more streets than any mayor before him.

Hutchinson's vision for the city created Charleston Town Center, ensuring that the retail center of the Kanawha Valley would remain "downtown" rather than move to the suburbs. I worked with him when our firm was hired by Forest City, the Cleveland development giant that built Town Center. I am certain Hutchinson recommended me for the job. Hutchinson was one of the great mayors of Charleston—he never received enough credit for his visionary service.

On March 17, 1980, longtime third district Democratic Congressman John Slack died in office and Hutchinson successfully ran for Slack's seat. Hutchinson's chief of staff began the hiring process for the new congressman's office. Hutchinson's wife Berry then visited D.C. and the chief of staff found he would have to fire some of the newly hired and very attractive secretaries— it was a demand from Berry, who called the women "Baby Dolls". Somehow, the story made it back to Charleston and her admonition was reported in the local papers.

Sadly, John served only from June 1980, until January 3, 1981, when Republican nominee Mick Staton defeated him. Staton successfully used as an issue that Hutchinson had missed several key congressional votes while vacationing on Hilton Head Island in South Carolina (the "Baby Doll" story also became an issue that hurt John). Staton himself would serve only one term. Bob Wise ran for and was elected to replace Staton, returning the congressional seat to the Democratic Party. Wise would then serve nine terms in Congress.

CHAPTER 34

The State Capitol

CHARLESTON'S DOWNTOWN HAD NOTHING ON the activity at the other end of Kanawha Boulevard. The illicit dealings at the statehouse in the 50s and 60s were rampant. Carter McDavid, a former UPI staffer, was Attorney General C. Donald Robertson's press secretary. Carter was hired by CRA when he left the state job he held. Carter told me he was asked several times—by those who eventually were indicted and served prison terms—if he would like to be in on the deals being made. Carter said it all sounded perfectly legitimate to him (he would have insisted on legitimacy) but he turned the offers down because he lacked the hefty entry dollars required to participate. Carter said it was one time that the paltry salary he was being paid was a blessing. Carter was an honest man.

Then there was the state legislator who left the Governor's Mansion one night with a bag full of money to dispense in a southern West Virginia election war.

The legislator got in his car with the money, had a heart attack, and died. Later in the evening State Capitol security guards checked the car—parked in the circle outside the mansion—and discovered the dearly departed behind the wheel. Urgent calls were made and, somehow, the car was found the next morning in another circle—this one just outside the north side of the statehouse where legislators parked their cars. Inside the automobile was the dead legislator. The bag of money was nowhere to be found.

The cavernous walls of the statehouse in years gone by hosted a hotbed of beautiful girls hired from the hills and hollows. They were housed in small cubicle offices in the building's basement. They were referred to as the "Mole People" and they generally left the office by 3:00 in the afternoon, after their nails had dried, readying for an evening with a state department head.

The penthouse of the downtown Daniel Boone hotel was tightly linked with the legislature. One Friday night there was a large gathering in one of the bathrooms of the luxury suite. A birthday party was being staged for a member of the House of Delegates by his fellow committee members.

Somehow, the *Charleston Gazette* got wind of the story, second hand, and the following Monday morning the newspaper printed details of the evening. The story carried an eyewitness report that a local prostitute called *The Porpoise* had submerged her bottom in a bathtub as members of the legislature looked on, fascinated, as she lay naked and prepared to perform a special expertise.

The eyewitness said in the *Gazette* report that the lady upon whom the legislators were fixated proceeded to fill her "nether regions" with water. She then pushed her hips together, spouting from the aforesaid "nether regions" a large gush of water—straight toward the ceiling. Applause followed. Needless to say, many Monday *Gazette* newspapers were kept out of sight of the wives of legislators who had witnessed this marvel of nature.

My good friend from my hometown of Keyser, Bob Harman, represented Mineral County in the 1950s. Bob relates the story of fellow delegate T.I. Varney of Mingo County as a "leaner". Bob said he left the House Chamber one day to speak with a lobbyist and when he returned, he walked down the center aisle of the House, encountering Varney, who was leaning precipitously from his number 100 aisle seat, face beet red, blocking Bob's way.

"Excuse me, T.I.," Bob said, attempting to pass.

"Harman, come here," T. I. beckoned.

"Yeah, T.I.?"

Whereupon T.I. showed Bob a pistol he had on his person. T.I. pointed to nearby Delegate Heyward Chambers and said, "See Chambers over there?"

"Yes, T.I.," Bob responded.

"I'm think I'm gonna' shoot him right between the eyes!" T.I. said.

"I don't think I'd do that, T.I.," Bob said.

T.I. holstered his pistol.

Delegate Chambers was watching the encounter and asked Bob what T.I. had said to him.

Bob said, "He told me to have a good day."

Harman roomed at the old Ruffner Hotel during his time in the legislature and one evening as he and fellow delegate Bill Nicely returned to their rooms, they heard loud moaning and groaning coming from yet another delegate's hotel room several doors down.

Concerned, they hurried to the room and burst in. The sounds of distress were coming from the bathroom. There, they found a fellow delegate in the bathtub, encased in a sea of ice that was packed tightly around him, preventing his escape. Delegates Harman and Nicely were stunned, but were able to pull the poor fellow from the ice pack.

They later learned that the elected representative had an early evening argument with his girlfriend who waited until he was taking a bath to haul hotel ice into the room, tossing it into the bathtub as the startled bather slid down into the tub to protect himself. Bad mistake.

Bob said legislators of that era loved their drink (available down at the Liquor Commissioner's office) and their chew. There was a full bar behind the House Chamber but one tippler who represented three counties preferred to hide his own booze in various public bathrooms near the Chamber—behind toilets and anywhere a pint could be stashed. Yet another aged legislator carried with him a spittoon and a hearing aid that was a horn that he held to his ear to catch the voice of orators of the Chamber. He would place the spittoon on the floor at his desk, chew tobacco and spit the tobacco juice dead center of the spittoon with a loud ping that resonated throughout the House of Delegates.

CHAPTER 35

A Phone Call Refused

At WSAZ-TV I was fortunate to swiftly migrate from coverage of Charleston City Hall, the police beat and feature stories to politics and coverage of the West Virginia statehouse. Bill Marland, Governor W.W. "Wally" Barron's predecessor, was the state's first governor to encounter television coverage and WSAZ's Bob Horan told me that Marland conducted his news conferences as he always had, by leaning back in his chair, putting his feet up on his desk, grinning, and saying, "What can I do for you boys?"

Marland served as governor from 1957-1961 and left office an alcoholic. He disappeared from the public eye after stepping down. The *Chicago Tribune* found him—he was driving a cab.

The *Tribune* story wound its way to West Virginia through the state's foremost investigative reporter, Jim Haught of the *Charleston Gazette*. A *Tribune* reporter told Haught he thought he had found Marland driving a cab. Jim asked the *Tribune* reporter to call the *Gazette* city desk—collect—when and if the story was confirmed.

The call came on a Sunday when Ed Peeks was manning the *Gazette* city desk. No one had alerted Ed of the potential blockbuster call and when the operator said, "Collect—will you accept?" Ed refused to accept the charges. The Associated Press in Chicago then picked up the *Tribune's* story and sent it out over the wire early Monday morning. Bulletin bells began to ring on the Teletype in the newsroom of the *Charleston Daily Mail,* and the *Mail* gleefully broke the story that afternoon, scooping the *Gazette.*

Wally Barron followed Marland in office and the first encounter I had with him was at a Christmas party at the Governor's Mansion. Barron, from Elkins, was always cordial. I shook Wally's hand and he asked, in a nasal voice, "How old are you, son?"

"I'm 22, Governor," I replied. Wally shook his head and said, "Nobody's 22."

Fifty-five years later, at 77, I have to agree with Wally—nobody's 22.

During Barron's tenure Jack Kennedy was assassinated. That day, after completing the 1:00 television newscast, I checked the wire for any late developments, found none, and headed out the door for lunch at the Press Club.

The club receptionist came to my table and asked me if I knew anything about the President being shot. I laughed and told her that was baloney; I had just left the station, and there was no such story on the wire.

A few minutes later, the receptionist came back and said the radio was saying the President had been shot in Dallas. I walked to the front desk, heard the report, and dashed out the door toward the station.

I gathered a sound crew and we rushed to the Governor's Mansion where Governor Barron was just getting the news. We followed the governor to the statehouse and I interviewed him on the way; shock was everywhere. Barron knew Kennedy personally because of the importance West Virginia had to the President as a result of the 1960 presidential primary. Barron was devastated and had little to say except that West Virginia had lost a great and true friend.

At Christmas each year Barron, a former liquor commissioner, would call a news conference and, at the end of the session, say, "Boys, Walter has a little Christmas cheer for you." Whereupon Walter Ferguson, the African American messenger for the governor's office, would come through the door with two suitcases. Walter, a short little guy—no more than 5-2, if that—was always a cheery fellow. He knew all about the Governor and his office and once witnessed two members of the Board of Public works engage in a fist fight in the Governor's office as Wally Barron sat behind his desk, accepting a Coke from Walter, who had been summoned to bring the governor a soft drink. Wally drank the Coke and watched the fight and Walter departed.

Walter grinned widely at us as he opened the suitcases and begin passing out fifths of liquor to those of us in the fourth estate.

I did not imbibe much at that point but I grabbed a bottle of *Rebel Yell* that Walter offered. I returned to the station with my liquor and proudly showed it to Ken Kurtz. Kurtz frowned and said, "You can't take that."

"Why not?" I asked.

"That's not ethical, free booze from a politician."

Well, he was certainly correct but I did not know how to return it to a statehouse closed for the holidays. I, therefore, put it on the mantle at my apartment and somewhere along the line the contents disappeared. I never gave Wally a break because of the *Rebel Yell*.

CHAPTER 36

Wally Barron

GOVERNOR W.W. BARRON, A FORMER MAYOR of Elkins, left office in early 1965 and opened a law office in Charleston. There was talk on the street that Wally would again be a candidate for governor in 1968. That rumor was put to bed when he and five members of his administration were indicted in February of 1968 in what was called "The St. Valentine's Day Massacre".

Reporters rushed to the federal courthouse when word came down that a grand jury had indicted six men on bribery-conspiracy charges relating to dummy corporations. The five were Clarksburg automobile dealer Alfred Schroath; Bonn Brown, an Elkins attorney and confidant to Barron; State Road Commissioner Burl Sawyers and Sawyers' number two man, Vincent Johnkoski; former State Finance Commissioner Truman Gore, and Governor Barron. The prosecution charged an elaborate kickback scheme for vendors doing business with the state. Prosecutors alleged documents signed by the group indicated they would share equally in the profits.

In the trial that followed, state vendors testified they sent checks to the dummy firms. Surely, Barron was going to jail. Not so: the presiding judge apparently determined that Barron's case was on a little different basis than those of the other defendants, and was said to have seriously considered a directed verdict of acquittal on the basis that the governor acted routinely in signing the agreements without intent of wrongdoing.

The jury was in session for 18 hours and found Barron innocent and four of the other six men guilty. A mistrial was declared for Gore on the eighth day of the trial. Gore remained under indictment but he was not affected by the verdicts of the other five men.

The Associated Press "Flash" bells rang as Opal Barron clutched both hands to her face when she heard the verdict of "innocent" read by jury foreman Ralph Buckalew. I interviewed Barron's lawyer, Robert G. "Joe" Perry, who said he was confident throughout the trial that Barron would be acquitted and he was not at all surprised by the verdict. Stanley Preiser, lawyer for both Sawyers and Johnkoski, told us reporters that, "There was not enough evidence on which to convict, unless the jury was pre-brainwashed as to rumors and had pre-convictions on their minds."

Charleston Gazette staff writer, statehouse reporter, and historian, John Morgan, wrote in the August 31, 1968 *Gazette* the following:

The verdict against Sawyers and Johnkoski apparently meant that the jury believed Isadore Lashinsky, star witness for the U.S. government. Lashinsky, a Charleston businessman under *indictment for income tax evasion, testified that he left $50,000 in sealed envelopes during visits in Johnkoski's office during 1961-63, the period in which the alleged conspiracy flourished. The witness, who testified under immunity from prosecution, said the money was left as commission payments on gross business he did with the state.*

Barron was again indicted in 1970 for allegedly rigging purchasing contracts. He was saved once more when a state Supreme Court decision threw out the indictments.

Then, rumors began that the jury in Barron's original trial had been rigged.

In February of 1971 a federal jury indicted both Barron and his wife, Opal, on charges of bribing the jury foreman. The indictment claimed Mrs. Barron had passed $25,000 in cash in a brown paper bag to the jury foreman as a payoff. The jury foreman pleaded guilty. Mrs. Barron's name was dropped from the indictment and Wally pleaded guilty to conspiracy, bribery, and obstruction of justice. He was sentenced to 25 years in prison but served only four.

I filmed the exit from the courtroom as Wally and Mrs. Barron ran the gauntlet of reporters. Sad day it was to know bribery had occurred and that Opal, a gracious lady whom every reporter liked very much, had allegedly played a part.

After he served four years in jail, Wally and Opal moved to Charlotte, North Carolina, where he died in 2002 and Opal passed away in 2010.

CHAPTER 37

Hulett Smith

MAKING REPORTORIAL ROUNDS AT THE statehouse, I always looked forward to stopping by the office of Governor Hulett Smith's chief of staff, Paul Crabtree. Crabtree seemed to know everything that occurred out of the ordinary around the Capitol grounds and one day he told me he had to fire a department head that had created a problem.

The situation was that a pretty secretary had become the object of the department head's admiration and his quest had become semi-public. Crabtree explained that a commotion was heard late one afternoon in the agency head's office. As the ruckus grow louder by the moment, a concerned staffer swung his boss' door open, revealing the department head chasing his secretary around his desk, screaming at her, "What you need is a good horse f—k!"

Crabtree said, tongue in cheek, "We did not fire him for his intentions, but for his utter lack of finesse."

Jack Canfield told me that Crabtree once pointed to Governor Smith's first press secretary, Con Hardman, as he watched Con walk out of the statehouse and down the steps, saying, "Con descending, Con descending, Con descending." Crabtree was a wry and funny guy.

Hulett Smith was a fine man and good governor. However, he was a tough act when it came to news conferences and sound on film (SOF). I would regularly return from his news conferences and spend an inordinate amount of time trying to edit his comments; Hulett did not speak in separate sentences. He tended to run one sentence into the next and there were no natural pauses to edit the remarks. I often asked WSAZ-TV photographer Bill Kelley to give me twenty seconds of Hulett's SOF remarks—any twenty seconds—followed by thirty seconds of silent film that I could use to do a voice-over to summarize the governor's remarks.

Hulett regularly would stop by the statehouse pressroom to chat with reporters. This sometimes created news and we welcomed this informal contact with the genial fellow from Beckley. Some of Hulett's staffers frowned on the uncontrolled media access—but Hulett was not one to be confined.

Jack Canfield remembered those days this way: "There was a press room next to the press secretary's office. It wasn't unusual to see Governor Smith stop in and chat on his way out of the Capitol at the end of the day with the likes of Herb Little and Bob Mellace and Charlie Ryan and Ed Rabel—all outstanding writers and reporters."

Well, maybe we were not always so outstanding. On one summer afternoon Hulett stopped by our reporter's den and the questions began, with Hulett gamely responding. Occasionally, a disembodied voice would sound off with a question and the governor would glance around, wondering from whence the inquiry came. He nevertheless answered it, and then bid us good afternoon and departed. As Hulett left, a grinning Jim Ragsdale of the *Associated Press* slid out from under a massive desk where he had been hiding and we all broke into laughter.

A closely guarded news release was being prepared in the governor's office after Hulett was successful in convincing Angus Peyton, a well-respected attorney of a pioneer Kanawha Valley family, to accept a role as the governor's Commerce Commissioner. The partially finished press release was on Jack Canfield's desk when Strat Douthat of the *Associated Press* entered Jack's office. Jack turned away for a short time to retrieve something for Strat and Strat read the salient parts of the release upside down, a trait of all good reporters. Peyton's appointment was soon a scoop on the AP Teletype—before it ever left Canfield's office. Jack was not pleased, but I have to think the reporter in him understood Strat's methodology.

Smith was always a fashion plate. He once made the "Best Dressed Men of 1965" list of the Fashion Foundation of America, along with Cary Grant and President Johnson. Hulett lived a long and distinguished life and died at the age of 94. Canfield was more than an excellent press secretary for Smith. He was close to the Governor and Mrs. Smith and their five children, and he was very protective of the family.

Jack did not have an easy go of it as Hulett's main media man—he had to deal with the fallout of the indictments of

Smith administration officials appointed by Hulett's predecessor, Wally Barron. Years later, in a speech to political science students at WVU, Jack remembered the day: "You're sitting in the press office on Valentine's Day, you're a 27-year-old press secretary to the Governor, the Governor's chief of staff is on vacation at Sanibel with only one pay phone at a nearby grocery store and the phone rings. You get a call that the grand jury has just indicted your party's former governor on conspiracy for bribery charges—former Governor Wally Barron, plus his business associate and lawyer, plus a Clarksburg car dealer—and three of your own administration's department heads: the road commissioner, the finance and administration commissioner and the deputy road commissioner. So you have to dismiss all three. And while it is true that not one of the indictments related to anything that happened in the Smith administration—they were for incidents in the Barron administration—gloom set in. Especially if you were a Democrat on point with the press."

Jack said in his speech to the students "I don't think the basics have changed that much, though. It still goes back to three things: The Message. The Messenger. The Media. And simple declarative sentences in plain English."

Canfield later became a member of the House of Delegates and his fascination with simple, declarative sentences was heightened. One day he finished a floor speech with these comments: "As Delegate Sammy Dalton once said on the floor of the House of Delegates when we were in the middle of a hot debate, 'After all, Mr. Speaker, that's what our forefathers 'n ever-thing handed down all that stuff for.' "

On reading Jack's quote of Sammy, I thought of Jim Comstock who once described to me the manner in which West Virginians speak as—"Elizabethan English—English as she is spoke."

In October of 1968 I wrote a column for the *Beckley Post Herald* where I reported on a meeting in the reception area of Governor Smith's office with 30 state department heads, a guest, and the governor. The meeting was closed, but most unusual, with the session interrupted by rounds of applause from Smith's appointed team. The gathering behind the reception room doors could be heard down the halls of the statehouse. Upon inquiry, Smith's press secretary, Jack Canfield, told me it was just a political pep talk—the governor did that from time to time, he said.

The speaker was Francis Burch, Maryland's attorney general, who had been busy working with Hubert Humphrey, candidate for president. Paul Crabtree, Governor Smith's assistant, was present for the meeting and he told me that Burch informed the attendees that he, Burch, would have an excellent chance to become governor of Maryland, should Hubert Humphrey be elected president—taking Spiro Agnew out of the Maryland governor's chair.

Paul related that Governor Smith strode back and forth across the reception area during the meeting, saying it would take a maximum election effort to keep the state Democratic.

The man running for governor on the Democratic ticket was Jim Sprouse, and the Republican nominee was Arch Moore.

Smith, Crabtree told me, said those in the room should get the message out that Arch *meant it* when he said he would fire all the folks currently holding statehouse jobs. Crabtree informed me that Smith said the people at lower levels of state government needed to get out and work hard. Crabtree said it was a unity speech with no coercion on civil service employees.

He then reminded me that the Hatch Act had changed to the point that civil service employees could participate in politics more than they used to. In the column I called Crabtree *"Governor Number One"*, and Governor Smith, *"Governor Number Two"*. I was trying to impress that, in my opinion, Crabtree called a number of shots for the governor.

Well, I went, I must confess, a bit overboard in my column. I wrote that Governor Smith was "panting" for a position in the Humphrey administration, should Humphrey win. I waxed on, saying the political meeting took place under a "tinkling taxpayer's chandelier". I wrote that the department heads sat in the governor's "state paid and operated reception room" where Smith said Sprouse would be superior in every way to Arch Moore. I reported that Smith smiled passively. The *Post Herald* played it big—the headline on my column said, *"Democrats Hold "Big Rally" In Governor's Suite"*.

Not surprisingly, the governor and his folks did not appreciate my column and there was reaction in the office. Smith, ever the gentleman, just shrugged it off. But, Canfield and his assistant press secretary Nancye Bazzle were pretty angry with me. They chose not to be public about their distaste for my remarks, they simply took out their frustration by privately writing a wonderful rejoinder to my young and brash commentary.

Their creation has never been seen by anyone but Nancye and Jack—until now. They have given me the privilege of making public their hilarious spoof of a young Charlie Ryan, who fashioned himself an intrepid investigative reporter:

<u>Capitol Candor</u>
REPORTER PREVENTED FROM DISCUSSING POLITICS IN "NEW" CAPITOL

By
Mr. Clean
Defender of Unclean Politics

Charleston—A meeting took place at the statehouse last week that should not go unreported simply because it was so unusual.

At about 9 a.m. last Monday, the big gun of the Charleston Press Corps, Charles Ryan, drove up Duffy Street in his SAZ-mobile, and pulled up to his parking place, paid for by the taxpayers, and protected by a guard, also paid for by the taxpayers.

The guard smiled passively as the SAZ-mobile pulled into its space, and he watched as Ryan deftly opened the door and charged into the capitol corridors.

Ryan wore an assured smile as he entered the pressroom of the state capitol, maintained for the press by the taxpayers' dollar. He sat down on a taxpayers' chair, and picked up the taxpayers' telephone, and called the governor's press secretary—whose salary is paid for by the taxpayers.

"Jack," Charlie said, "I, as a taxpaying reporter, demand an interview with Governor Smith."

"I'll see what I can do," Canfield said, as he leaned toward his secretary and asked, "I wonder what Ryan's up to today?"

Within a few minutes, Canfield entered the pressroom and told Ryan:

"The governor will see you now, Charlie. You realize, of course, that this will have to be short, since the governor has been spending most of his time panting hard for a position in the new Humphrey administration."

"I understand how things are," Ryan grimly replied. "I spent several months here in Charleston panting for a job with a wire service; Then, I spent several more months panting to get out of the wire service. Then, I panted for St. Louis. Then, I panted hard for any kind of job with SAZ. You see what I got."

Canfield, press secretary Number One, smile gamely and said, convincingly, "I understand."

The two walked across the corridors, kept clean by the taxpayers' janitors, and entered the governor's reception room.

As they closed the big doors to the room, they heard the taxpayers' chandelier above their heads begin to tinkle.

"Uh, oh," said Canfield, cautiously.

"The last time that happened we were discussing politics in this room."

Ryan flinched.

They entered the governor's office where Hulett Smith was seated, going through the *Congressional Directory*, panting hard, trying, obviously, to figure out what position he would hold in the Humphrey administration.

"Hi, Charlie, how's tricks?" the governor said, winking.

Ryan flinched again.

"Governor, I know things have changed a little since our last visit, but I was wondering if you could give me your evaluation of the political situation?"

"Charlie," Smith said kindly, "You know I want to help the press whenever I can. But ever since I put the governorship under Civil Service, it has become very difficult, indeed, to discuss politics.

"And I wouldn't dream of doing such a nasty thing as that while I am seated here in this wonderful chair, provided for me by the taxpayers of West Virginia. I know you would not want me to violate the trust they have placed in me.

"You and I know how upset they were when they learned that their governor had talked about politics with his team back in October," the governor said.

"Yes, I remember that," Ryan said. "Let's see," he added, "that was the meeting you failed to invite me to attend."

At this point, Smith felt forced to smile, and explained:

"Yes, Charlie. That meeting was for members of my team. Had I known all along that you were on my side, I assure you, you would have been invited. Of course, that's all past history now. Under our new policy, we cannot discuss politics any longer— under the tinkling taxpayers' chandelier in the reception room."

"Well, then, let's move on to another subject," Ryan said, gamely. "Since you won't permit any discussion of politics, how do you expect the Democrats to get your program, proposed by the Democratic Party, through the legislature?"

"Charlie, my son," Hulett said, almost apologetically, "I'm sorry. I can't discuss that either. I remember the days when I used to call in the leaders of the legislature to talk turkey about legislation. But, alas, you mentioned the word 'politics' again, and I simply will not stand for such a distasteful subject to be discussed while I sit at my taxpayers' desk. They might resent their governor mentioning politics, you know."

"But, Governor, how can we run campaigns without politics?" Ryan asked.

"Well, Charlie, I guess we'll just have to appoint all our officials. You know, of course, that the governorship is now under

Civil Service. I am considering putting members of the legislature under Civil Service as well."

Ryan sighed, not even acknowledging the governor's remarks.

He lifted himself from the taxpayers' chair, and shuffled across the taxpayers' carpet, through the reception room, beneath the tinkling taxpayers' chandelier.

Later, in the taxpayers' pressroom, he poured himself a tall cup of coffee, made in the taxpayers' coffee pot, and picked up the phone.

He gingerly dialed Huntington, once he got the taxpayers' tie-line, and heard the unmistakable Brinkley-type voice on the other end.

"Bos?" Charlie asked with anticipation.

"No, this is Carl Haberly. You see, I imitate Bos Johnson, who imitates David Brinkley. Just a moment and I'll get Bos on the line."

Charlie waited.

"Bos, I wish the old days were here again," he sighed. "Ever since I wrote that column about the tinkling taxpayers' chandelier and the public rose up with such indignation that Hulett Smith would ever discuss politics in the state capitol, he refuses to discuss any political theory at all on public property."

"But, Charlie, didn't Underwood do the same thing? And Barron? I mean, like, what do you expect, tea parties every afternoon at 4:00?"

"No, Bos, that wouldn't be possible. You see, the taxpayers would have to pay for the tea, and..."

"Charlie, what brought this about?"

"Bos, it's the NEW politics. You see, it's politics without politics. It's a..."

At that moment, Mrs. Bazzle, taxpayers' press secretary Number Two, walked into the pressroom.

"I'm very sorry, Mr. Ryan," she said, sternly, "but I overheard you mention politics on this telephone that is being paid for by the taxpayers. You'll have to refrain from using such a word in this capitol."

Resigned to failure, Ryan stood up and threw his empty coffee cup into the taxpayers' trashcan.

He entered the hallway, where he could faintly hear a panting sound coming from the governor's office.

Defeated and rejected and dejected, he entered his SAZ-mobile and went on to seek more fertile ground elsewhere.

He has an appointment tomorrow with Spiro Agnew.

Jack and Nancye deep-sixed their excellent spoof and it remained in Nancye's file cabinet for the next 49 years. I wish they had demanded equal space from the *Post Herald*, allowing the "taxpayers" of the state to see how they had adroitly nailed a young reporter who may have been too impressed with himself.

I loved their creative and hilarious rejoinder to my printed words—and we are great friends these 47 years later.

While most folks thought highly of Hulett Smith, Attorney General C. Donald Robertson was not one of them. Denny Vaughan was an assistant attorney general in Robertson's office when Robertson was running for governor in the 1968 Democratic primary against Jim Sprouse. Denny said Robertson, known for his huge ego, had for some time sought the sitting governor's endorsement in the race. Hulett had stalled and Robertson became very angry that Smith would not quickly offer an endorsement to him.

Denny was sitting in the AG's office when Hulett called Robertson. Hulett informed C. Donald that he had finally decided to make an endorsement in the primary race and asked Don to come to his office. Denny accompanied Robertson on the long walk from the Attorney General's east wing office to the west wing where the Governor's office was located—Robertson doing a slow burn all the way.

Hulett welcomed Robertson and Vaughan warmly and asked that they sit. The governor smiled broadly, did some small talk, and said in a magnanimous tone that he had finally decided to endorse Robertson in the primary. Robertson, infuriated, rose from his chair on the opposite side of the governor's desk and practically spat at Hulett, saying with clinched jaw, and tight fists, "Hulett, I'd rather have a case of the clap!" and walked out.

CHAPTER 38

Arch Moore

JIM SPROUSE SAID HE KNEW Arch Moore was going to beat him in the 1968 gubernatorial race when Congressman Moore's helicopter crashed into a ball field in the tiny town of Hamlin in southern West Virginia on November 3, 1968, the day before the general election. The grisly crash resulted in massive media coverage and voter sympathy for the gutsy Moore who was carried from an ambulance on a stretcher, placed in a wheelchair, and wheeled into Charleston General Hospital.

On that day I heard the newsroom Associated Press Teletype bells begin to ring, designating a flash story: "Gubernatorial candidate Arch Moore's helicopter has crashed and Moore is being rushed to trauma care at Charleston General Hospital," the bulletin read. I summoned a photographer to break out the sound-on-film equipment and rushed to Charleston General Hospital, pulling into the emergency room ambulance entrance with tires squealing.

I knew from the wire stories that Moore's helicopter had crashed when striking a flagpole at the Lincoln County ball field. The helicopter, the news reports said, appeared to be backing up to avoid trees and power lines, and then struck a flag pole and spiraled tail-first 30 feet to the ground. Witnesses said the craft landed on a car, which lessened the impact.

Aboard the helicopter with Moore were Dennis Knapp, at the time a Common Pleas Court Judge in Kanawha County and a candidate for the West Virginia Supreme Court; Louis Wells of Gaithersburg, Maryland, the pilot; and Jack Stafford of Princeton, a prominent Republican and friend of Arch Moore.

When the ambulance doors opened in front of the emergency room entrance, I was there with microphone in hand, pointed at Arch Moore, film rolling.

Ryan: "What did you think of when you were coming down? What thoughts went through your mind?"

Moore: "Well, the only thing, Charlie, that I can say went through my mind was this, and it seems rather foolish—but I was determined to live. I was fighting all the way down that flagpole. I wasn't giving up anywhere along the line. I began to take inventory as we were lying there—first, moving my legs and then seeing if I could breathe. I had some problem breathing."

Moore exited from the ambulance with a broad, although ashen, smile hovering over a "thumbs up" that he flashed to us as we recorded the scene and broadcast it state and nationwide. Arch insisted he be placed in a wheelchair rather than enter the hospital on a gurney—in what I believe was an effort to show he had survived in splendid fashion and was fit to be governor. I also believe Arch moved to his "survival mode" when his chopper crashed, much as he had done when critically wounded in World War II. He was a man of incredible will and determination. He could compartmentalize a situation, as he would often do in his life. He suffered only minor injuries, as did the others on the helicopter.

Sprouse later told me he was driving from one campaign stop to the next on that day before the election. Jim said upon hearing a radio bulletin about Moore's crash his first instinct was to turn his steering wheel sharply to the left and plunge over the side of the mountain. Jim, and others, seemed to think the crafty Moore, if he was destined to have a helicopter crash, had scheduled it the day before the election. Timing was everything.

CHAPTER 39

Covering Arch

ARCH MOORE HANDILY BEAT JIM SPROUSE in 1968 and became the 30th governor of the State of West Virginia. Moore was a favorite of mine, and I believe he felt the same of me. He loved to bait the media. On one occasion Arch had banned reporters from a meeting of the Board of Public Works. WSAZ's Bob Brunner and I (I was at WCHS at the time) accosted Arch as he left the board room. Brunner jabbed his microphone at the governor and demanded to know why the meeting was closed, etc., etc. Arch looked at Bob and said, "Aw, grow up, Bob!"

It's not as funny in print, but, damn, it was funny at the time. I had the encounter on film and audiotape and I turned the audio over to WCHS morning disc jockey Al Sahley and, for months, in the middle of Sahley's programs Arch Moore would say, on tape, "Aw, grow up, Bob!" Brunner took it in stride and actually enjoyed it, quoting the encounter in his memoirs.

During the Nixon wage freeze, the orders came down at WCHS that my news budget had been cut. I began to ration film—the most costly item in my meager allocation of funds to run a newsroom. During the governor's news conferences I would carefully restrict the film being shot—as opposed to the former practice of freely rolling film as the governor talked.

Moore knew all. He was acutely aware that I was tapping my photographer on the knee when I wanted film to roll or stop. As he was making what he thought to be an important statement he noted my camera was silent. He stopped in mid-sentence and looked at me and said, "What's the matter, Mr. Ryan? Doesn't Rollins Broadcasting let you spend any money on film?"

I swallowed hard and chose to reply by saying, loud enough for the governor to hear, "Roll it!" Moore smiled.

Moore was a joy to cover. He loved to banter with reporters and would chastise us if we were not up to speed on political and governmental events and many news conferences became great sport because of the exchanges between reporters and Arch. A special nemesis was the *Charleston Gazette* and Publisher Ned Chilton who simply detested Moore.

On one occasion when Arch had accomplished one of his many wins in battles with the legislature he was congratulated, and one supporter reckoned that even the *Gazette* would have to give him accolades. Moore wagged his finger at the fellow and said, "No, no, no! If I, Arch Moore, were to hear from the Governor's Mansion the screams of a drowning child in the Kanawha River and rushed from the mansion, walked across the water, and saved the child, the headline in the *Gazette* the next morning would be, 'Moore Can't Swim'."

Arch called the *Gazette* "The Morning Sick Call" and I think Chilton and the *Gazette* staff kind of liked the digs. Ace statehouse reporter Fanny Seiler was the *Gazette's* hard-digging journalist and fire-breathing columnist who regularly fricasseed politicians; but Fanny had a soft spot in her heart for Arch because the governor knew the one thing Fanny could not abide was refusal to answer her calls—and he returned all of them.

Many a politician met his political death because they ignored Fanny. Moore's office door was always open to her as he confided to her many stories that were scoops —molding her into an asset. I think she loved the guy. Such was Moore's ability to cajole.

Arch was 5-7 but when he entered a room, immaculately dressed, he commanded it. He had an uncanny knack of remembering names and events and would grab your hand, shake it, and subtly pull you toward him. It was simply a remarkable experience.

Larry Tucker, president of the State Senate while Arch was governor in his third term, told me he asked for a meeting with the governor after he and Moore had butted heads during a general election. Upon entering the recently-elected Moore's office, Tucker removed his belt and placed it on Arch's desk, saying, "I'm ready for my whipping." Arch loved it.

West Virginia visionary wildwater rafting pioneer Dave Arnold once retained Arch when the governor was between terms. Arnold needed Moore's assistance—he had asked the CSX Railroad to grant his company an easement across a right-of-way of the railroad and CSX had refused. At the time, Arch was widely considered to be a candidate for re-election in the next election cycle.

Arch took Arnold's case and moved quickly to call his friend, CSX CEO John Snow. "Arch!" Snow greeted the governor— "John!" Arch replied.

Snow agreed to investigate and get back to the governor. Several days went by before Snow returned Arch's call, saying he was sorry, but the easement could not be granted.

There was a heavy silence on Arch's end of the line and Snow finally said, "Governor? Are you there?" Whereupon Moore replied, "Mr. Snow, the way I see it, the score is now—CSX, 1, Arch Moore, 0." And Moore hung up the phone.

Within five minutes Moore's phone rang and he answered it. On the other end of the line was John Snow who said, "Governor, John Snow. We don't like the score."

Arnold got his easement.

CHAPTER 40

Hike & Lysander

GOVERNOR ARCH MOORE ATTRACTED GREAT talent to his team. He was fortunate in the 1972 election to have young, handsome, Edgar "Hike" Heiskell, III, running for the office of Secretary of State. Hike was a political neophyte, but with his dashing good looks, wit, charm, sartorial splendor, and friendly demeanor, he caught the public's fancy.

"I Like Hike" was his campaign slogan and, at 32, he became the first Republican to be elected secretary of state in West Virginia since 1928.

Hike and I often reminisced about our early clash and his entry into the world of politics—a decision that led him straight into the jaws of political journalism, encountering the likes of Ned Chilton and Don Marsh at the *Charleston Gazette*, Bob Mellace at the *Charleston Daily Mail* and Charlie Ryan at WCHS-TV.

My first encounter with the dashing young man from Morgantown—a combat qualified F-102 fighter pilot —was shortly after Governor Moore recruited him to run for office.

Jay Rockefeller was secretary of state at the time but would leave that post to run for governor against Moore. Hike said he had caught 'the fever' after attending a top-secret meeting with Moore and a handful of his closest cabinet officials at The Greenbrier.

Hike said, " I faced a well-financed businessman from Beckley, Tom Winner, who had Rockefeller's blessing and traveled around the state in a big, shiny Winnebago motor home that dwarfed my Plymouth station wagon. Caught up in the excitement of the moment, it hadn't occurred to me that (1) it had been forty-four years since West Virginia had last elected a Republican as secretary of state, (2) Democrats outnumbered Republicans by 3-to-1, and (3) I had never been in a single one of the counties south of Route 60 and had no name recognition anywhere."

A former prosecutor in Monongalia County, Hike was a political nobody with just $38,000 to finance a campaign he secretly believed to be doomed—his war chest was way too small for paid television advertising, the mother's milk of politics. So it was that when a rumor of political skullduggery surfaced in the southern part of the state, Hike pounced on the opportunity for "free" media.

He said, "Three days before the election, I issued a press release in which I claimed that a notorious group of Democrats in Logan County had set aside a secret fund of more than $100,000 for the express purpose of buying votes on election day. I called for the State Police to descend upon the county and seize the money, and reminded readers that, as a former prosecutor, I was much more qualified than my opponent to take on the task of election reform in our beloved state."

Hike tuned in WCHS-TV's 6:00 newscast that night to reap the reward of "free" television exposure, only to be hit with a sledgehammer as my commentary at the close of the newscast questioned the factual basis for his allegations. Hike told me, "As I listened, you posed one question after another that showed I had not identified any of the alleged perpetrators. In essence, you were saying I had made the whole thing up! My psyche was wounded for the very first time, after a nine-month campaign."

Hike was quick to respond, asking WCHS-TV for "equal time" under the Federal Communications Commission Fairness Doctrine to answer my comments. Hike was eloquent in his "free" commentary response—he was one of those candidates that the camera loved.

He said the three minutes equal time just days before the election was worth thousands of dollars—critical to his election as secretary of state. Hike won with a margin of one percent, a victory that was thought to be virtually impossible, given his handicap of scarce dollars and a recognition factor that was incredibly low at the outset of the campaign.

Yes, he had the help of the Arch Moore-Richard Nixon Republican coattails in that 1972 election, but I agree with Hike that his commentary provided a push at the end of the election cycle that created an additional reason for southern West Virginia voters to "Like Hike"—awarding him a slim victory. Those voters were treated to his good looks, sartorial and personal style, tons of charm, and the ability to communicate through television in the manner of a John Kennedy—Hike was made for TV.

A native of Morgantown, Hike left office after three years to return to the practice of law where he went on to become nationally known as a fierce opponent to automobile companies accused of defects that were alleged to have caused roll-overs and sudden acceleration.

Hike passed away in 2016, leaving a lasting legacy of political involvement and public advocacy that was admired and appreciated by countless Mountaineers. He was a special friend to me—a friendship that was borne out of an initial confrontation in an era when Republicans seldom won political office in West Virginia.

He and I texted during his brief illness and his last response to me was simply a moving example of his prowess as a writer. He said: "Upside, liberated from law practice; time to reflect and write and have more time to speak with friends and loved ones. Would love to join you for a cup of espresso some morning. Be assured I am secure in my spiritual existence in this universe. Thanks for your concern and enduring friendship." They were beautiful words from a beautiful man.

Yet another Moore notable was Lysander Dudley who became Arch's commerce commissioner. Dud, as he was known by one and all, was a totally charming man who always had a smile. He and his wife were bridge-playing partners with Arch and his wife Shelley. Dud loved Broadway, even acting in many musicals produced by the Kanawha Players. Dud was thrilled when, during his term as Commissioner, John Denver recorded *Country Roads*. Dud worked the phones and made the contacts, cajoleing Denver to come to Charleston to perform. He then took Denver to Morgantown and Mountaineer Field at West Virginia University where Denver sang the song to thousands beside a beaming Lysander Dudley.

When Dud first took office he knew I was a persistent reporter who would probe unmercifully when interviewing a newsmaker. So it was that on the first occasion when I sought an interview with him on some controversial subject that Dud refused to open his door to me. I countered by doing a "stand-up" outside his office door, noting that Dudley would not open his door to media.

I did the same on the next night's newscast and each night for a total of four days—Dud called me on day five and said he gave in. I did the interview, treated him well, and reviewed the standoff with humor, effectively patting him on the back.

For many years after he left office Dud and I would speak by telephone from time to time. I sat watching Larry King one night and was moved to call the show when King was discussing Lyndon Johnson. Incredibly, my call was accepted almost immediately and I reminisced about Johnson calling the Washington NBC owned and operated station after 11:00 newscasts to bombast anchor Robert Goralski when Johnson did not like the tone of his report on Johnson's presidency.

My name was not used on the call but a few minutes after my conversation with King my phone rang and Dud said, "That was you, Ryan, wasn't it?"

We were great friends throughout his term and his service as president of the West Virginia University Foundation and beyond, until his death at 83 in January of 2015.

CHAPTER 41

Arch Stories

WHEN I ENTERED BUSINESS IN 1974 Arch Moore was in the middle of his second term. He always went out of his way to promote me when we crossed paths at various events and said complimentary things about my firm as he crisscrossed the state. He was extremely kind to my effort and me, partly because we connected as personalities, and partly because, I believe, he admired my spunk to go out on my own.

Arch died in January of 2015. Shortly after he passed, Becky and I were on a car ferry to St. Thomas, returning from St. John in the U.S. Virgin Islands. Once there we were to fly to Charlotte and then drive home to Hilton Head Island. On the ferry I received a call from Charlie Capito, the husband of Arch's daughter, the newly-elected United Sates Senator, Shelley Moore Capito, who told me Arch had passed. I gave my condolences to Charlie and asked he convey them to Shelley. Charlie said it was remarkable that Arch, 91, had waited until the day after Shelley was sworn in as a United States Senator, to die.

Charlie said Shelley had asked him to call me to see if I would be willing to come to Charleston to preside over a memorial service for Governor Moore. "I know it may be presumptuous of us to ask, knowing you are in Hilton Head," he said. I assured Charlie I was honored to be asked and would certainly be there.

The service was elegant and participants included Governor Earl Ray Tomblin, Arch Moore III, Senator Joe Manchin, Tom Tinder (Moore's Welfare Secretary), and myself. In my remarks I related my role in the *Third House* parody of the Legislature in which I played the role of Governor Moore with my hair colored white with baby powder. I was hauled into the House Chamber on a carrying chair worthy of a Pharaoh. I had my scepter in my hand—a commode plunger.

As we moved down the aisle toward the Speaker's podium I feigned striking Cabell County Senator Bobby Nelson around the head and shoulders. Bobby was a major Democrat and foe of Arch and the crowd got it—and Bobby was a good sport. I ascended to the Speaker's platform and gave a rousing speech with all the Moore phrases I could muster. He was known for, time after time, making a statement in a news conference, pausing, and following up with a terse look at the camera, and saying, "And I mean that in *every sense* of the word."

I, of course, pounced on the words many times in my parody, saying, "And I mean that in everyyyyyy sensssse of the word!" At the end of my speech I broke into song, singing, "If I Ruled The World." The *Third House* was loved by Arch—but not by some of the other politicians present—particularly Secretary of State Jay Rockefeller who was portrayed by newsman Bob Brunner—playing Jay as a bit swishy.

Arch was a mighty governor with mighty faults. He served three years of a prison term, pleading guilty to extortion, mail and tax fraud and obstruction of justice, but West Virginians seemed to agree that he could have been elected to a fourth term if he had been legally able to run again following his incarceration.

I was shocked when he pleaded guilty. He said, "This news will be greeted with a great joy by some in the state of West Virginia. There will be others who will be sincerely grieved by reason of their devotion to me and my family. I know I have their understanding and love. For that, I shall be forever grateful."

I believe that Arch, like many politicians of the era, bounced up against the ethical line and then crossed it in so doing—liberties were taken as he and other old pols believed they were immune to conventional mores. Arch fell victim to omnipotence and he paid a price that many other "line bouncers" did not.

After he served his term in prison he sought reinstatement of his license to practice law, claiming his attorney had given him poor advice that led to his guilty plea. It was not to be.

The Arch Moore the public knew would not have pleaded guilty—he would have been confident he could beat the rap. Some say he copped a plea because federal prosecutors also were threatening to bring charges, unrelated to his activities, against some of the governor's family members. I have no idea if that was true, but I firmly believe there wasn't a jury in West Virginia that would have convicted him had he pleaded innocent. If he had not gone awry, he would have been West Virginia's greatest governor.

CHAPTER 42

Jay Rockefeller

JOHN D. ROCKEFELLER IV STOOD in front of a mirror at Frankenberger's Men's Store in Charleston. Bob McDonough, who always wore a large white Panama straw hat, was Jay's political adviser and he laughingly coaxed Jay to try some lids. Jay considered a fedora but finally nixed the idea; the towering young man McDonough was mentoring did not look all that good in hats.

Rockefeller, however, did look good on a ballot. And Jay soon moved from his VISTA volunteer activities at Emmons, near Charleston, to the political arena. I had the privilege of covering him for many years as a reporter and associating with him as a lobbyist and businessperson.

Jay was not universally loved in West Virginia, however. Many thought of him as a carpetbagger who had come to the state to seek high office in a small state that could be bought. One particular incident showed how deep the feelings went when Charleston attorney and Republican councilman Bill Mohler was stopped on the street by a woman who thought the 6-5 Mohler was Jay Rockefeller. She was effusive in her praise of

Jay and his decision to come to West Virginia. Mohler heard her out, saying nothing until she came to the end of her salute. Mohler looked down at the lady, and decided to take advantage of the fact she thought he was Rockefeller. He addressed her with the saltiest of language and walked off.

When Jay was dating Sharon Percy, daughter of Illinois Senator Charles Percy, he was serving his first term in the West Virginia House of Delegates and he drove a Ford Mustang. He had it parked in the circle of the statehouse where legislators were assigned parking spots (the circle was eliminated many years ago). Jay, ever the student, carried a two-foot high stack of legislative bills to the Mustang, placed the pile atop the car's roof, opened the door, stuffed his 6-7 frame into the small vehicle, and drove off, with legislative bills flying through the air behind the Mustang, decorating streets around the statehouse. I stood there as a reporter and watched him do it. I then wrote a newspaper column relating the incident, attributing it to his mind being on Sharon rather than legislation.

After Jay and Sharon were married they owned his and hers Mercedes Benz. When Jay decided to run for secretary of state, both cars were sold, leaving House Speaker Clyde See to quip that he would not criticize his governor until he had ridden a mile in his Mercedes.

Jay and Sharon's first born, John Davisson (Jamie) Rockefeller V, created quite a stir in the state—today the parents and baby would be on the cover of *People* magazine as they departed Memorial Hospital in Kanawha City. Back then it was just Chet Hawes from the *Charleston Daily Mail*, Ferrell Friend from the *Gazette*, and me, using a Bell and Howell hand held camera, recording the event. Senator Percy was very nice to us and chatted amiably with me about West Virginia. He seemed at ease to just stand there and talk as Jay ushered the group into a waiting sedan. Percy joined the group and they drove away. They were happy parents and grandparents and nice folks. Not even a diaper flew from the top of the car.

To say that Jay was not quite like the rest of us Mountaineers with whom he came to live is an understatement. My good friend Tommy Knight left his employment as a *Charleston Gazette* reporter and joined Rockefeller's Secretary of State staff. Tommy said he was ruminating with Rockefeller one day about personal finances and how he could possibly meet his financial obligations; Rockefeller had the answer: "Why don't you sell some bonds?" Jay asked. Tommy and I had never seen a bond, let alone own one. It was to laugh, and we did.

When Jay took office as Secretary of State he named political operative and former Sistersville Mayor Pete Thaw as his Deputy Secretary of State. Thaw had campaigned for John Kennedy and his brother Bobby. Pete was a witty guy and astute politician. He also had worked for and liked Arch Moore, the sitting governor, whom Jay despised.

I was in the Deputy Secretary of State's office one day and Pete and I got into a discussion of the ill feelings between Jay and Arch, the sitting governor across the hall. Pete expressed his affinity for Arch, looked around with slight unease, and then smiled. He got up from his desk, took his cigarette holder out of his mouth and walked to the door. He closed it and walked back to the couch in his office. He kneeled on the couch, reached behind it, and pulled up a large framed picture of Arch Moore.

Pete had brought it with him when he went to work in Rockefeller's domain, but he knew better than to hang it. However, Pete said, he figured Arch had nine lives and might somehow figure in his future, so, he was not about to let it go. Pete was the go-to guy for reporters in Jay's office. We could not get enough of his wit and political acumen.

Pete moved on to become the State Director of the Comprehensive Employment Training Act and presiding judge of the state Racing Commission. He then retired from state government and successfully ran for the Kanawha County School Board where he continued to have some fun and fought for fiscal responsibility of the county's educational system.

Pete passed away in 2018. Becky Jones Jordon, Pete's fellow school board member, said, "Pete genuinely cared for the kids in the system and he wanted the best education we could give them. He was elected to the board to represent the people of Kanawha County, and he took great pride in that."

CHAPTER 43

Jay & Janet

I REGULARLY INTERVIEWED JAY ROCKEFELLER WHEN he was Secretary of State. Some of those interviews took place in the statehouse pressroom near his office. He was extremely tall compared to my five feet, eight inch height. I hated the "Mutt and Jeff" look when the interviews were aired and I was looking up, up, up. To resolve my vanity issue I finally pulled four West Virginia Blue Books from the bookshelf in the room, standing on them as I conducted my interview. Jay just smiled.

Jay ran for governor and won the primary election in 1972. Arch Moore beat him in the general election. Jay's mantra that "strip mining must go" did not help his effort. His decision to go all out against strip mining opened coffers of cash for Moore from the state's coal operators who contributed whatever was needed to beat Jay. Jay abandoned his war against strip mining in subsequent campaigns; the cash from coal also cured him of not spending money—he realized he would have to tap his personal fortune in future campaigns.

After a rather humbling defeat Jay accepted a position as president of West Virginia Wesleyan College in Buckhannon from

1973-1975. The Wesleyan chapter of Rockefeller's life began with one astute educator moving unilaterally to write some history. Janet Welch, a member of the faculty at Wesleyan, watched Jay's career with great interest as a supporter and friend. She was saddened by Jay's defeat but immediately saw opportunity for both Jay and Wesleyan.

Janet told me she placed a call to an old college chum, Bill Watson, Rockefeller's friend and chairman of the state Democratic Party. After lamenting Jay's loss with Bill, she explained that she was a member of a Wesleyan search committee that was engaged in seeking a president for the college—"Would Jay consider becoming a candidate for the Wesleyan presidency?"

She advanced her quest by telling Watson she realized if Jay applied and was accepted (she was certainly confident he would receive approval) everyone knew his stay might be for a brief period. "How so?" Watson asked. "Well," she replied, "we assume Jay will again run for office in four years. But, in the interim, the position would be a natural for him."

Janet said Watson asked if she was serious, and she replied, "Absolutely."

"Hold on," Watson said, and laid down the receiver. Within a few moments he was back on the line and said, "We are interested." That weekend Rockefeller and crew were on the Wesleyan campus to check out the territory.

Jay applied for and was offered the presidency—he took the job. His father was the speaker at Jay's inauguration and said he was pleased Jay was now in a line of work that provided more security than his most recent endeavors. Everyone laughed, including a chuckling Jay Rockefeller. Janet Welch, however, had the biggest smile in the crowd.

Jay did excellent work in academe, befriending faculty and students alike—attending basketball and football games, walking the sideline, and cheering his team on. One day during his tenure there I called him from the WCHS newsroom to get his reaction to some political story. When he answered the phone he said he and the family were having dinner.

"Dinner?" I said. "Who has dinner at 5:00?"

"Everybody in Buckhannon," Jay replied.

Jay did, indeed, adapt well. Janet Welch was prescient in knowing that Rockefeller had become a man who would do nothing halfway. He became a President who led and gave. Wesleyan benefitted tremendously under his tutelage.

CHAPTER 44

Jay Fires Me

ACADEMIC CREDENTIALS AND EXPERIENCE HELPED Jay Rockefeller when he left the Wesleyan president's post and ran for and was elected governor in 1976. He was re-elected in 1980. When he left office he was succeeded by —guess who? Arch Moore.

As governor, Jay, loaded with gravitas, continued to be an easy target for Speaker of the House Clyde See, a great wit and intellect. Clyde fricasseed everyone who came to his door. One year Jay fostered a significant piece of legislation that Clyde opposed. Rockefeller and reporters were bewildered that the bill, thought to be a done deal, died in the last hour of the legislative session. Clyde just smiled and said, "Fat possums move late at night."

In 1977 Governor Rockefeller selected a dynamite lady to be his Commissioner of the Department of Employment Security. At the time of her appointment Carolyn Smoot was the CEO of the Charleston Job Corps, a federal program designed to assist disadvantaged youth in finding employment. She directed a stellar program from the old (now gone) Kanawha Hotel at the corner of Virginia and Summers Street.

Smoot became one of the first female African Americans to be appointed a department head in state government. She was stylish, poised and extremely attractive. Beyond all that, she had high intellect and was a leader. I knew her in my journalism years covering the Job Corps, which received its share of criticism as young women who could not make the grade in the program were accused of various acts of a criminal nature as they migrated to Summers Street, known as Charleston's choice street of bars and prostitution.

Once I had opened my business I did some PR for Carolyn as she countered the calls for the Job Corps to close or move from Summers Street. When she accepted the call from the statehouse she asked me to do work for her there. She signed a state contract for the services and Rockefeller went nuts when he heard about it. He quickly nixed the deal and I was out on my ear with major coverage in the *Charleston Gazette, Charleston Daily Mail* and the Associated Press.

The late Jim Dent of the *Gazette*, an extraordinary talent who wrote a daily humor column and drew slashing political cartoons, gleefully noted my dismissal with his acerbic pen. His cartoon depicted the governor's office with the state seal behind an empty chair, above which was a great hole in the ceiling and a shocked statehouse worker peering down through the gaping hole at an aide.

The aide was explaining to an inquiring visitor who was staring up at the hole, "Oh, that?" The aide then points to the governor's chair beneath the hole, saying, "Well, you see, this is where the governor was sitting when he heard that Ms. Smoot had hired the PR firm."

I immediately called Dent and asked him if I could have the cartoon, which he presented to me without charge. It has graced my office wall from that day forward.

CHAPTER 45

Arch Needles Jay

WHEN JAY ROCKEFELLER TOOK THE GOVERNOR's office he told an aide he'd need a new desk because his long legs would not fit under Moore's old desk. Moore heard about it and told reporters with a "Tsk, tsk," that someone needed to tell Jay a new desk was not needed. All "High Pockets" needed to do, said the 5-6 Moore, was to turn the desk chair counter-clockwise, lowering it. Moore loved to gleefully pick at Jay, and he did it exceptionally well.

During Board of Public Works meetings when Jay was Secretary of State, Moore would bait Rockefeller, asking him about this or that arcane functioning of the Secretary of State's domain. The office had a number of different functions and Jay, looking to the big picture, did not have in-depth knowledge when it came to detailed responsibilities of the Secretary of State's office—something he had in common with many of his predecessors.

Moore took full advantage, and would turn to Rockefeller on many occasions and inquire about an issue within Jay's area of governance and smile as Jay squirmed and attempted to answer his question. The response was often incorrect and Moore would say, "Let me expand on that, Mr. Rockefeller." He then would give a lesson on the subject matter as Jay's face turned crimson.

In one such meeting Moore inquired of Jay as to the number of employees in his domain and, as Jay hesitated, his deputy secretary, Pete Thaw, jumped in and gave the correct number. Moore shot a frown to Pete and said, "I'm asking him (pointing to Jay), not you, Mr. Thaw!" This was a time of learning for a young man who had ventured into one of the most political of states. He was fresh meat for pols such as Moore. Rockefeller took it like a man and learned how to swim in the shark pool, honing his skills and ultimately taking his revenge as he went on to heights his tormentors would not achieve.

CHAPTER 46

Jay & Mondale

As governor, Jay Rockefeller especially excelled when Charleston attorney Tom Goodwin joined the administration as Rockefeller's chief of staff. Tom understood politics and he understood Jay. Together they were a formidable team. Rockefeller focused on jobs and began the campaign to attract Toyota to West Virginia. He was successful in starting the landslide of Japanese investment in the state. Without Rockefeller's persistence and skill, Toyota, and those Japanese firms that followed, would never have located in West Virginia. Jay also fought for clean elections, road improvements and chaired President Jimmy Carter's *Commission on Coal*. His was an impressive list of great accomplishments for the state he had come to love.

He did, however, always exhibit a penchant for pinching pennies. In his early campaigns, staffers were known to grouse that Jay carried no money and would borrow from them, sometimes forgetting to repay the debt. In the presidential campaign of 1984 Walter Mondale was running for President and Jay was up for re-election against Morgantown scion and owner of multi media outlets in the state, John Raese. During the campaign I was moderating an event in Elkins that featured Jay as the main speaker. We sat side-by-side at the dais and engaged in campaign talk.

Rockefeller told me that Senator Byrd's initial decision to bring Mondale to West Virginia during the campaign caused his (Rockefeller's) poll numbers to tank precipitously. Rockefeller credited the damage to the unpopularity of Mondale in West Virginia, running against the sitting President, Ronald Reagan.

Jay said he then had to spend a pile of money on TV ads to get his numbers back to where they were pre-Mondale. Rockefeller said a few months later he received a second call from Byrd, saying he was again bringing Mondale to the state. Jay, fighting for his political life against Raese, said he implored Byrd not to do it, that his poll numbers would again slide downward.

"He brought Mondale in again, and I had to spend all that God damned money," Jay said, his face reddening. So, he opened his pocketbook to get his numbers back to where he had a fighting chance against Raese. Jay narrowly won the race, but he had to spend $12 million to do it. It was an unheard of amount of election cash (mostly his own) in a state with 1.8 million in population and a two-thirds Democratic majority. Raese, the Republican, spent just $1.2 million and lost by only 52%-48%.

CHAPTER 47

Supporting Jay

MY WIFE BECKY AND I hosted two fundraisers for Jay
Rockefeller to support his Senate campaigns. In the first there
were forty or so people present at $1,000 each. Jay stood before
the group and thanked them for coming and their support—he
then thanked Charlie and Vickie for being host and hostess.
Becky just smiled but the Rockefeller aides were aghast. After
Jay's speech Aly Goodwin, his aide, took him aside and told
him he had called Becky "Vickie".

"No, I didn't," Jay said.

"Yes, you did," Aly said, digging in her heels.

"No, I didn't," Jay repeated.

"Did," Aly said, turning away.

In the second fundraiser Jay stood before the fireplace at our
home on Abney Circle and smiled at the assembly—he once
again thanked all the thousand dollar faces and us—this time
getting Becky's name right.

I was what I called a "Card Carrying Republican" meaning I was a "known" Republican—the fact had been in print many times. So why did I support Jay? Well, first of all, because he asked. He would call the office and ask to speak with me. It appealed to my vanity as it did to anyone answering Jay's call. "Mr. Ryan, Senator Rockefeller on line one for you," the receptionist's voice said. Heady stuff within the office as staffers noted the boss was on the line with Rockefeller. Second, I liked Jay. I called him "Senator" until the day he said, "Why do you call me 'Senator'? Why don't you call me Jay?" He was sincere and I called him by his first name from that moment on.

The third reason I supported him was out of great respect; Jay was a person who did not have to work a day in his life. Yet, he came to West Virginia, learned to love the state and its people, and worked his heart out for them. He and I were often on opposite sides of issues but I never questioned his sincerity. He was indeed, as his supporters claimed, "A politician who can't be bought."

He evolved from a gangly guy who knew nothing about the country west of the Hudson to one who knew just about everything concerning West Virginia—a place that became his home. I was surprised when he announced his retirement in 2014 but I saluted his decision to spend time with family as he passed the mid-point of his 70s.

CHAPTER 48

Jay's Compassion & Record

THERE IS A MAGICAL STORY about Jay Rockefeller. It centers on Rockefeller's passion for the Charleston Rockets, West Virginia's Continental Football League team of the 60s—when Jay was Secretary of State. Jay was a major advocate of the Rockets and would regularly watch the team practice. Jay struck up a relationship with the team's quarterback and the two often would go to lunch or dinner. Each time the quarterback found himself picking up the tab—Jay did not carry much money.

Finally, after a number of meals, the quarterback told Jay he could no longer afford to eat with him—he said he was barely existing, financially, as a Rockets' quarterback and could not continue to pay for Jay's meals. For the next three weeks Jay did not appear at practices or games. As the fourth week rolled around a manila envelope arrived in the team's locker room, addressed to the quarterback. When the Rockets' player opened the envelope he found a deed of trust—Jay had personally paid off the quarterback's mortgage.

Jay's legacy is strong—legislator, secretary of state, governor, senator. Through it all he was committed to the people of an

Appalachian state so foreign to one born of historical wealth that one could not imagine it to be his life's calling.

When Jay stepped down on that historic day in the United States Senate, it was a long way from a coal mine bath house in Raleigh County where miners with coal dust on their faces looked askance at the "Rockeyfeller" in their midst as he campaigned for office. Little did they know he would be their champion in years to come, fighting and winning for them federal benefits for their wives and children.

Jay served on a number of major committees in the Senate: Commerce, Science and Transportation, Intelligence, Finance, and Veteran's Affairs—putting him in a major national spotlight. In 1992, Ryan-McGinn and CRA were on pins and needles because Jay was considering a run for the presidency. We had a number of phone calls with his chief of staff, Lane Bailey (who later came on board at Ryan-McGinn and today has a highly successful Washington firm of his own that does business throughout the United States and internationally) as strategy sessions were taking place in Jay's office.

Jay finally decided not to make the run. I think it was his only shot at the highest office in the land and I think he could have been elected. Instead, he endorsed a governor from Arkansas and Bill Clinton became president. Jay would have had to spend all that (expletive) money again, but I believed then as I do now, that the name Rockefeller, and countless millions of dollars, would have put him in the Oval Office. There was some post-presidential talk about Jay as Clinton's running mate but that quickly died.

Jay went on to give major support to Bill and Hillary Clinton's health care reform legislation, dubbed "Hillarycare", and helped us bring Hillary to WVU's Health Sciences Center's *Appalachian Rural Health Care* conference in 1993. It was a grand affair with Jay, Dr. Bob D'Alessandri and Hillary raising hands together.

In 2010 Jay said of Barack Obama "He says I'm for clean coal and he says it in his speeches, but he doesn't say it in here (patted his chest), and he doesn't say it in the minds of my own people. And he's beginning to not be believable to me." Soon, however, Rockefeller and coal developed a rift as Rockefeller began to increasingly criticize the industry as it became more clear he would not run for re-election.

Jay was a great servant to the state, but if you were on the other side of an issue he favored, he would repeatedly jab his finger at you and tell you that you were dead wrong. To me, it was representative of a certain perspective that he simply could not avoid—that of a Rockefeller.

At his 80th birthday friends and supporters came from around the world to express their gratitude for a great servant of the state and the country. There can be no greater commitment to West Virginia than that made by John D. Rockefeller IV.

CHAPTER 49

Robert C. Byrd

I WAS ASKED IN THE 60s, by the Morgantown and Beckley newspapers, to write a weekly political column from the capital. Soon, I had contracted with six newspapers and later added Jim Comstock's *Hillbilly* to the grouping.

U.S. Senator Robert C. Byrd was often the subject of the political column and he included excerpts from several of my writings in his autobiography *Robert C. Byrd, Child of the Appalachian Coalfields*.

Byrd said in his book that he took speculation in my columns that Secretary of State John D. Rockefeller IV might decide to run to unseat him *cum grano salis*—with a grain of salt. He said there was never a direct statement by Rockefeller that he had any intentions of running against him. Byrd said it was the product of clever minds that had an axe to grind.

Byrd cited the following from my *Letter from Charleston* in the Morgantown *Dominion News*:

"Step right up folks and meet the new, 1968 Jay baby. Jay baby has not only that certain something this year but combines it with political sex appeal, sincerity, and class.

"John D. Rockefeller IV, candidate for secretary of state on the Democratic ticket, has changed as he campaigns rigorously for his Board of Public Works office. Kanawha County voters remember him as the retiring, almost shy young man from New York, who worked with the county's poor in a place called Emmons, and who gosh-all hated it when some flashbulb snapper from one of the national magazines considered him good copy."

At that point Senator Byrd probably could not resist commenting, "Ryan then gushed—"

"Rockefeller has been set apart from ordinary men and is treated as though endowed with supernatural and superhuman powers or qualities. He is a Kennedy, he is progress, he is Mr. Clean, and he is God. Few question his election as Secretary of State. If he so desires, he can be elected governor and, contrary to what select henchmen say, he could beat Robert Byrd in a senatorial race.

"Speculation has it that Jay baby was groomed by Charleston Gazette publisher W.E. (Ned) Chilton as the man to take out Byrd in 1970. Rockefeller was extremely close with Chilton when he came to this town but he is not now openly associated with the Gazette. Other speculation has Rockefeller running gracefully for the Senate seat of Jennings Randolph, who would retire at the end of his current term.

"The Jay baby team of former VISTA workers and Peace Corps volunteers is plummeting forward at a breakneck speed and some are beginning to resent it. One politician secretly confided that he was all for Rockefeller originally but now his "long-haired liberalism scares me." Another said, "He flocks to anybody who says he's poor. I think it's a guilt complex."

"It is necessary to conclude that these are growing pains for a young political star. It is hoped that the right steps and turns are taken so that neither the candidate nor the public becomes disenchanted."

Well, Senator Byrd was partially correct about "clever minds"—I and my good friend and fellow columnist Tommy Knight, who once was employed by Rockefeller, were regularly fed information by Jay's staff designed to fan the flames of a Byrd-Rockefeller contest. Tommy's reporting said that Jay mentioned a possible run against Byrd to his folks and that the office staff jabbered about their man's chances—jabber that said Byrd could be defeated.

Reading my column decades later, I am amused by my conviction as a very, very young reporter that Jay could have taken out Byrd. I have to assume that I believed Jay's money would speak, but I was probably enthralled by the Rockefeller name. In the many years since that moment in time I came to know that if there was a political "God" in West Virginia, it was Bob Byrd. But, I had a column to write— twice a week. So, at times, there was indeed some salt in the old mill.

It was a wonderful time of conjecture as West Virginia embraced the glamour of having a Rockefeller in the hills and Tommy Knight and I ran with the rumors.

Senator Byrd, a man for the ages, was entirely correct in his assessment of young Ryan and he never held a grudge.

CHAPTER 50

Jennings Randolph

IN 1925 JENNINGS RANDOLPH WAS associate editor of the *West Virginia Review*. From 1926-1932 the Elkins native was head of the Department of Public Speaking and Journalism at Davis and Elkins College in Elkins. In 1933 he took his skills to the campaign trail and was elected to the United States House of Representatives—but he was ousted from his congressional seat in the Republican landslide of 1946.

Randolph then became a professor of public speaking at Southeastern University in Washington, D.C., as well as dean of the School of Business Administration. After that he joined Capital Airlines, later United Air Lines, as a public relations practitioner. In 1958 he was elected in a special election to the United States Senate after the death of Senator Matthew M. Neely. He served in the Senate until 1985.

Charleston Gazette editor Jim Haught once told me the *Charleston Gazette* closed its Washington Bureau because every time the newspaper assigned a reporter to cover the state's congressional delegation one of the state congressmen would hire the staffer away. Some wags considered it to be a rare example of congressional efficacy—a prophylactic move on the part of the West Virginia delegation to keep the *Gazette* out of their backyard. Indeed, Haught himself had once been a press aide to Senator Robert C. Byrd, only to leave Washington with some disgust for the political scene, returning to the *Gazette* to become an award winning investigative reporter and, eventually, the paper's editor.

So it was that early on in CRA's nascent political consulting years that ex-newsman George Lawless of Senator Jennings Randolph's staff rang us up. Lawless had been a Gazette reporter and the paper's original *Gazeteer* humor columnist.

The occasion for Lawless' telephone call was Senator Randolph's directive that he and John Yago (another *Gazette* reporter Randolph had hired) were to ask three agencies to "pitch" their services for the senator's upcoming political campaign. I immediately said we would do that and Harry Peck and I set about developing strategy and creativity for the Randolph for Senate campaign.

Harry and I believed, after going through the pitch, that we had been asked to participate as a token agency so no one could criticize Randolph if he hired an out-of-state firm. And that's exactly what he did—he hired an out-of-state firm.

During our pitch Jennings sat in his chair behind his enormous desk. I sat in front of the desk. John Yago sat to my right in a chair several feet away. George was on Randolph's right.

Jennings eased back in his chair after small talk had ended and signaled I was to begin my presentation. I utilized an easel and began to unveil our creative plan and strategy. I would speak and look at the senator for reaction. He would smile as his chins bounced against his chest and seemed to ripple down his sizeable stomach—he would look at his aides and nod his head in the affirmative. The aides would smile back at the senator and at me. It was going, I thought, just great.

Twenty minutes into the presentation I looked up from my easel at Jennings—his chin was deep against his chest, his eyes were closed and little gurgles of sound emitted from deep within his form, which tilted slightly to the left—he was sound asleep.

I looked at John, whose eyebrows were raised in alarm as his gaze went from Jennings to me. I looked at George and our eyes met with "What the hell do we do now?" stares. Finally, we all fixed our gaze on one another, averting our eyes from the sleeping senator. Ten minutes passed as I pitched and they nodded enthusiastically, all of us trying to ignore the elephant in the room.

Our unease was finally broken when the stentorian tones of the senator crashed through the angst as Jennings sat upright in his chair and said, "Gentlemen! If you will excuse me for a moment!" Whereupon, the senator got up and left the room—and my pitch continued.

Five minutes later United States Senator Jennings Randolph bounded back into the room, full of extreme energy and verve.

I finished the performance and all of us bid happy goodbyes as Jennings presided in fine form.

I do not know what occurred when the senator left the room, but to paraphrase Meg Ryan's classic movie line— "I'll have what Jennings had."

CHAPTER 51

Jennings Randolph's Roll Call

CHARLESTON ATTORNEY TIM BARBER WAS visiting Senator Jennings Randolph's office with clients who were lobbying a bill in Congress and Randolph spent a lengthy amount of time with them. The old campaigner simply did not wish for his audience to depart and he waxed eloquently about the affairs of the day. Finally, Barber pleaded the group had to leave in order to catch a scheduled flight back to Charleston.

Jennings followed his visitors out of his office to elevator doors, chatting all the while. Just as the doors began to close someone mentioned the *Charleston Gazette* and a recent editorial criticizing Randolph. Jennings grabbed the elevator doors as they were closing and forced them open. He began to, red-faced, castigate the *Gazette*—at which point the elevator bell began ringing in protest.

Hearing the repeated dings, Jennings paused, raised a finger toward the ceiling, and shouted, "Roll call! Roll call! Gentlemen, I must depart!" He released the door and scurried off for a roll call made by an Otis elevator.

But, make no mistake about it—Jennings Randolph was the real thing. I covered Jennings many times as a reporter, and I always admired his positive attitude, his love of people and his Shakespearean presence. In the Senate he had met hundreds of famous people and most of them were featured in photographs with him as he clasped their hands and smiled for the camera. Those photographs covered every inch of the walls in his office, beginning at waist level and reaching to the top of the 12-foot ceilings.

Senator Randolph, while sitting on a dais as he prepared to address an audience, had a penchant for making certain his hair was neatly in place (it was always swept back from his forehead). He would lean forward and dip his fingers in a water glass near his dinner plate and wipe his palms across the sides of his head, slicking down his hair.

The senator, who loved nothing more than a day at the Charles Town Race Track, was loquacious to a fault and we reporters would regularly take bets on how long he would speak when taking the podium. One could hardly overestimate; he loved to talk. He was a jolly fellow, given to smiling broadly and saying, "Happy day, happy day!" as he waved hello.

A few years after Jennings left the Senate and Jay Rockefeller took his place, the local Charleston chapter of the Public Relations Society of America asked Jennings to come to its annual meeting to receive the chapter's award as a champion of public relations and speaking skills. Jennings was most appreciative and spoke at length to the annual meeting—he was fantastic.

I chauffeured Jennings to Kanawha Airport for his flight to D.C. There was some confusion at the airline counter and it was obvious the folks there did not know who this veteran of the first years of the Roosevelt administration was. I stood at the counter with him and said, time after time, "Senator, we'll have this figured out in a few minutes." Time went by and there was no resolution, "**Senator,**" I bellowed, "I'm sure they'll have this worked out. Thank you **Senator**, for leaving Washington and your duties as a former distinguished **United States Senator**, to be with us."

My bellowing message finally got through and an entourage arrived to host the United States Senator aboard the flight to Washington.

The right to vote at 18—the 26th amendment to the United States Constitution—directed at veterans of World War II—probably would not have occurred without the voice of Jennings Randolph. The Randolph-Sheppard Act of 1936 gave the blind preference in federal contracts for food service stands. Randolph co-authored the Federal Airport Act that created the Civil Air Patrol and introduce legislation to establish a Department of Peace to manage international conflicts. His tenure was long and impressive. FDR and he were elected at the same time—he left Congress the year Ronald Reagan began his second term.

CHAPTER 52

Ken Hechler

CONGRESSMAN KEN HECHLER OF HUNTINGTON was a gifted politician who won his seat in Washington by taking on and beating the Kee family legacy. He filed against Congressman Jim Kee of Bluefield who had succeeded his mother in the 5th District seat. Mrs. Kee had gone to Congress after her husband, James Kee, a seated congressman, died. The name Jim Kee was iconic in his district.

Hechler ran against Kee in 1972 after the 1970 census eliminated one of West Virginia's congressional districts, merging it into the 5th district (now also gone). The combined district contained both Beckley and Bluefield—home to the Kee family. The new district contained 65% of Kee's old territory and Kee was considered a shoo-in for re-election, even though he had missed 359 of 1,964 roll call votes (the median lifetime missed roll call votes for congressmen in 1972 was 10.1%—Kee's was 18.3 %).

Hechler beat Kee going away. I felt I had helped Hechler in his campaign as a result of a one-on-one session I filmed with Kee in the latter days of the election calendar. From the beginning,

Kee stumbled badly through the interview. Normally a sound bite on the evening news would run, at best, no more than 50 seconds. As I reviewed the Kee interview I became convinced that viewers should really understand the condition the congressman was in.

I ran a full five minutes, most of the interview, on the 6:00 newscast that night. It was unprecedented to devote such time to one story. I made no editorial comment about Kee's performance, I simply said I had interviewed Kee earlier in the day and rolled the film. Watching the re-play I thought the interview would shock viewers as it entered the homes of thousands of 5th district homes. I believe it did and I believe there was voter reaction at the polls. Hechler was ecstatic that I had run the piece and I felt justified in having done so.

Later in the campaign Hechler brought to me his now legendary television commercial where he and his staff played out a one-minute parody of *My Fair Lady*, with Hechler bouncing around the stage singing "Get *Me To the Polls on Time!*" I ran the entire commercial on the 6 and 11:00 news. It was too good to relegate to just commercial time.

Hechler crisscrossed his district in a red Jeep with his name emblazoned on it and I could not help but feature the Jeep and the flamboyant congressman on many newscasts. He came to Charleston as coal miners fought to receive compensation from Black Lung disease and stood at the speaker's podium in the House of Delegates when a vote neared on the Black Lung bill. Our cameras were grinding as Hechler told the coal miners assembled in the gallery, "You are the real heroes of this movement and you should no longer work and die like animals."

Hechler had waved a big slab of bologna when he addressed miners at the Charleston Civic Center (he pronounced it "baloney") as he discounted arguments against making Black Lung a compensable malady. This time he had no bologna in hand, but as he warmed to his audience he could not resist taking a shot at UMWA President Tony Boyle and US Secretary of Labor George Shultz, saying, "The reason I didn't bring my baloney today is—George and Tony—*they* have the baloney!"

Hechler eventually left Congress to run for governor and he lost. In 1984 he ran for the office of Secretary of State and won, staying in the office through 1990. The native New Yorker had come to West Virginia after serving in the United States Army during World War II where he served in the 9th Armored Division that captured the Ludendorff Bridge. Hechler later wrote the novel, *The Bridge at Remagen*, which was made into a blockbuster film in 1969.

Leaving the Army he became a White House assistant to President Harry Truman where he wrote speeches for the president. While employed by Truman he also worked for Adlai Stevenson's presidential campaign. Stevenson lost and Dwight Eisenhower was elected. Hechler told me after he watched Ike's inaugural parade he went back to his office in the White House, expecting to be fired. He said he had to wait a while—he continued to work there for six months until, one day, an Eisenhower staffer wandered into his office and inquired as to how Hechler came to be on Eisenhower's staff.

Hechler explained that he was not on Ike's staff; he was on Harry's. He was shown the door that very day.

Hechler told me that he attended each year a reunion of White House speechwriters and was present when John F. Kennedy's legendary speechwriter, Theodore Sorenson, was being lambasted by his fellow Democratic speechwriters for supposedly collaborating with Republican columnist Peggy Noonan on a book she was writing. It was post Clinton-Lewinsky and Hechler said Sorenson rose from his seat, slammed the table with his fist, and said, "Let me make it perfectly clear! I did *not* have *textual* relations with that woman!"

Hechler lived to be 102. He was an original. I liked him immensely.

CHAPTER 53

Ken Kurtz

AT WSAZ-TV, MY FIRST ASSIGNMENT from Ken Kurtz was to film a scheduled Sunday toppling of tall smokestacks at a Union Carbide plant in South Charleston. The camera I was provided was a 16 MM Bolex that was wound by hand. On that Sunday I wound the camera to the point to which it would not wind beyond and waited for the explosions that would detonate at the base of the three tall stacks.

Boom! The explosions erupted and I pressed the button on the camera to begin the filming. Nothing. I pressed the button again—and again—as the stacks fell before my eyes, seemingly in slow motion. Nothing. The camera would not work. There was no re-do—the stacks were gone, just a pile of rubble. Why did the Bolex malfunction? Well, as I piddled around with the winding mechanism, I realized I had wound the camera the wrong way.

I spent the rest of that Sunday assuming I would be fired come Monday. It was a restless night heading to Monday morning and I dreaded the afternoon when I would tell Kurtz my story of pitiful ineptness. Ken showed on schedule and I fessed up, ready to clean out my desk. He listened to my predicament while reading copy from the *UPI* Teletype and said, "Oh, okay, we'll scratch it from the lineup," and ripped copy from the chattering machine.

"That's it?" I thought. No real reaction at all. Just a part of doing business. I was relieved, to say the least. My career was back on track.

Ken anchored the 11:00 pm newscast and he kept a schedule that saw him arrive at the station in early afternoon, work through the 11:00 slot and then listen to his police radio long into the night; he freelanced as a photographer for the Charleston papers and the *AP* with a very expensive Hasselblad and a number of long lenses. I emulated him to some extent, buying a Rolleiflex camera (called a Rollei) and shooting stills. Both Ken and I developed our own film in the station's dark room. Many of our stills were used on air, but the majority of Ken's were sold to the *Gazette*.

As time went on I also found Ken had his moments. He would leave a myriad of notes for co-worker Nancy Haught, a take-no-prisoners gal who assisted Kurtz, telling her to do this and do that. Nancy, wife of *Gazette* reporter Jim Haught, would take the notes, attach them to a long string of Scotch tape and hang the strip of tape from the ceiling—it almost reached the floor. At the bottom of the string she added her own note, which said, "NO!"

Nancy was not alone in her frustration. One particularly trying day with Kurtz I went into the bathroom to apply my pancake makeup prior to anchoring the 6:00, and ended up banging my head against the wall in frustration. I thought of Ralph Price, who once had Kurtz on the newsroom floor, banging Ken's head on the tiles.

Seeing *my* frustration, Nancy constructed a cardboard five-inch high wall that encircled the large desk at which I sat. The desk, in the middle of the newsroom, served as my place of business but it also was used to layout the evening newscast—sheet after sheet of news stories, lined up on the surface of the desk. The cardboard wall was emblazoned with the words, "Anti-Kurtz Wall".

Yes, he was at times a challenge, but Ken Kurtz was an extraordinary newsman with unique characteristics. He shot across town with his Keds on, covering news like a lawn mower chewing grass. He was full of energy and of the highest intellect. Looking back, it was a pleasure and honor to work with and be mentored by him.

CHAPTER 54

Peter Beter

WSAZ-TV News Director Bos Johnson was a Charleston native and was in the first broadcast journalism graduating class at WVU. He was a mentor to hundreds of journalists who passed through his newsroom in his twenty years at the helm. He was my Ben Bradlee and he taught me well, embellishing the rules of the game I had learned in journalism school. "When in doubt, don't," was a rule Bos imparted. That single phrase served me through twelve years of journalism and throughout my professional life.

One Saturday evening I anchored both the 6:00 and 11:00 Charleston newscast with Jim Mitchell anchoring the Huntington end of the broadcast. Mitchell and I did the lineup for the early newscast by phone at 5:00, as was the custom. Mitchell was an elegant anchor with curly black hair, a wonderful sense of humor, and great delivery. On this lineup conversation he teased me by saying, "Ryan, I won't tell you what it is, but my lead is one you are gonna' love."

"Okay, Jim, surprise me," I said.

The 6:00 news opening rolled and Mitchell was first up with the lead. Jim looked at the camera with his signature small smile and intoned, "A new name in the news tonight in the West Virginia gubernatorial race. A Huntington resident has thrown his hat in the ring. His name? Peter Beter (pronounced "Beater")."

Mitchell paused slightly and the grin grew a trifle larger as he plunged into the story. I was beside myself in Charleston and it was hard to maintain my composure when Mitchell threw the newscast to me, with a larger smile.

Following the newscast, news director Johnson was on the line to Mitchell, boiling. Mitchell fielded the angry Bos by saying, "Bos! What can I do? The guy's name is really Peter Beter and it's pronounced 'Beater'!"

Bos thought for a moment and instructed Jim to use Beter's middle initial to mitigate the name of the candidate. Mitchell agreed.

At 11:00 Mitchell came on the air with the smile just a bit larger; he assumed gravitas as he said, "A new name in the West Virginia gubernatorial campaign tonight. Huntington resident Peter *D.* Beter, has announced his candidacy for the top post."

Bos accepted defeat and did not call Mitchell.

Peter Beter visited the Charleston newsroom often during his campaign, assuring me that West Virginians up the hollows loved to see him in his Cadillac and his thousand-dollar suits.

"The people of West Virginia want to see their governor well-dressed," he told me. On one occasion I admired an expensive alligator belt Peter wore. He ripped it off his waist and tried to give the belt to me. I told him I could not accept it and a week later he arrived in the newsroom with his wife Lily and a cracked coffee cup. The cup had been given to him, Peter said, by a resident of Cabin Creek. He assigned to the old and damaged cup a sentimental value that he seemed to think represented the hardiness of rural West Virginians and he wanted it to be mine. I accepted the cup because it was a wonderful gesture, and one without monetary value.

Peter knew his name got attention but he suffered it gladly. Peter told me no less than United States Senator Jennings Randolph had told him to never change his name. "It is a political name! A name voters will always remember!" Peter said, quoting Randolph. Senator Randolph knew whereof he spoke—during the time Jennings was a United States senator, known far and wide in West Virginia, a guy by the name of Rudolph Jennings ran each presidential election year as a candidate for representative to the Democratic convention—he won, going away, each time.

CHAPTER 55

Emil Varney

ONE SATURDAY MORNING WSAZ-TV PHOTOGRAPHER Emil Varney and I rushed to Wayne County, West Virginia where a young boy had been sitting on the side of an abandoned water well, tossing rocks into it, when the sides of the well collapsed. The boy, about eight-years-old, tumbled into the opening in the ground and fell fifty feet into shallow water where he was trapped under heavy stones that fell on top of him. Emergency calls went out and when we arrived at the scene of the entrapment there were rescue crews, ambulances and local newspaper reporters.

Emil and I were the only broadcast folks on site and we filed reports for WSAZ-TV throughout Saturday and Sunday. I also filed for *Monitor Weekend Radio,* a 1960s service for NBC radio affiliates that provided weekend entertainment and hourly newscasts, relieving its affiliates of local programming.

I alerted *Monitor* to the ongoing story shortly after Emil and I arrived on the scene, suggesting to the *Monitor* producer that he could hold his audience throughout the weekend with the compelling story. He bought my pitch and the two days of reporting captivated *Monitor's* national radio audience as NBC pulled out all the stops, interrupting regular programming for my account of the boy's rescue.

The little boy was trapped for most of two days and was finally rescued without serious injuries. He survived in timely fashion—just as the weekend was ending and *Monitor* went off the air. The weekend of apprehension over the boy's entrapment brought some excellent audience ratings to the network and it richly rewarded me with a check for $800.

It was high cotton for a lad making $6,000 a year. I immediately borrowed another $800 from the WSAZ-TV credit union, enabling me to make a down payment on my first home—a $24,000 purchase. I sold the home five years later for $50,000. Those were the days.

Emil and I did many stories on the rage of the day—flying saucers and aliens. Emil takes delight in remembering our early '60s interview with a fellow who owned an appliance store in Cross Lanes near Charleston. The excited merchant called WSAZ-TV and reported he had seen a flying saucer land in the westbound lane of Interstate 64, which was being constructed at the time. By the time we arrived on the scene the story had gotten bigger. The man spoke to Emil's rolling sound-on-film camera and related, in no uncertain terms, that the flying saucer had opened and an alien had emerged, walking from the saucer and engaging the appliance dealer in conversation.

I reported the encounter on that evening's newscast. Emil's remembrance is the poor fellow found that the report of his siting caused him to be roundly ridiculed in weeks that followed. The appliance dealer closed up shop and moved away. Emil and I cannot remember if the alien was in search of refrigerators, stoves or some other appliance. Emil says the area of I-64 where the alien and saucer were supposed to appear is today the site of numerous wrecks. Hmmmmm.

In 1966 Emil and I traveled to Point Pleasant in search of West Virginia's Mothman. The humanoid moth-like creature was a man-sized bird that was related to supernatural events in the area and, later, tied to the Silver Bridge disaster at Point Pleasant. The first sighting was near Clendenin when five men digging a grave said the creature flew over them. In Point Pleasant a couple reported a similar creature with glowing red eyes and ten foot wings near the TNT area—the site of a former World War II munitions plant.

It was a story made for TV and Emil and I camped out in the old TNT plant, filming dark corners of the building where no man dare go. We saw—absolutely nothing. But, we interviewed some folks, got some reactions, and, the network bought it. I did a cut in on the 1:00 weekday NBC news hosted by Nancy Dickerson for which I received a nice check from the network. I loved that Mothman.

Today, one can Google a video on the Internet of a Mothman episode on "Lost Tapes." The TV program features interviews I did with several people at Glenn in Clay County and melds those interviews into the Mothman story. The video shows me interviewing eyewitnesses of a UFO siting. I am standing on a road in Clay County, saying to the camera, "Last night, a strange and eerie thing happened." A woman appears on camera, saying, "It was right in the tree tops, going real fast."

Then, "Lost Tapes" interjects an actor playing the role of a news reporter hyperventilating about the Mothman. In the real interview there are three boys—I say on camera, "Last night in Glenn, Clay County, three boys saw what they describe as an unidentified flying object."

I ask them, "What happened?" One replies, "I thought it was a car light." A Mrs. Banes appears on camera and says her daughter saw the object actually land. I report that the UFO was seen from a distance but searchers have not been able to find it. One of the boys looks into the camera and says, "I never seen anything like that before."

With a smile on my face I sign off with—"Now, improvised search parties are attempting to find *it*—just what *it* is, no on knows for sure."

Apparently "Lost Tapes" knew what *it* was, however—it was video footage with which they could titillate an audience.

CHAPTER 56

Liquor By The Drink

I HAD RUN, AT 22 years-of-age, for election to the Charleston Press Club's governing board and was elected as the youngest board member the club had ever had—a distinction I will forevermore hold since the Press Club was shuttered in the 70s, a victim of liquor by the drink legislation. I take solace in knowing that at the same time I was a board member of a bootleg club, future Charleston mayor and Kanawha County sheriff Danny Jones, at 15 years of age, and by his own admission, was dispensing liquor across city bars. Danny and I were just part of a large dilemma about the Devil's drink in the Mountain State.

To resolve said dilemma, an effort was made in the 60s to, through a constitutional amendment, alter West Virginia law that liquor could be sold and used—but only in private places. The state sold its liquor in state owned stores and bootleg clubs proliferated—they were the only venue in which one could get a drink outside a home. The constitutional amendment to make liquor available in restaurants was voted down and the proponents of liquor in clubs went back to the drawing board.

Another path was then created—a path that wound through legislative action. Assistant Attorney General Denny Vaughan drafted legislation to create a "Private Club Liquor Law"— churches and bootleggers found themselves rowing the same boat as both constituencies fought the legislation—and lost. The legislation that was passed required that a club register with the state as a private group of members who were each issued a membership card. The club then had to ask for the patron's membership card before serving a drink.

Within a few years everyone sort of forgot about the stipulation that a club (all restaurants decided they were private clubs) with a liquor license had to card "members" and discontinued issuing memberships—one could just walk in and have a drink. So far as I know, Denny Vaughan's masterpiece legislation requiring membership in the establishment one visited for an alcoholic drink was never updated.

Prior to the liberating liquor legislation, Charleston's Press Club and Army-Navy Club were called, quite accurately, "bootleg joints" by the Reverend L.E. Crowson of South Charleston. The crusading Methodist minister was a one-man army in chiding law enforcement that a blind eye was being turned toward the elite clubs where the members were the upper crust of society.

In 1967 Charlie Connor of the *Charleston Daily Mail* reported that Crowson once told his congregation he had become a vice spy, hiring an undercover agent out of his own pocket and going with him between 2 and 4 in the morning to a number of illegal gambling and liquor dives in Charleston. He said he observed extensive gambling and liquor activity, purchased some liquor on his own and got rid of it on his own. He preached nine sermons on "The Law of God" and said a considerable part of the mess in Charleston originated with the church—that "institution" church members did not want to confront God's law "which addresses such matters." Crowson said youngsters were affected—that Charleston teenagers had been "beguiled and bewitched."

Crowson told his congregation that some club owners were bragging that they had uncovered a drunk driving charge against him. Crowson said he would not dignify the accusation with a rebuttal.

Crowson's frequent target, the Press Club, was a great deal for us "ink stained wretches." We were Level 1 club members, automatically eligible to join by paying a paltry sum for membership with no dues.

Judges, lawyers, members of the Legislature, and businessmen, etc., were Level 2 members. These folks had to *apply* for membership, be approved by a board vote, and pay a hefty inauguration fee and monthly dues. They considered it a bargain—a drink in public without recourse.

The subsidization allowed those of us in journalism to rub shoulders with society, drink, and have a filet mignon, martini and dessert for about $5. We were subsidized by Charleston's finest—and thought nothing of it.

Ken Freed, with whom I worked at the AP, recalled in a *Facebook* posting that the Press Club liquor sales worked this way: "If you wanted your own brand of booze, say Johnny Walker Black, you bought it from the State Store (or from Shug, the bootlegger, after-hour jazz bar owner), and you gave it to the Press Club bartender. He served it to you for $.50 to cover service and what was a 'set up (ice, glass and water).'

"If you just drank the club's stock (purchased from the State Store as a private club like the Union Carbide country club), you paid $.60 a set up. If you wanted a cocktail (Bob Wells liked a brandy alexander—or five), it was $.75."

Into this strange arrangement came, regularly, the Reverend L.E. Crowson who ginned up (so to speak) enormous media attention by boldly and colorfully decrying the bootleg press club (and all such operations) in newspapers and on radio and TV (yes, we covered Crowson big time—talk about biting the hand that fed us).

After several Crowson onslaughts, efforts were made in political circles to save face. The Press Club manager would receive a discreet call from an unnamed source who would alert the manager that the club would be raided (either by State Police or the Sheriff's office) at a certain time of the day or evening. The "raid" was devised to assure the public that illegal saloons would not be tolerated!

Upon receiving the call, the club manager communicated to his members that their lockers containing booze would be secured and no alcoholic drinks would be served for two hours before and two hours following the scheduled raid. The "raid" then took place through unlocked doors with a subsequent quiet walk through the club. No one inquired about the lockers on premise and a few hours later the city's judges, lawyers, journalists and other assorted members began to once again bend an elbow.

Delegate Bob Harman of Mineral County was having dinner at the Press Club with a power company lobbyist one evening in the 1960s when the club manager came by his table and politely asked if he and the lobbyist could leave—*immediately*. The manager said he had just received a call from the Sheriff's office that the club would be raided in a few moments. "I was hustled out and had to leave half of my steak," Bob said.

On one occasion (an anomaly), Sheriff's deputies actually showed up at the Press Club *unannounced* and presented a warrant authorizing them to immediately raid the club. The quick thinking manager told them, "Governor Barron's daughter is at the bar on the second floor," (she really was). Whereupon the raiding party declared their warrant was flawed. "We'll be back in a half hour," they said.

Kanawha County restaurant and bar operator John Smiley noted, quite rightly, that there was a double standard. While the Press Club and Charleston's Army & Navy Club merrily served John Barleycorn to the city's upper crust and media with a realization they were inoculated from harm, Smiley's operations in the "Badlands" near St. Albans were regularly raided in Elliot Ness fashion. Smiley garnered lots of publicity by picketing the Press Club. Our cameras rolled as he railed against the inequity.

The golden days of private clubs came to an end when the liquor-by-the-drink legislation was passed. The mystique was gone—and so was the Press Club. It was sad to see the old lady on Kanawha Boulevard go. She was to the immediate left as one crossed the South Side Bridge from downtown toward South Hills.

The building was originally a garage that was built to handle heavy tonnage as it parked cars on four floors. The entrepreneurial media of the time purchased the building in the 1950s and gutted it, creating a beautiful dining and drinking venue. Then, Tom Corey and the Rollins Cleavenger and Rollins accounting firm bought the old lady.

She is now a combined office and luxury apartment complex owned by insurance mogul and entrepreneur Frankie Baer. Old timers that pass by the building remember her benevolently as their bootleg saloon that hosted legendary local and national journalists, while liberally watering Charleston's finest.

CHAPTER 57

Bos Johnson

IN THE 1950s WSAZ-TV HAD established a satellite facility in the state capital in order to capture more sales in the Charleston market. The station built a microwave hookup and news director Nick Basso set up a two-city newscast with anchors in Huntington and Charleston and "ping ponged" between the two cities its 15-minute broadcast.

During the 1960 West Virginia primary, David Brinkley sat in the WSAZ Charleston studio and reported on John Kennedy's activities of the day. Brinkley watched the WSAZ ping pong and a few years later, when NBC began to think about developing a news program called "The Huntley Brinkley Report", the network sent producers to Huntington and Charleston to study the WSAZ setup. Their final product completely mimicked the Nick Basso design.

Then, in 1963, NBC decided to expand the Huntley Brinkley report to 30 minutes and WSAZ made the same move. To a person, everyone wondered how we could possibly fill 30 minutes of airtime with local news. It was a naïve time.

The WSAZ newscasts now use a sophisticated system that allows each city to decide which stories to air in each region the station reaches in its tri-state coverage area. That sophistication had as its genesis the astute innovation of those WSAZ pioneers of the 50s.

Bos Johnson succeeded Basso as WSAZ's news director. He was unquestionably the most trusted voice and anchor in the market we served and was, as president of the Radio & Television News Directors Association (RTNDA), known nationally as one of the country's premiere broadcast journalists. Bos, as RTNDA President, presided over President Richard Nixon's last televised news conference in 1974.

Television news came of age in the 60s and 70s and Bos was the Walter Cronkite of the Tri-State. It was Bos who told the heart wrenching stories of the Silver Bridge disaster and Marshall University plane crash. His voice was the link that viewers sought the night of November 14, 1970. I was sitting in the Sterling Restaurant on Capitol Street in Charleston when someone approached me and said there had been a plane crash in Huntington—the plane had carried the Marshall football team.

I rushed to the WCHS newsroom to anchor coverage through the night. Bos was already on the air and I played catch up. No one could have topped the presence that night of Bos Johnson. The historical kinescopes of his broadcasts that sad night are preserved in the film libraries of the West Virginia Culture Center. If one wants to see award-winning reporting, all one need do is Google those broadcasts. Bos, for his part, said that night he covered, "the saddest news story of my career."

Bos eventually moved from his Huntington newsroom to a position as professor of journalism at Marshall University. There, he continued to train journalists in the fine art of ethics and the responsibility of getting the story straight and without embellishment—always covering both sides of the story. I, and all of us who came under his wing, owe him a tremendous debt of gratitude for influencing our lives in a manner that made us better men and women. When the Brian Williams scandal broke at NBC News I thought Williams would never have had a problem if Bos Johnson had tutored him.

Bos died in November 2014 at age 85. He shaped broadcast news as one who understood how excellent journalism could be brought to the small screen. He was selfless—an ego big enough to command respect and attention but small enough to give guidance and sustenance to his community. His profession, and the young men and women who looked to him as a mentor, owe him much.

CHAPTER 58

The Associated Press

My years at WSAZ TV were interrupted when I left to join the Associated Press in West Virginia. Charlie Monzella, AP state broadcast editor, recruited me to replace him as he moved on in the vast AP world. I admired Charlie and the guys I worked with—Herb Little, Strat Douthat, Jim Ragsdale, Ken Freed and other top journalists, but I lasted at the *AP* only six months because I could not tolerate being inside an office eight hours a day.

I felt compelled to take the job the AP offered because I believed I had to work in print journalism to establish my credentials as a *real* reporter—and the prime example of stellar journalism in the world was the Associated Press.

My job as the broadcast editor was to rewrite the news wires—stories directed to newspaper Teletype machines—received with a "clackity clack" noise that conveyed urgency and the occasional ten bells that indicated a "Flash", the most important of news bulletins. The news wire editor, after satisfying the needs of state newspapers, would pass his stories to me and I would rewrite them in broadcast style for radio and television subscribers.

When the newspaper copy was tossed on my desk I dutifully and quickly rewrote it and passed it to the grizzled *old* ladies (probably 50 years of age) who placed it in a paper holder beside their Teletype and begin to type my story. For the first two months they regularly would whip my copy out of the holder and toss it back on my desk, saying, "Learn to spell!" And I did. My spelling had been atrocious but, thankfully, I became well schooled in the necessity of spelling at AP University.

The AP Bureau Chief at that time was a fellow by the name of Bob Wells. Bob arrived at work mid-morning and spent an hour reading paperback novels. At 11:00 he broke for lunch, clambered down the staircase at the *Charleston Gazette,* where the AP bureau was located, trundled across the street and on to Kanawha Boulevard where he entered the Charleston Press Club and began his three-martini lunch.

I reported to the AP at 6:00 a.m. and worked until 3 p.m. My lunch break corresponded with Bob's habitual lunch hour of 11 a.m. and once I had filed the 11:00 "split" for radio and TV broadcasts, I was down the stairs and off to the Press Club to join Bob, a heavyset fellow, at his table. I did not drink much liquor at all in those days, and never at lunch, and I marveled at Bob's capacity.

With each martini Bob became more loquacious and began to spin off marvelously entertaining stories of his years with the AP. During my lunch hour reporters from the city would drift in and join our table, eager to listen to Bob. I departed at noon but Bob continued to eat, drink, and tell stories, returning to the AP office at 2 p.m.. He then left for home within the hour.

He didn't spend much time in the office but Bob was a wire service original who, with his indomitable spirit, probably did more to keep his AP newspaper and radio-TV subscribers happy than did most bureau chiefs. When he left West Virginia he was assigned to Berlin as the European editor of AP photos.

CHAPTER 59

Mannington & A. James Manchin

On November 20, 1968, disaster struck the Farmington Number 9 mine of Consolidation Coal Company in Marion County. First word of the story came across the Associated Press wire shortly after 5:30 a.m. with "Flash" bells ringing to tell the world that an explosion had rocked the mine with so much force it was felt twelve miles away. The blast (we would eventually know) killed 78 trapped coal miners.

WSAZ photographer Emil Varney and I hurried to the mine site on the day of the explosion and were immediately turned away by Consolidation security guards stationed miles from the scene. We could see in the distance the black smoke rising from the Llewellyn portal and filmed the gruesome scene that would become iconic in the history of coal mining. We gathered as much information as we could and quickly ferried our black and white 16mm film to Charleston for the 6:00 news and NBC exposure. We had no facilities for instant and live coverage in the 60s.

Emil and I began a vigil that saw us at Mannington for most of a week. Late in the first day, as we again unsuccessfully tried to gain access to the Llewellyn portal site, a large black Cadillac came chugging up the road and Marion County legislator A. James Manchin rolled down the window, hailing Emil and me. Jimmy, in his best Fiorello LaGuardia style, asked how we were doing.

"We can't get through the guards at Llewellyn, Jimmy," I said.

"Get in!" the large black mane of Italian heritage bellowed, with a yank of his head. Emil and I obliged, piling into the car. Jimmy gunned it and up the mountain we went to the barricade. The guard raised his hand in a "Stop!" motion and walked briskly to the car.

Manchin rolled the window down, leaned out and waved— "Hello, my friend!" he shouted.

"Oh, it's you, Jimmy," the guard said.

"We need through that gate, Jerry, my friends and I!"

"Sure, Jimmy, hold on!"

The gate swung wide and Emil and I were at the portal where no other media were allowed.

Manchin looked over his shoulder at the guard as we drove through the gate and muttered, "That son-of-a-bitch was against me last time around"—meaning the fellow had not supported Jimmy at the polls. It was vintage Manchin.

Jimmy escorted us the rest of the day to any off-site we requested, using his personality, friendships and larger-than-life persona to pave the way. He then inquired where we would stay that night (motels were miles away). We said we had not thought about it in our rush to get to the site, obtain coverage, and dispatch our film to Charleston and NBC.

Jimmy put up his hand to silence us and drove us to his brother's home, the house of John Manchin where Emil and I bunked on the family room floor after a sumptuous Italian dinner cooked up by Mary Manchin, mother of future governor and United States Senator, Joe Manchin. Those things you never forget, and I'll always be grateful to Antonio James Manchin, Joe's dad and mother, John and Mary, and the entire Manchin family for their kindness to Emil and me.

The next day the huge mine fire continued to spread with flames shooting 150 feet into the air. We learned the numbers from Consolidation officials: 99 miners were in the mine at the time of the explosion and only 21 made it out, leaving 78 miners trapped inside.

As is always the case when people are trapped and relatives wait, media turned to the families for interviews. I approached the grieving wives of the trapped miners with great care. I asked first if they would *agree* to be interviewed rather than thrusting a microphone in their face. With those who agreed to talk, I chose my words with care. Many reporters crossed the line, asking hurtful questions such as "What's it like to know your husband's trapped down there?"

As explosions continued to rock the mine I gently and carefully sat beside a woman whose husband was trapped and asked her if she was willing to share any thoughts at this moment. She agreed and I asked about her husband's number of years in the mines and his attitude toward mining. I asked if he had any fear for the danger of the job. I have always been proud that I dealt with those terrible interviews with decency and care for all concerned.

CHAPTER 60

Tony Boyle

UNITED MINE WORKERS OF AMERICA President W.A. "Tony" Boyle arrived at Mannington and Emil Varney and I set up our sound-on-film equipment, preparing to cover the message from the UMWA head. We had no inkling what Boyle would say, but we assumed he would harangue Consol for an unsafe mine and express grave concern for the trapped miners and their families.

Most of the country was shocked with the words we recorded from the man who was charged with the well-being of union coal miners. Boyle stood in front of hundreds of media as cameras rolled, recording history, capturing in black and white the Dickensesque figure of Boyle in a wide black fedora and overcoat, telling the amazed reporters, "We must recognize that this is a hazardous business, and what has occurred here is one of the hazards of being a miner. As long as we mine coal, there is always this inherent danger of explosion…this happens to be one of the better companies as far as cooperation with our union and safety is concerned."

Media contrasted the Boyle statement to that of John L. Lewis in 1947 when 111 miners were killed in an explosion in Centralia, Illinois. Lewis, coal dust on his face, said, "Coal is already saturated with the blood of too many men and drenched with the tears of too many surviving widows and orphans."

The Mannington mine was eventually sealed, leaving 78 miners entombed for eternity. The historic disaster sparked mine safety reform and was the beginning of the end for Tony Boyle's reign at the UMWA.

Jock Yablonski

IN 1969, JOCK YABLONSKI ANNOUNCED his candidacy for President of the United Mine Workers of America. He did this in opposition to Tony Boyle following Boyle's infamous defense of coal operators at the Mannington Mine disaster. Thus began a campaign of extreme interest in West Virginia, and I glued my newsroom to it.

Tony Boyle came to town and ensconced himself in the penthouse of the Daniel Boone Hotel—the same suite of rooms used by Elvis Presley when he played Charleston. I learned from informants that Boyle was at the "D-Boone" and I sent reporter John Montazolli to the hotel with orders to find and interview him.

Montazolli, a strikingly good-looking young guy sporting long hair of the time, was very much of Italian ancestry. John called me from a pay phone booth at the D-Boone and said Boyle was not to be found, that he was apparently in his suite and no one knew when he would come out.

"Go knock on his door," I instructed.

Montazolli thought that would be futile but he and photographer John Bradford made their way to the penthouse door and Montazolli knocked hard. Around Montazolli's chest, Pancho Villa style, hung a battery pack to power the lights photographer Bradford would use if Boyle's henchmen agreed to an interview, of which we thought there was fat chance.

So, the scene was: A very Italian young man standing in the doorway with what looked for all the world like a heavy ammunition belt crisscrossing his chest. The door to the penthouse opens and there stands Tony Boyle himself.

Montazolli was shocked that Boyle had answered his knock, but started to make his pitch. Boyle was startled even more as his stare went from John's eyes down to what looked to be an ammo belt. Boyle's face went ashen as he quickly slammed the door in Montazolli's face. Boyle would not meet with us from that moment on.

Unlike Boyle, Yablonski sought media and was a good and lively subject in print and on the air. Short in height and burly with large bushy eyebrows, a large nose and gravelly voice, he was the coal miner embodied, but with the moves of a fighter. I interviewed him many times and came to like him very much.

I invited both Boyle and Yablonski to debate live on WCHS-TV and radio. Boyle refused, Yablonski accepted and I placed an empty chair in the studio next to Yablonski with Boyle's name on it. Each question I asked Yablonski was answered—and then I would ask the empty chair for Boyle's response. It was quite effective and good TV.

Yablonski lost what was considered to be a rigged election. He conceded but on December 18, 1969 he asked the Department of Labor to investigate the election for fraud. Just weeks later, December 31, Yablonski, his wife and daughter were attacked in their farmhouse near Pittsburgh.

Three hired goons invaded the home and, first, shot and killed the daughter, Charlotte, 25. Yablonski and his wife Margaret were awakened by the gunshots and Jock went for a shotgun by his bed. He never made it. He and his wife were shot dead. Yablonski's son Kenneth discovered the gruesome murders five days later.

I tore the AP flash bulletin from the Teletype and rushed to the announcing booth, interrupting an on-air program. I had to control my emotion as I read the bulletin—Yablonski, his wife and daughter—all brutally murdered.

Hundreds of investigators were assigned to the case and seven people went to prison, but not Boyle. He was convicted of the murder much later—after a UMWA official in Tennessee squealed. For "Tough Tony" it was over—he was sentenced to life in prison, where he died.

CHAPTER 62

Isadore E. Buff

DR. I.E. BUFF WAS A mighty crusader who fought to establish that pneumoconiosis was a life-threatening disease brought on by breathing coal dust, a disease that affected every underground miner, eventually disabling him or killing him as he struggled to breathe. Their lungs literally turned black, causing Buff to name the malady "Black Lung".

Buff was an ideologue who fought the coal companies through publicity. His offices were not far from the WCHS-TV studios where I was news director. He had white hair that billowed from his head. In his sixties, he had a ruddy complexion that got redder as he ranted and raved in front of our microphone and camera. He was considered a kook by most. The Kanawha County Medical Society renounced his crusade with a resolution condemning activities by those in the medical profession that might incite coal miners without scientific evidence

My WCHS-TV co-anchor Roy Brassfield and I gave Buff plenty of airtime. We covered his progress as he campaigned and he was our go-to guy if the day's news was short. "We need another sound piece, Roy, what do you think? Buff?" I would ask.

Roy would agree and then call Buff who hurried to the station where Roy or I would interview the man who always had something to say, knowing media needed to feed the monster of regularly scheduled newscasts. Nevertheless, he was always a good interview. He would condemn mining companies, doctors, the medical associations and anyone else he thought neglected mining safety. He gave them hell without regard to his personal safety or legal repercussion.

It would be proven that Buff was, without question, correct in his assessment of Black Lung's cause and the coal industry's resistance to protecting or compensating its miners from the insidious disease. I believe we helped, through our intensive coverage, Dr. Buff's successful crusade to change the industry.

Buff's campaign came to a head in 1969 when thousands of miners marched on Charleston to support the Black Lung Association and a legislative bill to recognize coal dust as hazardous and to compensate miners' families who had lost a family member to the disease. The UMWA ordered coal miners not to participate under threat of expulsion from the union. They refused. Buff, wearing a hard hat, addressed the hundreds of miners, calling himself a "Medical Bandit", to the delight and thunderous applause of the coal miners who were ripe for a legislative fight.

CHAPTER 63

The Third House

THE BLACK LUNG 1969 LEGISLATIVE session was grim, as was the humor. Miners placed a coffin on a gurney in the Capitol building rotunda—complete with a mannequin dressed as a coal miner. Lying in state, the mannequin was a perfect reminder of death by pneumoconiosis. The coffin was inserted neatly into one of the second floor alcoves that surrounded the "well" between the House and Senate Chambers.

The *Third House*, the parody of the Legislature staged by reporters who covered the statehouse, was presented the final week of that session. It featured such antics as a reporter in the house gallery with a sign around his neck designating him as a fat cat lobbyist. He looked down with disapproval on his face as the House Judiciary Chairman (played by reporter Ralph Murphine) spoke in opposition to a bill the lobbyist wanted passed.

Fictitious legislator Murphine began to change his mind about the bill in mid-speech as the fellow playing the lobbyist floated fistfuls of play dollars down from the gallery—dollars that drifted softly onto Murphine's head. Murphine began gathering the bills, stuffing cash in every pocket, accepting one after the other of the lobbyist's demands, finally bellowing "Uh, uh, Mr. Speaker, I have chaaaaaged my mind and I fulllllllly support the bill!"

The audience loved it, save the House Judiciary Chairman. Following the play the crowd dispersed and we reporters were invited to House Speaker Ivor Boiarsky's office for a round of drinks and self-congratulation on another great *Third House*, as authored by the *Gazette's* Jim Dent.

When the Speaker's party ended it was past midnight and we were well-oiled. Tommy Knight (a reporter at the *Gazette* at the time), an Associated Press reporter (a woman whose name I have forgotten), and I, migrated to the now totally empty rotunda and giggled as we approached the coffin containing the mannequin. We wheeled the gurney carrying the coffin from its alcove and began to spin it around the second floor of the statehouse, pushing it from Senate to House, laughing uproariously.

"Elevator," Knight yelled and we rushed to the elevator, pushed the button, and transferred the coffin to the first floor, running it up and down the corridor from the Attorney General's office in the east end of the state Capitol to the Governor's office in the west end. The Capitol was empty of anyone but we three errant and drunk reporters, save one solitary Capitol guard who arrived as we began our second roar down the corridor to the AG's office.

The guard recognized us and took pity. He instructed us to return the coffin to its resting place and get the hell out of the building. We burped our appreciation and, after putting things in order, removed ourselves to the statehouse lawn where we finished the night of celebration. Were we to do that today we would be put in chains with our names at the top of the page of tomorrow's *Gazette*.

House Bill 1040, declaring Black Lung a compensable disease, passed later that week with a young legislator from Wyoming County, Warren McGraw, championing the legislation. House Speaker Boiarsky called for the historic roll call and the electronic board began to register the vote of each delegate. Our cameras rolled, recording the words of the Speaker as the big board flashed green. Boiarsky called out, "Ninety-five 'yes', five absent and not voting, I declare the legislation passed." Later, Congress would pass the national Coal Mine Health and Safety Act.

Isadore E. Buff died March 14, 1974, at the young age of 65. I attended his funeral. He was a crusader to be admired and every miner who receives a federal check to help ease his affliction from black lung has a white-haired, slightly stooped, and certainly mischievous Dr. I.E. Buff, to thank.

CHAPTER 64

Presidential Coverage

WHILE AT WSAZ AND WCHS I covered three United States Presidents: Lyndon Johnson, Jack Kennedy and Richard Nixon.

In the 1960s I traveled with Governor Wally Barron (aboard the state's Aero Commander airplane) to Pittsburgh and Morgantown where President Lyndon Johnson made a campaign stop at the Pittsburgh airport and then flew on to Morgantown to dedicate the new Hart Field airport. I covered Johnson again at Summersville, West Virginia when he dedicated the Summersville Dam.

In Summersville I was up close with Johnson and he reached out a giant hand and grabbed mine, shaking it as I asked some question that was probably inane. It was an experience. He clasped my hand (in my other hand was a Bell & Howell 16 mm camera) and held it for what seemed an eternity. His gaze was fixed on me. I felt the magnetism of the man and it had impact. I have since read most every Johnson biography; he fascinates me.

Jack Kennedy came to the West Virginia State Capitol and said on a rainy day to a thousand people on the statehouse grounds, "The sun may not always shine in West Virginia, but the people always do." Ken Kurtz and I were anchors for the live broadcast as we sat on a WSAZ mobile unit adjacent to the steps to the statehouse where Kennedy made his speech—we made comment as I held an umbrella. It was a big deal—Kennedy had come to thank West Virginians for putting him in the White House; a Catholic was thought to have had no chance to win in the heart of the Bible Belt and his success in West Virginia was thought to be significant in the final election.

My Nixon coverage took place when he was campaigning for President in 1968. He was a guest on a joint telecast of WSAZ's *At Issue and* WCHS's *Viewpoint*—both public affairs Sunday half-hour news shows modeled after *Meet the Press* and *Face the Nation*. Bos Johnson represented WSAZ, political editor Bob Mellace the *Charleston Daily Mail*, statehouse reporter Tommy Stafford the *Charleston Gazette*, and I, WCHS TV. We shook Nixon's hand, engaged in small talk and showed him the way to the WSAZ studio. The tape rolled and Bos introduced our guest—and four pretty good news guys went at "Tricky Dick." Mellace was a great political reporter and those who were stung by him referenced the reporter by saying, 'Malice from Mellace'. Mellace, representing the Republican newspaper, cut him no slack. Tommy Stafford was the Democratic newspaper representative and he was as tough as Mellace.

Nixon turned out to be an excellent guest and fielded the toughest of questions without breaking a sweat, as he had in his debates with Jack Kennedy. Nixon had obviously shaved just before the interview, eliminating the famous dark beard—he had learned from his debacle in the Nixon-Kennedy confrontation. We exchanged pleasantries after the show, again shaking hands and talking politics. It was heady stuff for a 24-year old.

During his brother Jack's term, Attorney General Bobby Kennedy came to Charleston. I followed closely by Bobby's side as he made the political rounds. I was pressed close to the Attorney General in a packed elevator at the Kanawha Hotel. He was gracious and did not seem to mind that a reporter was up close and personal.

During the elevator ride he turned to his aide and I heard him whisper, "What's the name of the local FBI agent?" The reply was that his first name was John. Kennedy nodded his head that he understood and when the elevator doors swung open he exited and turned toward the agent, saying, in his best Boston accent, and with a handshake, "John, thanks for all you are doing for the Department here in Charleston."

Then, Bobby brushed his hair from his forehead, flashed a Kennedy smile, and strode into the hotel's eloquent ballroom, waving to all. A standing audience applauded for more than a minute. As Bobby spoke to the large luncheon crowd, little did I realize his life would end across the country in a hotel kitchen, leaving a gaping hole in the heart of the nation.

CHAPTER 65

St. Louis

IN 1967 I RECEIVED A job offer from KTVI-TV in St. Louis. I was extremely aggressive in trying to move up the broadcast food chain—believing at 27 that I was behind schedule in climbing to a major market—with the ultimate goal of becoming a network correspondent. I took the job, becoming a street reporter for KTVI—called a "Word Man", in the parlance of the time.

The years in St. Louis were eventful. I covered City Hall and the colorful mayor of St. Louis, Alfonso J. Cervantes (a midwest Fiorello LaGuardia); the St. Louis County Administrator, True Davis; the Missouri governor, Warren Hearnes; and the burning of East St. Louis, Illinois.

On May 25, 1968 Vice President Hubert Humphrey came to St. Louis to dedicate the now iconic "Arch" that marks the Gateway to the West. Humphrey spoke on a rainy day that could not deter thousands of Missourians from attending the dedication of what has become one of America's treasures. I reported on the historic dedication while marveling at the view from the apex of the Arch.

The years 1966 and 1967 were filled with race riots and the burning of major portions of the country's largest cities. Firefighters and news people were fair game for those who were rioting. In the St. Louis market we were called on daily to cover the unrest in East St. Louis—where rioters were shouting, "Burn, Baby, Burn!" On one occasion I was covering an arson that blazed high above the city's skyline when my film crew and I were accosted by a gang that surrounded us and began to advance, clubs and rocks in hand.

We were saved. Not by police but by some very brave firemen who waded through the crowd and took command. The crowd shrank back as a fire captain shouted at them to disperse. He had no gun, but he a lot of bravado and I will always be grateful to the men of the East St. Louis Fire Department.

CHAPTER 66

Musial & DiMaggio

THEN, THERE WAS BASEBALL. WHEN out with a film crew in St. Louis I would invariably get a call via our shortwave radio from Easy Ed McCauley, sports director at KTVI. Easy Ed had been a star basketball player for the St. Louis Hawks in the fifties. He asked that I divert my film crew to Busch Memorial Stadium and we dashed off to answer his request—and a lunch in the press box above the playing field. Before chowing down, I would walk out on the field to watch Easy Ed interview various members of the St. Louis Cardinals as famous names all around me went through pre-play drills: Bob Gibson, Tim McIver, Johnny Romano, Orlando Cepeda, Julian Javier, Lou Brock, Curt Flood and Roger Maris—to name a few.

However, the piece 'de resistance was in that press box where I ingested some mighty fine food. Stan Musial came by. We shook hands and engaged in small talk. Wow! A few feet from where I stood, West Virginia's Jay Randolph was doing play-by-play—the voice of the baseball Cardinals. Jay also did the football Cardinals broadcast. He broadcast those games from a perch high above the field that was open to the elements, giving him the feel of the game.

Once, when broadcasting an out-of-town game, Jay felt hemmed in by a broadcast booth that was glass enclosed. After taking isolation as long as he could, he grabbed a chair and smashed the window before him, saying to a startled stadium official, "Bill me!"

Another interesting baseball experience was meeting Joe DiMaggio in, of all places, Clarksburg, West Virginia. I was there to do business with a client and I was staying at the downtown Gore Hotel. I went out for an afternoon run and saw a figure that looked like DiMaggio. I questioned myself as to whether it really was Joltin' Joe, but as I drew closer I was convinced it was indeed the Bronx Bomber.

I walked up to him and said, "I don't usually do this but when I see an icon on the street corner in Clarksburg, West Virginia, I just have to say hello."

He grinned and shook my hand. I asked him if he was there for the Italian Festival, which was underway that week. He said no, that he often came in to fish with a well-know coal operator Jimmy LaRosa.

CHAPTER 67

Governors, Five Alarms & Tom Mix

ALABAMA GOVERNOR GEORGE WALLACE CAME TO St. Louis as the American Independent Party candidate and I landed a one-on-one interview with him in the KTVI studios. Off-camera, Wallace chewed on a cigar, but when the film rolled he removed his stogie and urged voters to "Stand Up for America!" Wallace was a tough little guy and our news director, Geoff Smith, had covered him in Birmingham, the Alabama capital, before moving to St. Louis. He was not a fan of Wallace and I was proud Geoff chose me to do the interview with the man who had declared "Segregation forever!"

Texas Governor John Connally came to the state to stump for Jimmy Carter. I interviewed him as he rode on the back of a convertible through the state capital, Jefferson City. Just four years before, Connally had been in a convertible with President Kennedy in Dallas when Lee Harvey Oswald ended Kennedy's life with a rifle shot from the Texas School Book Depository in Dealey Plaza.

Movie character actor Horace McMahon was an interesting interview. He came through town plugging the Frank Sinatra movie, "The Detective." McMahon was in the movie as a fellow cop with Sinatra. When the camera was off he had a terrible tic in one eye. I wondered how the guy could make a living in the movies with such an obvious handicap. Once we began to film the interview, the tic abruptly stopped. When the interview was over, the tic immediately returned.

St. Louis, for some reason, was a big "fire" town—after my first five-alarm fire report on the riverbanks of the Mississippi, I went out and bought fur-lined boots, a heavy jacket and cap. The winters were frigid, topped only by the summers, when the humidity shot through the roof.

While at KTVI, I was privileged to do frequent feature stories. The Ralston Purina Company was headquartered there and I asked to review the company's archives where I found the original radio scripts of the *Tom Mix Radio Show* (sponsored by Ralston and Checkerboard Square), a program that rivaled the hit radio program *Jack Armstrong, the All American Boy*. I reported for five consecutive days on the trivia of the Tom Mix programs. The St. Louis D'Arcy Advertising Agency of the 1930s wrote the scripts for the show. It became great camp back then to listen to the program and wait to hear the names of the villains. The D'Arcy agency wrote into each script—as villains— prominent St. Louis attorneys of the time.

In the stacks of Ralston Purina memorabilia I found a Tom Mix secret decoder ring, awarded to members of Tom's "Straight Shooter's Club". In my last report—live in the studio— my filmed segment ended and I held up the decoder ring and said,

"If anyone watching has a decoder ring, hang on to it—they are indeed rare."

We switched immediately to our weather guy, Don Beecher. Beecher looked slightly amused. He reached in his jacket pocket and said, "Lucky me, I just happen to have one. I've carried a secret decoder ring for years." True story. The news director was pleased—good TV.

St. Louis was a great experience and I agree with Tom Becherer, a KTVI producer and fellow reporter of the time, who said it was one of the greatest jobs he ever had. But, a station airing Bugs Bunny as competition against our 5:30 newscast had better ratings and the writing was on the wall. Staff cuts were soon to be made. Bos Johnson had a position coming open in Charleston and he offered me the job. I accepted and packed my bags.

Within six months of my return to WSAZ-TV I was offered the job of news director across town at WCHS-TV. I struggled a long time over the decision—Bos had rescued me from a tough situation and I worried I was going to offend him if I took the job. I finally decided to accept the WCHS offer because I wanted the experience of running a newsroom—and the pay was better. I said goodbye to a station I loved and once again thanked Bos, who believed enough in me to hire me three times.

CHAPTER 68

News Director

I TOOK ON THE CHALLENGE of raising low ratings to fight the champ, WSAZ-TV, and relished in doing it. I engaged stringers (freelance photographers) throughout our coverage area, redesigned our news set and hired additional reporters to provide enlarged coverage in the Charleston-Huntington market.

I anchored the 6:00 news with Roy Brassfield whom I hired out of Logan, West Virginia. I hired Jane Martin as our "Weather Girl" and launched Bill Richards and Frank Annand as the 11:00 anchors. I called our newscasts "Newsday" and ground out exclusives by creating a public affairs program on Sundays. Additionally, we were required to produce a documentary each month—quite a task for a newsroom of less than ten people.

I was sitting at home one evening watching the 11:00 newscast with Richards and Annand. I had moved Richards from his role as weathercaster to anchor and had forbidden him to do commercials, determined to change Bill's on-air persona to news anchor. Richards, however, loved doing commercials. Two weeks into his transformation, at approximately 11:10, I watched Bill break for a commercial only to see him immediately reappear aboard a Honda motorcycle. Bill was jumping up and down on the Honda, gleefully exclaiming its many features, grinning to beat the band. At the end of the commercial break his face again appeared on camera—as solemn "newscaster" Bill Richards.

I was seething, waiting for the newscast to end so I could call Bill and raise hell. Bill, the most genial of fellows, just shrugged it off. I did, however, succeed in keeping him off Hondas for the rest of his run until we replaced him at 11:00 with Brassfield. Bill went back to commercials and did an excellent job as WCHS radio news director as I began to concentrate fulltime on the TV end of the news operation.

Co-workers chief photographer Dick Johnson, staff photographers John Bradford, and Bill White, and Larry Sonis, my Huntington reporter, were solid professionals. I hired Larry straight out of Marshall University. I was greatly impressed with him and he was the real thing: bright, decisive, brilliant. A great catch—but I did not realize he did not have a driver's license. For the first month he caught the Huntington transit, complete with 100 pounds of camera gear, to get to assignments. Unbelievable.

Once Larry got his license and could drive the WCHS-TV cruiser, things improved dramatically. Larry eventually transferred to Charleston and covered the morning news reports and co-anchored the noon news with me. We had a marvelously great rapport. It was helped along when, one day, Larry found a banana in a refrigerator used on the set of the morning talk show. He observed the banana each day, testifying as to the daily rot of said banana. He would bring it to the set and, just before I went on the air, hold up the banana, sending me into convulsions of laughter. When the banana finally withered into nothing and Larry had no banana to hold, he would simply say, "Banana," just before the mike was opened, and I would lose it.

Larry and his siblings were sensational. Their mother, Mary, would regularly stop by the WCHS newsroom after newscasts and they would engage in badinage, dropping "F-bombs" at a time when the word was not so freely and publicly used. Mary said her husband had died when the children were just infants and she determined she would bring them up in a manner guaranteeing they would be tough and competitive—salty language was a part of that. She raised superior children.

Larry, a dear friend, ran for and was elected to the West Virginia House of Delegates where he successfully led the fight to abolish closed committee meetings and open state documents to the public. He eventually moved to Florida and founded a public relations firm. Unfortunately, he died a young man. I remain friends with his two sisters, Debbie and Tina who, with similar brilliance and humor, keep Larry's spirit alive.

News stringers in West Virginia, Ohio and Kentucky provided a wide geographical coverage map for my effort to overcome WSAZ-TV—or at least put a dent in their ratings. Raamie Barker, in Logan County, was an outstanding stringer. Raamie was the best, delivering one scoop after another to us, beating WSAZ to the punch. Years later Raamie became the top aide to West Virginia Governor Earl Ray Tomblin. I first met Earl Ray when invited by Raamie (whose fulltime job was as a school teacher in Madison, West Virginia) to speak to his high school Civics class. Raamie introduced me to his star student—young Earl Ray Tomblin—who would become West Virginia's governor in 2010.

While Raamie held the honors as the most outstanding news gatherer in the field, another standout was our stringer in southeastern Ohio. This fellow had better camera equipment than WCHS-TV and he delivered great material. He also would treat us with tidbits on the end of any film reels that had not been fully used. In other words, he might shoot 75 feet of a 100-foot roll on some news story, and then finish with 25 feet of stuff he'd shoot around the house. Most of the "stuff" was film of naked women in a hot tub at his home.

Needless to say, we could not wait to process his film to watch his tidbits, which we named "Tit-Bits". I lived in great fear that somehow the stuff would get on the air. I was not, however, so fearful that I ordered the stringer to cease and desist.

CHAPTER 69

Textbook Wars

THE GREAT KANAWHA COUNTY TEXTBOOK War exploded in 1974 while I was at WCHS-TV. The year presented one challenge after another as to whether certain stories and accusations should receive major, minor, or no coverage; the entire landscape seemed to be filled with folks who would make outrageous claims and toss verbal bombs onto burning events.

In March 1974 the Kanawha County School System's English Language Arts Textbook Committee recommended, as part of West Virginia's elementary school curriculum, more than 300 books for use in elementary schools—books that were controversial in that they were multicultural and expressed the egalitarian concept that all people are created equal. School board member Alice Moore, wife of a fundamentalist minister, objected to many of the books and quoted from one, *Autobiography of Malcom X*—wherein Malcolm X referred to Christians as "brainwashed." She asked for 325 books to be made available for her review and told media she had found quotes from Black Panthers Eldridge Cleaver and George Jackson to which she objected.

In May, Moore charged at a board meeting that the textbooks she had examined were, "filthy, disgusting trash, unpatriotic and unduly favoring blacks." The Kanawha County Parent-Teacher Association weighed in on her side and a group of local parents did as well. The national media descended upon Kanawha County.

WCHS was a CBS affiliate and the CBS crews used our station to edit their reports and chat with my co-anchor Roy Brassfield who did the heavy lifting of coverage of the sizzling hot story. A CBS photographer was attacked and Walter Cronkite weighed in with radio commentary.

WCHS-TV general manger Curtis Butler and I watched the violence erupting in the station's viewing area, and we decided something had to be said. I worked with him to develop a commentary and he bravely editorialized that the textbook selection was well-balanced—asking for reason and acceptance and use of the books on the school board list. Alice Moore attacked Butler and me in an equal-time editorial in which she recited excerpts from one of the books, titled *At Lunchtime, A Story of Love* in which a school bus of young people engage in sex.

She hardly needed the extra time; Brassfield, who became news director when I left WCHS to open my business, interviewed Alice Moore so often they came to know one another well. Roy liked her as a person, as did most folks—she was smart and attractive and had a lilting southern accent—and a harsh tongue. She and Roy were guests of the Phil Donahue show, the era's blockbuster news interview program, broadcast from Chicago. Donahue devoted two broadcasts to the dispute.

Roy became a sought-after speaker and eloquently described to a group in southern West Virginia the threat of violence in WCHS' day-to-day reporting of the schoolbook story. He related that he and his photographer were making their way through a rather large gathering outside the Kanawha County Board of Education office when they were stopped.

Brassfield:

Three gorillas were standing in front of the door that led to the second floor stairway leading to the board meeting room. Unknowing, we attempted to go through the door.

One of the men said, "You aren't going upstairs."

I said, "Pardon me?"

He said, "You aren't going upstairs."

Again, I said, "Excuse me, we're going up to the board meeting."

At this point, one of the guys pulled from behind him a large metal pipe and said, 'I said you aren't going anywhere."

Being of reasonable intelligence, I said, "You're right."

Roy managed to make it outside and take another entrance into the building and cover the board meeting.

In the wake of the protest movement, a federal agent visited Roy's home and suggested he move his family out of town for a time. Federal agents followed him for several weeks.

Ku Klux Klan, Guns & Jail

ALICE MOORE WAS A LIGHTNING rod and the crackle and hiss from her and her supporters set Kanawha county on fire with threats, shootings, and bombings. Moore told media that the school board list included some textbooks that preached sedition. "I object to using materials in the classroom that encourage students to rebel," she said.

She charged that vulgar and profane materials were in the classroom. It was a tense time and each of our newscasts seemed to lead with a brewing cauldron of unrest that saw half of the county's students absent from school.

At school board meetings Moore was calm and collected with the exception of one episode where she and another board member clashed, shouting at one another while board president Russell Isaacs called for order. The NAACP and the Ku Klux Klan entered the fracas, rounding out a panoply of vested interests.

People went to jail and some startling interviews ensued. One protest leader told reporter Jim Reader of our cross-town rival WSAZ-TV that, after a night in jail where he had been in a room with four juveniles, one "colored boy was saved." The Reverend Ezra Graley said the night in jail was worth $10,000 to him.

Twenty-seven local ministers denounced the books and twelve thousand people signed a petition protesting the books. A walkout of students ensued, with more than 40,000 elementary school students staying home from classes.

Our cameras ground away as bombs were found at schools and one school was dynamited. Guns were trained on school buses, and students that continued to attend classes were harassed. Charles Quigley told the *Charleston Gazette* that he asked Christians to, "Pray that God will kill the giants that have mocked and made fun of dumb fundamentalists." Quigley said he wanted school board members Russell Isaacs, Harry Stansbury and Albert Anson struck dead.

Protestors picketed at schools and businesses throughout the county and especially at Heck's Discount Stores whose CEO, Russell Isaacs, was president of the Board of Education. In September thousands of coal miners went on strike to support the boycott, taking the controversy to a whole new level. Governor Arch Moore was asked to intervene but declined to send the National Guard or state troopers into the melee.

In November the school board met at the Charleston Civic Center with thousands of seats made ready for a maximum crowd. Fewer than a hundred people trickled into the cavernous theatre. Thousands chose to stay home, fearful violence might occur. The board, taking advantage of the low turnout, voted to return the books to elementary schools.

The protesters continued, however, with a battle cry of, "We have just begun to fight." But the vote held—with subsequent approval of Alice Moore's entreaties that guidelines be adopted to assure future textbook selection would be done with recognition of home sanctity and encouragement of loyalty to the United States. Future controversial books were confined to school libraries and parental approval before a student could check out flagged books. Alice Moore said she had accomplished more than she had ever hoped to accomplish.

The year of unrest wrote history the Kanawha County textbook controversy is thought by some to be a seminal moment in the then-emerging and now-continuing story of conservatives and evangelicals.

CHAPTER 71

Chilton, Comstock, Marsh & Hindman

AT THE HELM OF WCHS's news operation I tried to innovate in every way I could. I asked *Charleston Gazette* Publisher W.E. Ned Chilton III, on the left of the political spectrum, and the *West Virginia Hillbilly* publisher Jim Comstock, on the right, to write and present commentary one night each week—a fellow by the name of Eric Sevareid was doing the same thing during Walter Cronkite's nightly report and CBS' 60 Minutes was getting lots of eyeballs with its "Point-Counterpoint" series featuring James Kilpatrick and Shana Alexander.

Ned, a graduate of Yale, was a friend of and admirer of television personality William F. Buckley. Ned liked the idea of a television presence akin to Buckley's effort. Comstock cottoned to it immediately—he knew it could sell newspapers.

Out of that relationship I formed a strong bond with Ned and Jim. My politics were certainly 180 degrees from Ned's, but I admired him as a fire-breathing journalist who believed the duty of a newspaper was to comfort the afflicted and afflict the comforted. Ned delivered some hard-hitting commentary and Jim supplied superb whimsy.

When I entered business, the foundation I had with Ned and with *Gazette* Editor Don Marsh proved to be beneficial. Marsh and I had covered the statehouse together and admired and liked each other. Don was ten years my senior and his intellect and sharp wit made him a favorite of Chilton. Don would kid me as my business began to prosper, saying, "Better nouveau than no riche at all."

After I founded Charles Ryan Associates, Don wrote a witty column that bemoaned the creation of our *Charleston Daily Mail West Virginia Poll* that rapidly eclipsed the *Gazette's* fledgling polling efforts. CRA's Rex Repass, *Daily Mail* editor Sam Hindman, and I were the collaborators who created the *West Virginia Poll*. Marsh said in his column of metaphoric hand-wringing that Ryan had rapidly gone from public relations to politics and advertising, capping his expansion with public opinion research—creating a business so successful that music played when one was on hold (pretty special for the time). Not only that, Don said, Ryan drove a Mercedes. Don was extremely kind to me and I am quite aware I may have gotten some preferential treatment from him as editor of the *Gazette*.

Sam Hindman, then editor and later publisher of the *Charleston Daily Mail*, seized upon the poll with glee. Many called him "Shoe" because Hindman looked amazingly like *Shoe* in the cartoon series by Jeff MacNelly, as featured in the *Daily Mail*. Hindman was a newspaperman's newspaperman. He slouched through the newsroom and across the golf course, one of the funniest, talented, and most interesting guys I have ever met. When Sam ascended to the publisher's post David Greenfield succeeded him as editor and, together, they made a formidable team.

I often played golf with Hindman and Greenfield. Sam was famous for his score keeping. "Whaddya' have on that hole, Sam?" was the query upon leaving the green. "Par—sorta'," was Sam's reply.

Greenfield, an excellent golfer, often tried to coach me to a better game by saying, "Just use your God-given talent, Ryan!" It was not that easy, but things got better when Sam decided to publish a golf magazine. He hired a golf pro with a journalism degree and the golfer-editor often played with our group. I had the best scores of my life as he tutored me on every shot.

You had to love the Hindman approach to golf—an approach that saw all the bag boys come running when Mr. Sam appeared because he was roundly known to give $50 tips with regularity. Back then the publisher had a lot of latitude with his expense accounts as the *Daily Mail* and other newspapers peeled off a 35% profit each and every year.

CHAPTER 72

Chilton & The United Way

IN THE 1980s *GAZETTE* PUBLISHER Ned Chilton, who was prone to address close friends as, "Old Shoe", was on a rant against the United Way because the national organization was reported to be taking a huge chunk of its donated monies to pay inflated executive salaries. Charles Ryan Associates was doing pro-bono work for the local United Way as Chilton slammed away at the national headquarters. The national office told the locals and me it was sending three top executives to Charleston to dress Ned down—they asked that I arrange a meeting with Chilton so that they could set him straight and save themselves from Chilton's diatribe.

"You do not want to approach Ned that way. The only thing that will take Ned off the case will be some reform at national headquarters in regard to executive salaries," I advised them. Not to worry, I was assured, the Washington folks would chew Ned up and spit him out.

Came the day of the meeting and the three suits from the national organization and I arrived at the *Gazette*. We were escorted into Ned's office and left standing there. Ned was not to be seen, but we could hear him. He was loudly muttering, "Where is it? Where is it?"

Within a few seconds his head emerged from below and behind his desk and he bellowed for his secretary to help him find an electrical outlet for his coffee machine. He ignored us as he shouted, "Sumatra! Sumatra! Dark!" meaning he was going to brew up some pretty strong coffee and, oh, by the way, "Who wants some?"

We all said in unison that we loved dark, strong coffee.

"Sit, sit!" Ned shouted.

We sat.

"Donuts! Donuts! Glazed! Glazed!" Ned yelled at his secretary.

She left with a bound and I began to introduce the suits to Ned who stayed seated and grinned at them like a Cheshire cat.

After the introduction I went to the farthest corner of the office and sat down and waited for the fun to begin. I was working without charge, I had given my best advice, and it had been ignored. So I decided to just sit back and watch the fireworks.

Ned invited the suits to proceed as donuts arrived and coffee was poured. Glazed! Sumatra!

I had to give it to the suits. They pitched their hearts out and Ned sat and listened intently, eating donuts, drinking coffee, and scratching his stomach.

Whey they had finished Ned asked if they had said all they wanted to say and the suits nodded in the affirmative.

Ned leaned back in his chair, put his jean-covered legs up on the desk, displaying sockless alligator slippers, clasped his hands behind his head and said, grinning, "Are you sure?"

The suits glanced nervously at one another, sensing Ned was coiled, and again nodded yes.

Ned thereupon jerked his feet off his desk, stood up, leaned across the desk and barked, "Well, you've had your say, and now I'll have mine, and I say, F—k the United Way!"

The suits' faces went ashen and the meeting was over. Chilton grinned at us all the way out the door.

I had to love his style.

CHAPTER 73

Fiery Ned

NED CHILTON HAD A THING ABOUT telephone etiquette. When he called an office and a receptionist or secretary would say, "May I say who is calling?" he would go ballistic, huffing and puffing that the person he was calling was obviously an uppity sort and he, Chilton, would have none of it. I knew this and had cautioned my receptionist and all our secretaries who might answer an incoming call that they were to never ask who was calling—just take the call and put it through to the person requested.

However, I had recently hired a new secretary and I failed to apprise her of this CRA rule. So, I found myself the victim of the Chilton oddity when the new secretary, Maggie, asked who was calling when Chilton phoned to ask for a copy of a recent political poll we had conducted.

Chilton went off on Maggie and then me. I tried to settle him down but knew I had to do more to rectify things. Maggie, my secretary, was African American. Chilton was a champion of black employment at a time when professional positions were not filled by blacks in generous numbers. I quickly dispatched Maggie to Chilton's office to deliver a copy of the poll and told her to be certain to insist that she personally put the material in Chilton's hands. She did so and reported back that Ned was very nice to her. The telephone transgression was forgotten.

Ned had a habit of calling to personally deposit his unhappiness with news he heard around the *Gazette* newsroom. Upon learning that I had hired Republican House of Delegates Minority Leader Larry Swann to run our Clarksburg office he called me on a Saturday at home. Ned did not know Swann personally, but he was extremely irate that I had hired a ranking member of the House of Delegates, assuming, I am certain, that I had done so to gain favor for clients we represented in the lobbying sector of our business.

I was carrying groceries up two flights of outdoor stairs to the house and upon arrival at the kitchen picked up a ringing phone. It was Ned and he asked if I had hired Swann. I said that was true and he again went off, accusing me of doing something that was unethical and saying, "I'm coming after you, Ryan!" I responded that Swann was indeed a legislator and the House Minority Leader, but he was also a talented professional and, I said, "Oh, by the way, he can't live on a legislator's salary alone—he is entitled to a job."

Swann was a solid professional who would draw clients from the north central part of the state. He was a part-time legislator and, like all his peers, needed to be gainfully employed in the private sector, as I had pointed out to Chilton.

Needless to say, however, my weekend was ruined—the *Gazette* and its fire-breathing publisher were coming after me. I envisioned editorial outrage by Chilton and a beating that would affect my business in a devastating way.

Well, the attack never came. I believe Chilton's ire was quickly doused in the *Gazette* newsroom because, unlike Ned, most reporters and especially the statehouse newshounds, knew Larry and told Ned he was absolutely wrong in his conviction that Larry (or I) would misuse his Minority Leader position.

I was extremely proud of our hiring of Larry Swann and stood in great respect of him; he represented the best in the legislative arena and in our business. The lesson was that one's reputation withstands any unworthy attack or misunderstanding.

Ned Chilton feared no one—he did not give a wit about potential litigation that might be lodged against the *Gazette* and its forthright editorials. *Gazette* editor Don Marsh loved Chilton and his traits. Marsh, as the paper's editor with an office next to Chilton, would regularly hear Chilton initiate a *Gazette* investigation by bellowing into the newsroom, "Haught!" It was Ned's manner of summoning ace investigative reporter Jim Haught to hurry to Chilton's office to receive an assignment to "go after" yet another poor fellow the publisher thought to be a miscreant.

I thought Don Marsh to be a great journalist and extraordinary man. He was a superior and gifted writer with an intellectual sense of humor. Don and I traveled to Morgantown one day to address students at the WVU School of Journalism. On the way back to Charleston, we were ecstatic that we had each been paid a $100 honorarium. Don was in a great mood and told Chilton stories as I drove. Don said Chilton was on the phone one day with Congressman John Slack who represented much of southern West Virginia, when a heated argument occurred between the two men. Don said Chilton finally hung up on Slack, shouting into the phone, "Who the hell do you think you are? You're nothing but a goddamned Congressman!"

Ned was a top ranked squash player—a game I also played at Edgewood Country Club. Ned delighted in the fact that I had a bit of a temper on the squash court and I regularly smashed my racquet into the wall of the court, frustrated, when I missed a shot. I would then make my way to Ned's office where, surprisingly enough, Ned sold squash racquets. I could have purchased the racquet at Edgewood Country Club, but I may have reasoned that buying from Ned might give me a leg up with a man who could be quite mercurial in attitude. Regardless, Ned had the best prices on squash racquets.

Fact is, I liked Ned very much, and I respected his fire-breathing editorial page. I once asked the *Daily Mail's* Sam Hindman why the *Mail* was not more like the *Gazette*—crusading day after day in an effort to change something. It was an effective tactic and I wanted the *Daily Mail*, where my political convictions resonated, to emulate Chilton's methodology—pushing conservative positions day after day, until it altered the social and political landscape.

Ned died in 1987, coming off the squash court just after he had finished a match in regional competition in Washington, DC.

He was 65—way too young to pass from the scene. I mourned his loss and urged then-sitting Governor Arch Moore to attend his funeral. Moore took it under consideration, but chose not to pay his respects to his nemesis. It was a bad mistake.

CHAPTER 74

A Need to Earn

TIMING IS EVERYTHING, SO THEY say, and my timing was to enter business in the middle of a national recession that saw sky high inflation, interest rates of double digits, an oil crisis with long lines at gasoline pumps, and a stock market crash. What was I thinking?

I made the decision because I was barely getting by financially—the ownership of WCHS-TV and Radio, where I was employed, had firmly embraced the Nixon wage freeze that the President had imposed in 1971 and re-imposed in 1973—icing my annual salary at $10,500 for five years. Better, I thought, to see if I could be my own boss, make a decent living, and do something I would love.

"How to do it?" That was the question. The answer began to form one day in 1968 in a newspaper Governor Arch Moore called the "Morning Sick Call"—the *Charleston Gazette*. That particular day the *Gazette* was anything but a sick call for me—it was my tip sheet that created a path toward a new career.

I walked into the Strand Pool Hall on Hale Street in Charleston and ordered an early lunch at the counter. I opened the *Gazette* to see what else Richard Nixon could do to my earning power. An article that said entrepreneur Fred Haddad had opened his 12th Heck's (*Heck's* was a word formed by using the first letter of the names of the five founders of the discount chain) outlet in Point Pleasant, West Virginia caught my eye.

Haddad, and a fellow retailer by the name of Sam Walton, had the same idea—buy in bulk at a steep discount and re-sell the items at prices below those found in traditional retail stores. The business model proved to be highly lucrative. Heck's eventually faded away, but Walton's dream exists today as Wal-Mart and, ironically, Wal-Mart became West Virginia's largest employer.

I marched back to the television station and called Haddad. I asked if Heck's had ever considered a house organ. Fred replied, "What's a house organ?"

I responded, "A company newspaper."

"Oh, we tried that, it didn't work," was Fred's rejoinder.

"May I come over and talk about it?" I asked.

"Sure," he said.

I convinced Fred and Heck's vice-president Russell Isaacs to let me rekindle the Heck's house organ. Russell put me in touch with Wal-Mart's tiny offices down in Arkansas and the folks there were glad to send me copies of the Wal-Mart company publication, which became the model for what I called *The Heck's World*.

I recruited "reporters" at each of the Heck's outlets to take Polaroid pictures and send handwritten or typed notes about store employees and their activities. I rewrote the material as news stories and created captions for the pictures. I worked with Phil Fourney, publisher of the *Ravenswood News*, in printing the first edition, which I laid out with Phil's oversight.

With continued tutoring from Phil, I did the layout for two subsequent editions and then sought a "layout man" who could do the job faster. I hired Chuck Carpenter at the *Charleston Gazette* and applied my newly-found time to visit and win the house organ business of Purity Baking, Charleston National Bank and the West Viginia Funeral Directors Association. I added the West Virginia Trial Lawyers and for several years ground out house organs each month, matching my net income at WCHS-TV. My success caused me to believe I had found a niche I could develop if I were to add public relations services to my activities.

I visited the Heck's offices each Saturday and chatted with Russ Isaacs about my dream of starting a business. Russ gave me hours of his time and encouraged me. I owe him much. The problem was that I could not ethically add PR to my services while employed as news director for WCHS-TV.

I also shared my dream with an old friend, Charleston attorney Gene Hoyer, who gave me great encouragement. While undergraduates at West Virginia University, Gene and I often studied together. Gene became a very successful attorney and owner of several parcels of choice downtown Charleston real estate. He believed average intelligence and hard work equated success. If the intelligence level was a little more than average, so much the better, Gene said, with an engaging grin.

With encouragement from Russ and Gene, I took a deep breath and decided the only way to resolve my issue was *just to do it*—leave WCHS and open a business. So, even though folks thought I was crazy, I resigned my post and hung out my PR shingle.

I felt certain I would succeed if I could add at least one PR client. I found that client in Dean Lewis. Dean had a flourishing law practice and construction business. He had listened to my dream and encouraged me—he agreed to hire me at $1,000 a month to produce brochures and initiate a public relations plan for his construction company.

Dean was always available to me and mentored me through many times of concern. He was an incredibly able and successful intellect who was probably the smartest person I ever encountered. He worked hard, and so did I—but this time, with his help, I would be working for myself.

CHAPTER 75

Crazy Charlie

YES, A JOURNEY OF A thousand miles begins with the first step. Mine came when I opened the door of the office of WCHS-TV general manager Curtis Butler in August of 1974 and told him I was giving my two weeks' notice. After I advised Curtis of my plans he asked me to reconsider. Curtis said, in effect, that I was crazy. He said it in a very nice way, but the message was clear—I would starve.

"You are the fourth highest paid professional here," he explained. "Only the national sales manager, the chief engineer and I are paid more than you. Why would you give up a job and position such as you have in the community to do this?"

I explained that I felt I was, regardless of my lofty standing in the WCHS-Nixon wage freeze, starving. I told him if my venture did not work I could always return to broadcasting. I apprised him of my clients and my conviction that I could grow a sizeable business that would allow me to support my family in a far better way.

For ten days I would end my nightly Monday-Friday 6:00 p.m. newscast saying something like, "And that's the news this evening. In a few days I'll be leaving this post to open a public relations firm that will be known as *Charles Ryan Associates*. My thanks to you for viewing. Goodnight."

Curtis, God bless him, let me get away with it as I counted down the days over a two-week period. My future business partner of thirty-three years, Harry Peck, told me he watched with incredulity each night as I promoted my soon-to-be business to a tri-state audience, citing the days left before my firm would be launched. Harry said he decided to accept a job offer from me barely two months later, based on my nightly commercial. Harry thought I could sell my wares.

The years 1969-1974 at WCHS were indeed crucial to my success in business. When I left Channel 8 I had a profile in the Charleston-Huntington market and many friends who were ready to assist me in my quixotic quest.

I wrote a number of people in the business, political and legal communities, to tell them of my decision to open a firm. I did not hear from many of them but the letter blitz later brought response from a few key individuals who opened significant doors for me. For the most part, however, there was at the time of the two-week "goodbye" a continued belief in the journalistic community that I had gone off the deep end. "Poor Charlie, a nice guy, but what the hell is he thinking?" was the universal attitude.

Except for one guy. His name was Lu Leslie, a retired Associated Press Bureau Chief. I can see him now, stooped just a bit, in his seventies, ruddy red face and snow-white hair above his horn-rimmed glasses. Lu had made a living in retirement by freelancing public relations.

He came by my newsroom one morning to congratulate me on having the courage to step out and open a PR shop. He said there was a need in the market for such services and that I would succeed—*if* I followed his advice.

I asked Lu to sit down, eager to hear what he had to say. Lu pulled up an old wooden chair in front of my desk and leaned forward to impart his wisdom.

Here was the only fellow on the face of the earth that had not told me I was a fruitcake. As he opened his mouth to utter his words, I leaned toward him, waiting for the advice. He then spread nuggets of gold that guided me throughout 33 years of business.

"I have just two words of advice for you," Lu said.

"Two words?" I said, "Just two words?"

"Yes," the ruddy face replied, smiling.

"And—they are?" I asked.

"They are," Lu responded, "be—expensive."

"Huh?" I said, perplexed.

And then this kind benefactor explained what he meant.

"You are a journalist, as am I. I know from experience that when a journalist quotes a price for his or her services, he, or she, greatly devalues them. You think everyone can write because it comes naturally to you. You think everyone can 'sell' a story because it comes naturally to you. I am here to tell you that a huge majority of the American public does not have the skills you have. In order to not devalue yourself, charge rates you believe to *be expensive*—it will cause you to put a reasonable market price on your services."

I remembered Lu's advice throughout my career and was able to avoid the trap that would have awaited me had he not walked into my office. Years later when one of my associates would complain to me that he or she heard in the marketplace that we were "too expensive," I would smile and say, "That's correct. When they want the best, expensive is not a problem; that's who we are—the most expensive shop in town."

No one succeeds on his own; we stand on the shoulders of others. Lu Leslie's shoulders were wide.

I put my Oldsmobile Cutlass in gear and drove from my home on Hazel Road in South Hills to the downtown business district. It was eight in the morning, the Tuesday after Labor Day, 1974. The Sternwheel Regatta, the highlight of the holiday weekend, had just ended; the annual end-of-summer festival had brought thousands of people to town and the trash was still being cleaned up. I parked in the garage at the Charleston House Hotel on Kanawha Boulevard and walked toward Capitol Street. I passed the Charleston National Bank and my stomach churned.

I had actually done it, crazy or not; I had resigned at WCHS and I was on my own. I had rented a 10 x 10 office in the "Barber Shop" and there was no turning back. The "Barber Shop" was a grouping of twenty offices in first floor space at the head of Capitol Street. Attorney Timothy Barber owned the office I had rented. Tim ordinarily sublet the offices only to attorneys, but he made an exception for me.

Tim loaned me a desk and filing cabinet. I had only to purchase two pull-up chairs to face my desk, and my office chair. I was distraught when I learned Chesapeake and Potomac Telephone required a $50 deposit for my phone. Fifty dollars was hard to come by. I *did* have an electric typewriter. It was a small portable that I had purchased just months before opening the business. It replaced a heavy, very old Remington manual typewriter that had been in my basement office at home. The purchase became necessary because I had carried the bulky Remington to the second floor of the house, for some reason, and, carrying it back down the stairs, I dropped it.

It loudly bounced down the stairs, coming to a stop at the front door, indenting large grooves in the entry's floor. It had just missed baby Amy, who was standing to the side of the door, watching the activity on the baseball diamond just across the street. I was glad to buy a new typewriter, thankful that Amy had been spared the Remington collision.

Barber's law offices featured a storefront façade of Colonial design. The very attractive building had a sign to the left of the door listing all the lawyers in the building. Tim agreed I could place my shingle on the right side of the door, but he said nothing about size. *Charles Ryan Associates* was therefore emblazoned on a sign equal to the entire complement of attorneys listed to the left of the entrance. I was, after all, in the promotion business. Tim never complained, he just smiled that mischievous smile of his when he first saw my shingle—it *was* damned attractive—of Colonial design.

The attorneys in the Barber Shop were mystified by my presence and generally embraced the "Ryan is crazy" mantra. They could not discern how anyone could sell intangibles such as ideas, slogans, and the shaping of public opinion. Yes, they regularly charged for intangibles, but, by God, they were lawyers.

The office across from mine was the professional address of an attorney who favored John Barleycorn. He was sometimes found in the early morning hours in his office, stretched across his desk, his enormous head beet red in color, sleeping off activities of the night before.

Across the hall was another attorney, Bob Wise. He would, within the next 20 years, become governor of the State of West Virginia. Next to him was a fellow by the name of Bob Louderback, a sweetheart if ever there was one. Bob wrote the incorporation papers for Charles Ryan Associates. He and the other barristers delighted in stopping by my office door, sticking their head in, glancing around, chuckling, and asking, "So, where are the Associates?"

Bob also would regularly come by at the end of the working day, just before leaving the office. He would lean through the door, his lanky frame seeming to wrap around the doorframe, smile, sweep his arm toward the pile of papers on my desk, and say, "Time to go home—it'll all be here tomorrow." For the next 33 years I remembered Bob's words and the sweep of his hand as I would leave the office, worrying that I still had things to do, but finding comfort in his advice.

Tim Barber was yet another of those individuals who made it possible for me to succeed. Here was a person who had no reason to be so kind to me; it was just Tim's way. Tim loved to inject humor into all things and he possessed a personality that attracted a myriad of colorful characters to the "Barber Shop."

Downstairs in the Barber Shop basement was an apartment that flooded one night and a young lady, nude, had to be rescue as she clutched overhead girders in the unfinished ceiling, raising her legs in the air for fear she might be electrocuted if she were to descend into the water where lamps and electric cords were still operational.

I regularly sat in Tim's office as colorful politicians such as A. James Manchin and Rudolph (Rudy) DiTrapano, a highly successful litigator, chairman of the state Democratic Party, and a colorful figure in and out of the courtroom, entertained with stories of political campaigns and courtroom hijinks.

It was a classroom, really, with professors who lived large lives and approached each day with gusto. It was an exhilarating environment for an entrepreneur and I was privileged to experience it.

CHAPTER 76

Harry Peck, Mary Marks & Connie Porter

ONE WEEK AFTER HANGING OUT my shingle I received a call from Larry Tucker, president of the Farmers & Merchants Bank in Summersville, West Virginia. Larry asked if I could do advertising as well as public relations. I assured him I could and then realized I needed help; I knew nothing about advertising.

I contacted and hired as a freelancer Steve Baer, the director of advertising for Frankenberger's Men's Store on Capitol Street. From that relationship more advertising clients came on board and I was looking for full-time help. Joe Farris at WCHS radio recommended I talk with Harry Peck, the only advertising guy around, Joe said, who knew anything about broadcast advertising.

On one of the best days of my life, Harry came to see me at the "Barber Shop". I told him I needed him, but I could not afford him. We then talked through some possibilities of employment. Harry came on board the beginning of May in 1975 with the agreement he would keep half of whatever he brought to the table. Harry was a ball of fire and within a short time he accepted the position of CRA Executive Vice President—with salary and benefits. Harry often complained, humorously, that he should have kept the original deal.

With Harry's arrival and acumen we began to grow in the advertising sector as the two disciplines of advertising and public relations complemented one another; Harry was the consummate advertising man and I was the PR guru. The partnership signaled our first move from Capitol Street to 1510 Kanawha Boulevard, East, a grand old home three doors east of Ruffner Avenue.

A week into my business launch I realized I needed to hire a secretary. I advertised for my first hire and received a resume from Mary Marks. I threw it into my reject pile because I noted that she was a Marshall University journalism graduate and over-qualified to be a secretary. She called me and inquired if I had received her resume. I explained that she, as a journalism graduate, was over-qualified for the position I had open. Mary asked if she could interview, regardless. She came in and I hired her on the spot. It was the best business decision I ever made.

I had an arrangement with an attorney who was an office mate to split Mary's salary with him; she would work half the time for him and half the time for me. After about a month I realized the attorney was never going to pay his share and I terminated the relationship.

Mary was a godsend and I could not have succeeded without her. She did the books, acted as receptionist, wrote press releases, kept my calendar, provided tremendous wit and

humor and gave me great encouragement. Especially important was the fact that Mary could collect. When a client was
slow to pay Mary would go to his or her place of business, sit
in the reception area and follow the slacker when he or she
left the building, dogging the person, asking for payment. I
later told people that Mary would follow her target, pull up
the miscreant's trouser leg and sink her teeth into a walking
calf, making her subject drag her everywhere until the client
handed over the money owed us.

She was Superwoman and collected *all* the debt. Mary left me
after five years to enter law school. She confided to me she had
no doubt she would do well, jerking her thumb over her shoulder toward some of the attorneys in the Barber Shop, saying,
"If these bozos can be attorneys, I sure can."

She graduated law school in a breeze, was highly sought by
those who knew her skills, and decided on a career in banking. Regrettably, she died young of cancer. I will always have
a heart full of love for her and her memory. I would not have
succeeded without her dedication to my effort. Years later,
when we moved CRAoffices to the BB&T Tower on Summers
Street, we named our main conference room the "Marks
Room" in loving memory of Mary.

The business grew—one day I received a call from Charleston
Mayor John Hutchinson. He asked for an appointment and
arrived at my office with his assistant and a few community
leaders. They wanted to hire CRA to assist in expanding the
Sternwheel Regatta, the city's Labor Day weekend festival that
centered on the Kanawha River.

Harry Peck relates in his wonderfully witty memoir "*Who Authorized This?*" that we were given about seven days to come up with a marketing plan. Harry wrote: "So, Charlie and I got a six pack and came to work on Saturday. It was hard for us to believe that they were turning the whole city over to us, and the sky was the limit. We just had to find a way to pay for our ideas. After a couple of beers, the ideas started flowing. Let's expand it to six days— no how about a week—no let's start off the Saturday before Labor Day with a parade through downtown and fill in the rest of the week with events that we can dream up."

Into this mix of aspiring creative came Connie Porter. Connie, in her late twenties or early thirties, was originally from Romney, West Virginia, a town my dad always pronounced "Rumney", so I called her a "Rumney Girl." Connie was our bookkeeper and salvation with numbers. She was a lifer and would stay with CRA through retirement. I am eternally grateful to the gracious and loyal Connie, whom I later dubbed, after *Star Wars* became a hit, C2P2. Connie loved it.

Our success with the Regatta was noted, and our numbers were, thanks to C2P2, correct, and more clients came on board.

CHAPTER 77

West Virginia Water

I ENTERED THE CONFERENCE ROOM of West Virginia Water (the name at the time) on the top floor of the People's Building on Summers Street in Charleston. I was two months into my venture in American capitalism. Around the table sat at least twenty executives and at the head of the table was a handsome, young, and dynamic president of the company. His name was Jerry Smith. He would rise to the top of West Virginia American Water's nationwide system. He was a force with which to reckon.

The West Virginia arm of the American Water Works System was faced with a PR problem. The conservative *Charleston Daily Mail* was editorializing against West Virginia Water's plans to build a new, multi-million dollar water treatment plant. The newspaper called it a "Taj Mahal." Public sentiment for the project began to erode and the West Virginia Public Service Commission, that would rule on the initiative, was reviewing the plan.

My letter-writing effort prior to leaving WCHS had resulted in a referral to Jerry by none other than one of the state's most distinguished barristers, Paul Chambers of Jackson, Kelley, Holt and O'Farrell—the oldest and largest law firm in the state. Paul was the water company's outside counsel and his recommendation carried enormous weight—he was a true "Big Foot."

Paul had briefed me on the situation and I came to the meeting of executives— in the largest conference room I had ever seen—fully prepared to explain a public relations plan that would quench the *Daily Mail's* criticism and garner public support.

"What can we do?" Jerry asked. I was prepared.

"Introduce a series of media visits, began public tours of the new plant, make editorial board visits." I replied. I then laid out a comprehensive media strategy.

As I pitched Jerry and the somber executives around the West Virginia Water Company conference table, I thought of the *New Yorker* magazine cartoon on my desk that showed Columbus presenting to the Queen his maps of the new world, begging for money to go explore. The cartoon was called "The Pitch".

I was Columbus reincarnated, making the "pitch" to West Virginia Water. On that day Lu Leslie was a spiritual presence beside me and I was determined to be expensive. Jerry listened to what I had to say, nodded approval, and said, "What do you think this will cost?"

I felt the perspiration on the palms of my hands, took a deep breath and, remembering Lu's words, said, "One thousand dollars a month in retainer, plus expenses and markup on pass-through items." I then waited for a response, hoping I had not embraced Lu's mantra too enthusiastically.

"That's about what I thought," Jerry said. "Let's do it."

I maintained professional composure, simply nodding my head in acceptance of the job. What I really wanted to do was rush from the room, open a window and shout "Yahoo!" I had my first big corporate client.

I hurried back to my office on Capitol Street and called my mentor and client, Dean Lewis. "Dean!" I said into the black telephone on my office desk, "guess what?"

"What?" he answered.

I then told him the story—West Virginia Water had signed on as my client—at a thousand dollars a month.

Dean laughed and said that was just great. He paused, and then added, "We don't need no more public relations."

Lesson learned—be prepared for a client to leave the moment it walks through the door. Dean had been more than kind; I had delivered good service for the six months I was on retainer with his construction firm, but I was not in their budget.

Dean gave me the lifeline to land that first major client. He became my lifelong friend—without him I never would have had the courage to go out on my own. It was a priceless gift, given with no thought of a return. Dean, now deceased, was an exceptional and giving person. He is always in my thoughts and in my heart. I owe him a successful, fulfilling career. Every person who ever received a paycheck from CRA owes him a debt of gratitude. He will never be forgotten.

The public relations plan for the water company?

It was initiated and within a relatively short time the media bombardment of the new plant abated. I was proud of the fact that decades later the plant was doing exactly what we said it would do---provide quality water service to the Kanawha Valley that would endure for generations.

It was not until 2014 that the aura of good feelings about West Virginia American Water was shattered. The company that year encountered fierce media criticism and public outcry after a discharge from an old Pennzoil tank farm upriver from the water treatment plant occurred, sending pollutants into the public water supply—leaving thousands fearing for their health. Meantime, they had only bottled water to drink, and in which to bathe, as they waited in great apprehension for test results of the water they had consumed.

CHAPTER 78

Harold Lambert

IN THE ROOM ON THE day of the pitch to West Virginia Water was the company's public relations chief, Harold Lambert. As I made my presentation I was worried that Harold might take offense that Jerry Smith was bringing in outside counsel.

My worries were for naught; Harold was the consummate professional. He welcomed me with open arms and we became fast friends. Harold was twenty years older than I and when he retired at the mandatory age of 65 he came on board with CRA. His work for clients and counsel to those outside and inside the firm was invaluable. In later years we would honor Harold as we had honored Mary Marks, naming one of our new conference rooms in the BB&T tower "The Lambert Room".

Harold was the quintessential old-time PR guy. His tactics were from the ground up and he always produced, shooting pictures, assembling slide shows, writing press releases, buttering up news people and writing with passion and wit.

Harold published poetry and homilies that are priceless. Here are three I especially liked:

>~*There's a great deal of comfort in knowin' you ain't never gonna' amount to nothin'.*
>~*You can take the coal miner out of the coal mine, but you can't take the pink flamingo out of his front yard.*
>~*Some divorces are made in heaven.*

In his book *Is the Mockingbird Still Singing?*, Harold penned many wonderful poems, including the following.

>~**The Joiner:**
>*He joined the Elks and joined the Moose,*
>*The S.A.R. and others;*
>*He met with all societies*
>*And claimed most men as brothers.*
>*For fifty years he joined and met,*
>*And pallbore—till at last,*
>*His brother-men had all died off;*
>*His life was in the past.*
>*For a few years he brooded on,*
>*Bereft of comrade-men.*
>*Then he bought a gun, and with a bang,*
>*Joined the lodge again.*

CHAPTER 79

Failures & Lessons

As our agency grew, I had the opportunity to meet Dick Kreusser who owned an agency in Indianapolis. Dick's agency was called Handley Miller, founded in 1961 by Richard N. Miller and former Indiana governor Harold W. Handley. Dick bought the firm from them. He was originally a copywriter at Handley Miller and the agency had struggled after Dick took the reigns.

I believed there was an opportunity to partner with him in a market of two million people—providing us room to grow and giving Dick additional managerial prowess and public relations expertise. Alas, it was not to be. We had extended ourselves over considerable territory and client service was a problem; had we done the partnering in the age of the Internet, I believe we might have succeeded in Indianapolis.

I licked my Indianapolis wounds and learned my lesson and went back to the grind. I considered my failure flawed strategy rather than a huge mistake, and I finally learned that, before opening in new markets, I needed to listen more to Harry Peck. We were fortunate that our later Washington and Richmond initiatives *worked*—they did so with Harry Peck's caution.

CRA Vice President John Auge always said we in the creative business, even in the toughest of times, were the chosen few. It *was* one of the toughest games in the world, but one in which we could arise each day wondering what was in store—knowing great things could happen.

I added to John's focus on creativity the importance of the "pitch". I sat down immediately after every pitch and wrote down what went wrong and what went right. I tried to learn from every win and every loss.

And—from time to time, there were losses. Every agency experiences them and we surely had ours. I always stressed "staying power" during those periods and I insisted on retaining loyal people. There were times that executive staff and I took pay cuts in order to keep our loyal talent.

Longtime CRA employee Linda Cook came to my office one day just after we had lost a meaningful client and gave me a cork with *CRA* emblazoned on top of it. She had attached a note that said, "No matter how rough the waters, CRA always rises to the top!" The gesture was tremendously meaningful to me—a testament to the backbone of one employee and representative of our staff's determination.

In tough times I would walk around the office, whistling, making joyful small talk, attempting to display total confidence. CRA built a culture—a culture that had at its core integrity, hard work and dedication to a company's men and women and its clients. That culture gave us staying power.

CHAPTER 80

My Dad Passes

MY LIFE WAS CONSUMED BY growing a business. My focus on that was halted with the death of a parent. Following his retirement, my mom and dad moved to Red Lake Florida, near Gainesville, where my half-brother Bill and his wife Ann lived. I stayed in close touch with Mom by phone, especially when my father became ill, suffering from congestive heart failure following a minor heart attack years earlier. My trips to Florida were few, something I regret.

It was August 9, 1977, and I was running up the steps to our second floor office. I received the news from our receptionist—my father had died.

My dad lived to be 79 and is buried in Hawthorne, Florida. He was a loving father who could be distant at times, but I now understand that, knowing what he went through as a young man, beating an addiction, losing and regaining a family, then raising a second. He was a great man of whom I am very proud.

Following Dad's passing, Mom moved from Red Lake into Hawthorne. She paid half the down payment on an elegant little brick home, and I paid the other half. I also signed papers that gave her the right to live in the home in perpetuity. I then made all the house payments until she died.

Mom existed on Dad's railroad retirement (there is no Social Security for retired railroaders) so I sent her money each month to augment her income. When she died I discovered that she had banked every penny of it and she then willed those dollars back to me.

It was so Mom. She did without some things to do that, for sure. She had an old Buick that she and Dad had purchased brand new in Charleston in the '60s. One year, my great friend Dean Lewis and I flew in his aircraft to Gainesville and Mom met us. It was quite a walk to the Buick after we parked the aircraft.

"Mom, why did you park so far away?"

"So I won't have to back up."

"What's wrong with backing up?"

"The car won't go in reverse."

"So, you can never back up? That's ridiculous!"

"No, no, you just have to *plan ahead.*"

I took Mom to a dealership and we bought a car—one that would back up.

Hawthorne was a tiny town but with more infrastructure than Red Lake. Several of Mom's friends lived in Hawthorne and one, Kate Duke, was at Mom's house so often she eventually moved in with Mom. Kate was a blessing. Mom's other friend was a great gal by the name of Vivian Wagner. Vivian was older than Mom and was a fireball who had served on town council and was always wrapped up in some activity of note in Hawthorne.

Vivian and Mom were members of the First United Methodist Church and Mom was the founder of its Thrift Shop. If you are ever in Hawthorne, Florida, stop by the Methodist Church and look at the building adjacent to the lovely white chapel—the name emblazoned across a large sign on the lawn says, "Mabel Ryan United Methodist Women Thrift Shop".

CHAPTER 81

Mabel Ryan—A Remarkable Woman

My MOTHER HAD A GREAT sense of humor. For years she carried with her a picture showing a bottle of Joy dish soap beside a bottle of Pride detergent. She never met a stranger and would break into conversation by saying, with a big smile, "Would you like to see a picture of my pride and joy?" The answer was always yes, with the expectation of seeing a baby picture, whereupon Mom grabbed her pocketbook and whipped out the photo of the two bottles—Pride and Joy.

Kate Duke became Mom's caretaker after Mom contracted lung cancer—a terrifying surprise to me because Mom had not smoked in 40 years. Kate cared for Mom like a sister, and my wife Becky and I came to love Kate and will always be indebted to her.

Becky and I visited Kathy Tashie (Bill and Ann Ryan's daughter) and her husband at their home in Charlotte, North Carolina fifteen years after Mom's death. I had not known until then how much Kathy loved Mom. Mom was not her grandmother by blood, but Kathy always considered her "Grandma". It was a result of Bill and Ann and their family regularly visiting at Red Lake where Mom and Dad became close with Dad's grandchildren.

It had been a long and eventful journey from Mom's childhood home at Seven Islands in Tucker County, West Virginia to Gainesville, Florida when Mom passed away in 1997 at the age of 82. When Mom was in her final days my sister Hellice arrived at Mom's house before Becky and I. Mom dearly loved Becky, and Hellice related to us that Mom would repeatedly ask, "When are Charlie and *my* Becky coming? And then Mom would say, "Bill, I'm ready. Come and get me."

Hellice said after Mom made several calls to my dad she could take it no more and told Mom, "Mabel, stop doing that. If Bill comes to get you, you'll miss Charlie and your Becky when they arrive." Hellice said Mom looked at her, laughed, and said, "You're right," and stopped calling for Dad.

Mom was being cared for at home by Hospice and had not spoken for several days. Kate was by her side and placed her hand on Mom's arm, saying, "We're going to miss you, Mabel." Whereupon Mom opened her eyes, looked at Kate, and said, "Why? Where are you going?" We all broke into laughter.

As for Hellice, she was the perfect bedside companion as Mom prepared to pass from this life. Hellice had also sat with her sister Anna Margaret in her last moments. Hellice was aware of the "death rattle" as Anna Margaret struggled to breathe. A bright light appeared before Anna and Hellice felt frozen in place, watching as the light encompassed her sister. The light, she said, spread side-to-side and then collapsed to the center and shot skyward.

At that moment Hellice was convinced Anna Margaret had passed and she moved to her side and touched her hand. Anna Margaret stirred and her eyes opened. Hellice worried she had interfered somehow, that Anna Margaret had been meant to leave at the movement the light shot skyward. Anna Margaret passed within a few minutes after Hellice's remarkable experience. Hellice asked a minister why she had witnessed the light that covered her sister. The minister said, "Because you were blessed, Hellice."

Hellice's experience did not repeat during our vigil with Mom, but I am sure it was on her mind as she, Mary Virginia, Becky and I said our goodbyes.

I loved my mom dearly—I cherish her memory—and I am certain Dad heard her call and that they are together.

CHAPTER 82

Ryan Reader/Motion Masters

EACH YEAR CRA SAW GROWTH and we added Joe Gollehon, Hale Gay, Ann Fly, Dan Woodrum, Jim Reader, Carolyn Perry and Jerry Handley to our staff. They joined Harry, Mary and me as we signed a lease to rent additional space in the old Kanawha Boulevard mansion that housed our firm—the new space was the attic of the antebellum home. There, in winter, our attic dwellers would freeze because of a faulty furnace, and in the summer, suffocate because the window air conditioners were not up to the job. Summer also featured the arrival of mice and yellow jackets that considered the attic to be their domain. Among those attic dwellers was Rex Repass—who came to us in 1979.

That year I visited Washington, DC to participate in a client meeting. It was decided during that meeting that the client would hire a public opinion research firm and launch a $10,000 study. I returned to Charleston and announced to our folks that I was going to start a public opinion research firm—$10,000! I had dollar signs in my head.

I hired a young woman who had promise and we very quickly obtained a project with West Virginia University. One week before the research was due she came into my office, crying. She was way over her head and said she was quitting. I had to scramble and I hired a freelancer to finish the project. I lost my shirt on the job, but delivered a quality product. It was then that I decided I needed a professional researcher.

I thumbed through applications in our jobs file and found a jewel. He came in for an interview and I hired Rex Repass who held a master's degree in public opinion research from the University of Tennessee. He was absolutely sensational and I decided to create a public opinion research subsidiary that I named "Ryan Repass Research". Rex eventually bought the company from me and today "Repass Research" is a world-class firm with offices in Cincinnati and a nationwide practice. Rex is a close friend and one of my most stellar hires. To this day he references his start at CRA. Rex epitomizes what loyalty, integrity and friendship are.

Jim Reader also brought with him the tools to form a new company subsidiary. Jim, with fifteen years in broadcasting, and a voice to match, took over our media training (a service we provided throughout the country) that I had been conducting and hired Carolyn Perry to begin producing film and video commercials and company films. The firm was "Ryan-Reader". Jim hired Diana Sole several years after he took the reins at Ryan-Reader and she was fabulous. We eventually sold Ryan-Reader to her and she took the company to a whole new level. The company is in business today as West Virginia's foremost production house, Motion Masters.

In 1980 we made a major move to accommodate CRA and its subsidiaries. We leased 5,000 square feet of space in the Heck's

Building on Kanawha Boulevard. The move doubled our rent, but we prospered. We then expanded to 8,000 square feet, leasing the third floor of the building, then, the fourth floor and penthouse—the entire building was ours save the second floor (the building had three floors with a street level parking lot under it designated as the first floor), leased to Midwest Steel.

CHAPTER 83

The Huntington Office

_⌐ᴏ

JOE GOLLEHON WAS A SOLID public relations professional who worked for Union Carbide Corporation. He and I got to know one another as I began to do media training for Carbide executives in the then-sprawling South Charleston Technical Center. As we chatted from time to time, Joe expressed interest in joining our firm. Joe was a big ticket item for me and I hesitated. The Carbide folks were good to us and I got signals Joe would be an asset to CRA that could bring even more Carbide business.

I made the offer and Joe accepted and a great friendship and partnership was born. I later asked Joe to lead our Huntington office, purchased in 1984 from longtime advertising executive John McCormack.

McCormack was a forceful Irishman who drank and smoked in a manner that lived up to his ancestry. He was a colorful figure with beautiful white hair and mustache and a rosy red complexion. He asked Gollehon one day, "Joe, what's the first thing you do when you return home in the evening?" Joe said he wasn't sure—he did different things each evening—and he asked John what it was that he did.

John smiled, stretched back in his office chair, and said, "Joe, the first thing I do each evening is open my front door and accept a martini that has been prepared for me."

John was known for hiring the prettiest girls out of Marshall University—all of whom wanted to work for the dashing advertising man who had clients throughout West Virginia, Kentucky and Ohio—a client base dominated by banks.

McCormack was engaged by the John F. Kennedy campaign to assist them in winning southern West Virginia in the 1960 presidential primary. McCormack flew with Kennedy in small, chartered planes as the candidate traversed the southern coalfields. John sometimes slept in a seat behind Kennedy as the days on the campaign trail grew long. Affable and totally outgoing, John developed a relationship with the candidate.

McCormack, of the Roman Catholic faith, was totally frank as he whispered in Kennedy's ear; he did not sugar-coat the challenge Kennedy had in Protestant West Virginia. The good news for Kennedy was that McCormack understood the territory and its people—his classic advice was a great asset to his fellow Irishman who won the hearts and allegiance of the coalfields.

My dad and mother stood proudly behind my sister, Mary Virginia, and me. We were off to church, dressed to the nines.

Ryan Collection

My father, about to leave for work, as my sister and I stand beside him—my upward gaze and engineer's cap demonstrate my awe of my dad.

Ryan Collection

A train crew under the command of my grandfather, far left, in white coveralls. My father is the young man second from right, wearing a cap and a rather stern look.

Ryan Collection

The Maple Avenue Gang: Third from right, standing, second row, Jim "Munch" Mahood; far left, I am holding a toy car, with a patch in my jeans; standing, next to me, my sister Mary Virginia. Kneeling, Jerry Pifer.

Jerry Pifer

Left to right, my dad, William Donaldson Ryan; my
granddad, Benjamin Franklin Ryan; my aunt, Mary
Beatrice Ryan Rowan, and her husband Jim Rowan.

Ryan Collection

My sister Hellice and her first-born Nancy, sitting with
our dad on the porch of our home in Keyser.

Ryan Collection

I was at 17 at WKYR, my hometown station in Keyser.
I was disc jockey, announcer and newsman.

Ryan Collection

In 1960 Eleanor Roosevelt campaigned in Morgantown for
John F. Kennedy. I had penciled my questions on a note card.

Ryan Collection

Secretary of Labor Arthur Goldberg came to Morgantown
when I was 21 and I scored a one-on-one exclusive interview.

Ryan Collection

President Lyndon Johnson works a rope-line in Morgantown at
the dedication of the Walter L. (Bill) Hart Airport. I emulated
Emil Varney with both film and still cameras in hand.

Emil Varney

David Brinkley does a "standup" during the
1960 West Virginia Presidential primary.

Emil Varney

Emil Varney films John F. Kennedy in 1960—he was with
Kennedy so often that Kennedy called Emil by his first name.

Photographer Unknown

President Kennedy and Governor Barron on West Virginia Day, 1963—the rain poured and Kennedy said, "The sun may not always shine in West Virginia, but the people always do."

Emil Varney

Ken Kurtz and I at the state capitol, covering the JFK statehood speech. Kennedy said, "I am proud to come here today to join you in saluting the birth of this state."

Emil Varney

Emil Varney recorded historic photojournalism that shaped West Virginia in the '50s and '60s.

Charlie Ryan

I was 22 and thrilled to be co-anchoring the Ashland Oil News Picture. The newscast was in black and white and 15 minutes in duration.

Emil Varney

WSAZ-TV News Director Bos Johnson (left) interviewing
Governor Wally Barron, circa 1962. Bos, a television pioneer,
built WSAZ-TV into one of the country's best news operations.

Emil Varney

Richard Nixon, Bos Johnson, and I during a joint taping
of WSAZ' TV's "At Issue" and WCHS-TV's "Viewpoint",
as Nixon campaigned for President in 1968.

Emil Varney

Charleston Mayor John Hutchinson (right), with
Hubert Humphrey, campaigning in West Virginia.

Emil Varney

Circa 1963, seated, left to right, Ed Rabel, WCHS-
TV, and Charles Ryan, WSAZ-TV. Standing, far right,
Emil Varney—to his right, Rabel's cameraman.

Unknown

Lunch at the Charleston Press Club, 1965—seated
left to right: Herb Little, Associated Press; Ralph
Murphine, WSAZ-TV; Ed Rabel, WCHS-TV; Carolyn
Boiarsky, WCHS-TV; Charles Ryan, WSAZ-TV.

Leo B. Gardner

Governor Hulett Smith was outstanding in his role
as the state's chief executive—handsome, urbane and
one of the best-dressed West Virginia governors.

Emil Varney

A crowd waits in Wayne County in southern West Virginia in
1965, where a young boy was trapped in a well for three days.
Emil Varney and I covered the story for NBC television and radio.

Emil Varney

I covered the West Virginia Legislature for Jim
Comstock's *Hillbilly* in the 60s. Comstock
called me "Hillbilly's second best writer."

Emil Varney

Charleston Gazette cartoonist Jim Dent penned this
political comment when Governor Jay Rockefeller cancelled
my CRA contract with Carolyn Smoot, Commissioner
of his Department of Employment Security.

James Dent

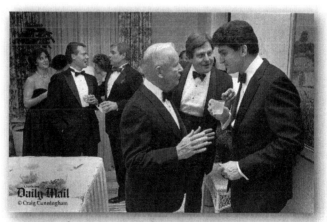

Governor Arch Moore and then West Virginia State Senator
(later United States Senator) Joe Manchin enjoy exchanges at
the Governor's Mansion as State Senator Buffy Warner looks on,
circa 1987. Directly to Moore's left is State Senator Bob Burke.

Craig Cunningham, Charleston Daily Mail

Jay Rockefeller campaigning with kids, circa 1975.

Emil Varney

I often interviewed Jay Rockefeller while standing
on two copies of the West Virginia Code.

Charles Ryan Associates

Governor Wally Barron, far right, launched a cleanup campaign in 1964. Charleston Mayor John Shanklin (third from left) assists in sweeping Capitol Street. Far left, I was obviously enjoying the event.

Emil Varney

The WCHS-TV 1970s news team: Left to right, sports director Wade Utay, weather forecaster Jane Martin, news director, Charles Ryan, weather forecaster Bob Grassi (Wilson to viewers), and my co-anchor Roy Brassfield.

WCHS-TV

Governor Cecil Underwood loved the pageantry of the political life. Here he smiles and waves while participating in a parade—with state troopers to either side of his limousine.

Underwood Campaign

Governor Cecil Underwood and First Lady Hovah were guests in our offices and at our home on a regular basis. We came to know the Underwoods as family and will always treasure our relationship with them.

Charles Ryan Associates

Governor Underwood's Kitchen Cabinet in post-election celebration of his win over Charlotte Pritt: Left to right: Harry Peck, me, Robert Samples, John Brown, Steve Haid and Gary White. Sitting, left to right, Bill Phillips and Hovah and Cecil Underwood.

Ryan collection

Mike Roark (center), mayor of Charleston. Far left, Danny Jones—a future Charleston mayor. Far right, Homer Hanna, chairman of the Kanawha County Democratic party.

Photographer unknown

My partner Harry Peck and I enjoyed many years and experiences together. The business and the friendship taught us respect, trust and loyalty—essential ingredients in any successful partnership.

Charles Ryan Associates

The incredible 1980s CRA creative team: Standing, left to right, Jody Malcolm, Phil Evans, John Auge, Tad Walden, Harry Peck and Rick Mogielski; kneeling, Ty George, on stool, Linda Cook—I was proud to work with each of them.

Charles Ryan Associates

I presented my book *The Pullman Hilton* at the same time world-renowned author Pat Conroy signed his books on Hilton Head Island in 2015. He was the ultimate cheerleader for writers and gave me a great hug as we posed for the camera.

Pamela Martin Ovens

Becky and I in our Canaan Valley vacation home with Amalfi—our lovable and totally spoiled Maltese, whom we nicknamed "Velcro".

Entrance Magazine

Becky and I with George W. Bush as the President
visited Charleston with Karl Rove. I asked
Rove to "take care of our guy." He did.

Bush Campaign

The family at St. John in the US Virgin Islands. Left to right:
son-in-law Chad Porter, daughter Jennifer Porter, grandson
Blake Porter, myself, Becky, granddaughter Lily Porter, son-
in-law Steve Tweedy, daughter Elizabeth Shandon Tweedy,
granddaughter Lauren Tweedy, and grandson Ryan Tweedy.

Steve Simonsen Photography Inc.

CHAPTER 84

CRA Encounters Gaston Caperton

GASTON CAPERTON, THE 31ST GOVERNOR of W.Va., was born February 21, 1940—seven days before I arrived in the world. Gaston was certainly born with a silver spoon in his mouth, but he managed to excel on his own. He attended Dexter School in Massachusetts, Episcopal High in Alexandria, Virginia, and the University of North Carolina at Chapel Hill. After graduation he returned to Charleston where he eventually managed the insurance firm of McDonough, Caperton and Goldsmith, later to become solely owned by his family and then by Gaston alone.

The insurance firm grew under Gaston's leadership to the place where it was the 10th largest privately owned brokerage of its type in the country. Offices were originally at the corner of Kanawha Boulevard and Dunbar Street downtown. In the 1990s Gaston built a large, modern building on a hill overlooking the state capitol and moved his business there, employing hundreds of people.

In the 1970s, Gaston asked me to come up with some ideas for the annual Jefferson-Jackson Dinner, the Democratic

Party's big annual event to tout its candidates and platform. I pulled out all stops and the CRA creative team worked several days to come up with a proposal to retain as a headliner for the event, Jimmy "J.J." Walker. Walker, at the time, was nationally known as the star of the CBS comedy *Good Times*. We pitched the "J.J." in his name as the Jefferson-Jackson tie-in and figured the Democrats could have him as the lead-in to the boring politicians that would ultimately drag onto the stage.

I climbed the three stairs of the old mansion that then housed McDonough, Caperton and Goldsmith and sat in Gaston's attic office to explain my idea that had required considerable agency creative hours. Gaston smiled throughout the meeting and concluded by saying "no" to the pitch. I was disappointed but assumed CRA would at least be paid for its effort. Not so. Gaston simply thanked me profusely for my ideas. I learned then that political campaign work *of any kind* was fraught with risk.

In 1988 Caperton decided to run for governor against Arch Moore. Caperton was not expected to win—he had never run for political office and was a novice campaigner. Money spoke, however, and Gaston won the election. Gaston served a second term when he defeated the Republican challenger Cleve Benedict, who had not a chance of winning.

As governor, Gaston reduced a huge state debt by raising taxes (something he had pledged while campaigning that he would not do) and creating a budget surplus. He built roads, prisons, and promoted economic development. Education, however, was item number one for him. Gaston was dyslexic and had a burning desire to help educate children, motivated by his handicap. He funded 58 new schools and raised teacher's salaries. He championed computers in the classroom and later in life would be called a visionary who changed education in America.

Gaston was a great friend of Smoot Fahlgren, founder and owner of Fahlgren Advertising in Parkersburg. We bid for state contracts against Smoot, feeling we'd never win with the Gaston-Smoot connection. We were correct. We did not win. Gaston was always glad to see me but I never had the connection Smoot enjoyed. One of our executives used to imitate Gaston as we prepared to bid against Smoot, saying Gaston's reaction to our bid would be, "But, but, but—what about Smoot?"

Gaston's time in office had one black mark—the West Virginia Lottery. The Director of the Lottery, under Governor Caperton, was Butch Bryan. Bryan went to prison for bid rigging and steering a $2.8 million advertising contract to the Fahlgren Martin Agency even though it did not have the best rating for the job. He was convicted of mail fraud, wire fraud, insider trading and lying to a federal grand jury. Charles Ryan Associates, the Fahlgren Martin Agency, and the Arnold Agency were among those seeking the advertising contract during Caperton's term.

There were eight months in 1991 that were quite chaotic for the ad agencies involved in the bidding. Federal investigators interviewed me in my offices in Charleston during the investigation of Bryan. My attorney was present for the interview. Much of the questioning I got was in reference to Governor Caperton. After the interview it was my thought that the Governor might indeed be indicted, based on the questions asked. That, of course, did not happen, but the 1991 Lottery fiasco was a stain on Caperton's administration.

Gaston was the first West Virginia governor to be divorced in office. His wife and Miss America runner-up, Dee, was a beauty with a mind of her own. She set up shop in the statehouse and let everyone know she was going to have a role in state government. It was not to be. The Capertons became estranged and Dee left her digs near the statehouse press office. She and Gaston were divorced in 1990 and she died in France in 2000.

When he left office in 1999 Gaston became President and CEO of the *College Board*. He served there with distinction and established a national profile. When he retired he returned to Charleston where he was widely considered to be a candidate for the United States Senate against Shelley Moore Capito. Caperton surprised most folks, including me, by choosing not to run.

His was an outstanding career and West Virginia is indebted to him.

CHAPTER 85

Cecil Underwood For Governor?

Just prior to CRA's move to the BB&T Tower we suddenly found ourselves once again in the middle of politics. A college friend of mine from Elkins, Bill Phillips, had recently retired from a government career in Washington. Bill and I had remained friends since graduating Potomac State College in 1960. Bill was the most complete political animal I had ever known. He lived and breathed politics—Republican politics. He was simply superb as an analyst and strategist in the political trenches.

It was October, 1995 and our daughter Jennifer was a Princess in the Mountain State Forest Festival (Bill and Jenny Phillips had sponsored her). Bill and I settled in, each with a glass of Bill's favorite Glenmorangie Scotch, and he told me of his conversation the previous night with his old friend Cecil Underwood. Bill related that he had told Cecil he should again run for governor in 1996.

Cecil listened to Bill with great interest. Bill described an Underwood renaissance—if Cecil were to be elected in 1996 at the age of 74 he would not only have been the youngest, but he also would become the oldest governor ever elected in the state.

I told Bill I greatly admired Cecil, but my doubts that he could be a viable candidate in the 1996 election were borne of the fact that he had run for governor many times since that first term and always failed.

I said, flat out, that Cecil could not win. Bill, the consummate political operative, brilliant, a lifelong friend to Cecil and Hovah Underwood, believed in Cecil while I was skeptical of his ability to woo voters—in my defense, I was not alone. However, Bill was so persuasive in his arguments that he convinced me I was wrong. I signed on and, just as Bill had predicted, and with Bill's guidance, Cecil did indeed become not only the youngest, but also the oldest governor ever elected in West Virginia.

But, it was not easy. Cecil's opponents in the 1996 Republican primary were former astronaut Jon McBride, a Charleston native who had grown up in Beckley and then moved to Lewisburg, and David McKinley, a member of the House of Delegates from the northern panhandle.

At Bill's urging, a number of high profile West Virginians joined the Underwood effort. In Summersville, West Virginia, was a dynamic young business leader by the name of Bill Bright, president of Bright of America. Bill was a Republican of profile and easily warmed to the idea of an Underwood campaign. He quickly coalesced state business leaders and staged a luncheon at the Charleston Marriott to launch the idea that Underwood should be the GOP nominee. More than 200 men and women showed up in support of Cecil.

Phillips said, "I looked around the room that day and, seeing the number of known Democrats in attendance, including previous and current holders of public office, I knew this thing was real and we could win." After the luncheon Bright launched the "Governor's Council" that brought weight and gravitas to the idea that Cecil Underwood was a viable candidate for governor.

Phillips reached out to Corky DeMarco and Laura Brotherton who formed "Democrats for Underwood", which became an important and productive element in the Underwood campaign.

Cecil blew astronaut McBride and legislator McKinley away, winning the primary election by a large majority. McBride was an interesting sort and captured newspaper space in the *Beckley Register Herald* on August 4, 1998. The *Register Herald* said his wife accused him of shoving her into a ceiling fan in their home during a disagreement between the two. His wife later recanted, the newspaper said. McKinley eventually did very well—achieving election to the United States House of Representatives in 2010.

CHAPTER 86

"You've Got To Beat That Woman"

SOON AFTER CECIL UNDERWOOD BECAME the Republican nominee for Governor, Becky and I were at "Tent City" at a West Virginia University football game when Governor Gaston Caperton, the sitting Democratic governor who had, eight years earlier, defeated Arch Moore, took me by the arm and led me aside. Caperton said to me, with intensity in his voice, "You've got to beat that woman!"

The woman to whom he referred was Charlotte Pritt, the Democratic nominee for governor and Cecil's 1996 opponent, who had run a write-in campaign against Caperton eight years earlier. Gaston seriously disliked Ms. Pritt. With that conversation, I thought we were going to win.

After the primary election, the brilliance of Bill Phillips shone bright; he organized a "Kitchen Cabinet" to guide the campaign. It consisted of Bill, as the campaign chairman; Gary White, CEO for Buck Harless' lumber and coal empire; Dr. Steve Haid, a legislative lobbyist and a Democrat with deep ties to the state's education community; John Brown, a public relations practitioner; Robert Samples of Ryan Samples research (CRA's public opinion research firm); CRA executive vice president Harry Peck, and I, as the agency guys.

Bill's skill in assembling the group was unmatched and Gary White (who later became interim president of Marshall University following the untimely death of Steve Kopp) was a backbone of the group with his knowledge of the coal industry and what some wags called the "people in the little white houses"—a reference to the general population who would eventually determine the winner of the governor's office.

Democratic nominee Pritt was an attractive and smart woman, and former state senator. She had served in both the West Virginia House of Delegates and Senate and had established her credentials as a major liberal. *So* major that we believed she was out of step with the two-thirds majority Democratic registration in the state. Nevertheless, it was going to be a tough race that would require lots of money, something Cecil never had much of in his oft-repeated runs for public office.

CHAPTER 87

Tom, Hoot & Buck

IT IS SAID THAT MONEY is the mother's milk of politics, and it is true. Bill Phillips recruited fundraisers who were stars that could milk the political udders dry. The Underwood Finance Chairman was well-known and immensely likable insurance executive Tom Wilkerson of Charleston (whose wife Sandra always referred to as "Mr. Wonderful").

On his committee were Bob "Hoot" Hooten and James H. "Buck" Harless, both self-made multi-millionaires. Hoot owned Hooten Equipment Company that had put most of the refrigerated units into restaurants and supermarkets through-out the state. Buck was a coal and timber giant and had worked the Republican fields for many years. Tom, Hoot and Buck knew everyone in West Virginia who had a dollar to give.

During those grueling months of campaigning the fundraising team would meet on a weekly basis at John Wellford's corporate offices in his Northgate park development near Kanawha Airport. CRA media buyer Caryn Durham and I attended those meetings and one morning as Caryn was sitting at the conference table making final notes on a campaign media buy,

Hoot came in and sat down beside her. Hoot was a brusque guy on the surface and a lovable fellow under that façade. He looked at Caryn and said, "Darlin' go get me a coffee."

Caryn never missed a beat. She continued to jot down the cash needed for the next media buy and said in an aside to Hoot, without looking up from the numbers, "No, Mr. Hooten, but while you're up—would you bring me a Diet Coke?" Hoot's eyes got real big as he got up from his chair. He returned with his coffee and placed a Diet Coke for Caryn in front of her. Caryn looked up at Hoot, smiled sweetly and said, "Thank you, Mr. Hooten." Hoot, ever the gentleman, said, "You're welcome, darlin'."

Tom, Hoot and Buck and their committee raised the needed in state cash, and money came from outside conservative groups who wanted to see a Republican win in West Virginia in 1996. Between the primary and general elections the Underwood campaign spent more than $1.2 million (not a lot when compared to Jay Rockefeller's campaign expenditures, but Cecil did not have millions in personal wealth as Rockefeller did).

CHAPTER 88

Wrong On The Issues, Wrong
For West Virginia

THE WEST VIRGINIA STATE VICTORY Committee, an offshoot of the National Republican Senatorial Committee (NRSC) produced an ad that was disowned by Cecil Underwood but certainly did much to elect him. The Committee's ad charged that Pritt had a liberal record that was way out there—off the charts. It said Pritt had proposed teaching first graders about condoms, voted to permit the sale of pornographic videos to children, and voted to allow convicted drug abusers to work in West Virginia's public schools.

It further charged that Pritt voted against honoring the men and women of West Virginia who fought in the Gulf War by voting to allow the burning of the American flag and that she opposed requiring students to begin their day with the Pledge of Allegiance. The spot ended saying "Charlotte Pritt—Wrong on the Issues, Wrong for West Virginia." The disclaimer that followed said, "Paid for by the West Virginia State Victory Committee, Mary M. Dotter, Treasurer. Not authorized by Underwood for Governor."

Underwood denounced the ad and asked the Victory Committee to cease its campaign. He was, of course, refused. And the ad ran through Election Day. Pritt sued the Republican National Committee for libel, asking for $10 million, and lost—eight years later.

The basis for the Victory Committee ad was an innocuous vote by Pritt while in the state legislature. Underwood was genuinely upset by the salacious nature of the ad and later volunteered to testify as a witness for Pritt in her suit against the Republican National Committee.

Cecil won the election 51.65% to 45.80% with Libertarian candidate Wallace Johnson picking up 2.5%. Bill Phillips said there were seven significant events/actions, or reasons Cecil won. He listed them as (1) breaking with transition—not moving into Republican Headquarters, (2) the Governor's Council, (3) early public endorsements by incumbent Democratic members of the State Legislature, (4) Democrats for Underwood, (5) the Kitchen Cabinet, (6) constant public opinion polling, and (7) the Underwood bus tour the final week of the campaign. Phillips said Cecil's 1996 election was the beginning of the two party system in West Virginia. Bill said, "This was confirmed in 2000 when George Bush was the first non-incumbent Republican candidate for President to carry West Virginia in 70 years."

CHAPTER 89

Underwood's Inauguration

FOLLOWING CECIL'S UNDERWOOD'S ELECTION, GOVERNOR Gaston Caperton cleaned out his office at the statehouse and his personal belongings at the Governor's Mansion, and moved out. He addressed the West Virginia Roundtable at Edgewood Country Club shortly after. With a wry smile, Gaston told us what former Governor Hulett Smith had told him as he, Gaston, left office.

"Gaston," Caperton quoted Hulett, "when you leave the governor's office you will move out of the mansion, move into your home, unpack the boxes, and then sit in your study, waiting for the phone to ring."

Gaston said Hulett paused, and then said, "Gaston—it won't."

"And it didn't," Gaston laughed.

I thought, sitting there, that the next four years would go swiftly by and soon Cecil would be cleaning out *his* office. I resolved to remember that our winning campaign was momentary and to not get caught up in the importance of being a *Friend Of The Governor*—what we referred to as a "FOG".

Bill Phillips urged me after the election to consider appointment as chairman of the state Republican Party. I told Bill I appreciated the confidence he had in me but I would be shooting myself in the foot with my CRA clients—many of whom were Democrats. Bill then asked if Becky and I would chair Cecil's inauguration. We were flattered and said we would gladly do so, not knowing what we were getting into.

Between Election Day in November 1996 and Inauguration Day January 13, 1997, Becky and I solicited workers for the inauguration, chaired at least 20 meetings of at least 30 people and hired the professional entertainers, food suppliers, and infrastructure personnel necessary for the gala at the Charleston Civic Center and Municipal Auditorium. The effort was huge and exhaustive. During that time I came down with a giant case of the flu and the committee meetings were led by Becky for at least ten days.

The inaugural events began the day before Cecil's swearing-in. Charleston's Municipal Auditorium was filled with an enthusiastic audience and several hundred clergy from around the state. Those present had been invited to celebrate the *Inaugural Service of Prayer and Celebration,* organized by Underwood's longtime friend and Huntington United Methodist Church Minister F. Emerson Wood.

Underwood was the main speaker at the event. A 50-member African American Choir, the West Virginia Wesleyan Concert Chorale, and a children's choir from Underwood's church, Christ Church United Methodist of Charleston, sang during the event.

Emerson gave what may have been the world's longest prayer, but he was not going to miss the opportunity to take ample time in requesting the good Lord to assist his friend Cecil. Cecil later asked Emerson to lead *Mission West Virginia*, a not-for-profit working with community and faith-based organizations.

We raised several million dollars to stage the inaugural. It was a lot different garnering donations for an inaugural than raising money for a campaign. The dollars flowed in and we staged the biggest and most expensive inaugural event in the history of the state. Democrats and the media roundly criticized us for doing so.

Becky and Janet Mani orchestrated the Inaugural Grand Ball at the Civic Center. They supervised flowers, tables, curtains, stages and anything else that was present in both venues within the large building. Coal magnate Lawson Hamilton was a close friend of Underwood and a major underwriter of the gala. Lawson paid for the talent, and what talent it was. *Peabo Bryson*, the *Temptations*, the *Bob Thompson Quartet*, *Santa Cruz, Souvenir*, and *Bo Thorpe's Orchestra*.

The day before the ball Lawson came to review the setup. Becky and Jan had decided it would be better if Bo Thorpe were moved to another location and so advised Lawson. Lawson pulled me aside and said, "Now, the girls are beautiful—but Bo stays here."

I informed Becky and Jan that the man who was paying for the show wanted it to remain in the room in which they were standing. They agreed that money talks and Bo stayed in place. Lawson loved Bo Thorpe and regularly enlisted him to perform at events at Lawson's favorite venue, The Greenbrier. And, as he often did at The Greenbrier, Lawson took the stage at the Inaugural Ball and belted out several tunes from the stage. Lawson could sing exceptionally well, and he delighted the audience.

The ball came off without a hitch except for one thing: Milan Puskar, a major contributor to the Inaugural purse and founder of Mylan Pharmaceuticals, was angry that his table was not where he wanted it to be. We hurried to move his group to *wherever* Puskar desired. Money continued to talk.

At one point Becky and I accompanied Cecil from one dance to the next and it was like walking with a monster celebrity. I shouted at Cecil, "You're being treated like a rock star!" He shouted back above the din, "I know!" and just shook his head as people reached to touch him.

I think it was such a loud and demonstrative outpouring of affection and praise that it shook him a bit. I introduced him from the stage where the *Temptations* were playing and he was given a thunderous ovation. Here was a guy who was supposed to be an also-ran, a guy who was not supposed to beat a Democrat. He was thought to have lost the race at 11:00 election night—with the media interviewing him as though he had indeed lost to Charlotte Pritt. Dean Lewis told me that he had gone to bed late election night, thinking Cecil had lost. He did not know Underwood, whom he had known and supported for decades, had won until he picked the *Gazette* off his lawn the next morning. Cecil was a hero.

CHAPTER 90

Finding Talent For Underwood

THE TASK OF FINDING DEPARTMENT heads was not an easy one. There were a number of Cecil Underwood's close friends who were eager to join the administration but not enough to go around. The day before the inauguration I joined Dan Page, Underwood's Communications Director, just outside the governor's office. We sat at dual computers, pounding out press releases as acceptance of various state government positions came straggling in. It occurred to me that this late assembly of cabinet secretaries might be very unusual, and then I realized it was probably the same for every administration, as governors went hurriedly from campaigning to governing.

Wandering through the governor's grouping of offices as they sat empty and void of any scintilla of documents left over from the Caperton administration was a weird feeling. Office after office was stripped of photographs, pens and pencils, and the normal comfort items one sees when offices are occupied. The walls bore evidence of framed documents that had been removed—leaving white spaces and nails that had held prized manifestations of the occupant's education or award received.

I walked into the office that had been occupied by John Perdue, Governor Caperton's Executive Assistant, who had just been elected West Virginia Treasury Secretary. Perdue had a sense of humor; in his office chair was a large drawing of a confused bureaucrat—depicted as a whirling dervish—with the caption, "In four years *you* will look like this."

Once Cecil was in office he asked those of us who had served as his Kitchen Cabinet to continue to serve in that capacity. We agreed to meet regularly with the governor to counsel him on major decisions in state government.

This, I believe, we did well. We would gather at the Governor's Mansion around the large dining room table and weigh the approach to be taken on challenges of the moment. Cecil was always open to ideas, but generally agreed with us only when he was mostly of the same opinion. On occasion, however, he would bow to us—if we stood shoulder to shoulder and confronted him. He had a strong will but recognized our value.

CHAPTER 91

Cecil & Hovah

CECIL UNDERWOOD WAS AN ELEGANT man—the most handsome of West Virginia governors. He knew he was attractive to women. "It has been that way all my life," he confided to those around him.

He was certainly attractive to his wife Hovah—she was Cecil's closest confidant and he valued her political judgment more than any other. Her veto of strategy was always taken seriously by Cecil and was seldom overturned. She was an intelligent and incisive participant in dinners at our home on Abney Circle as we hosted media personalities or executives with whom the governor needed a closer relationship.

As he and Hovah sat at our dining room table, the governor's driver, always a state trooper, sat in his limo in the driveway. We urged all the assigned troopers to "come inside", but they would always refuse. The troopers were professionals and treated Cecil and Hovah as though they were their parents.

Trooper Mike McCarthy accompanied Hovah whenever she went shopping in downtown stores or Charleston's Town

Center Mall. Mike would review each outfit "Chequers" boutique sales executive Diane Vaughan would select for Hovah and give his candid opinion. Diane and Mike did well—Hovah was always stylishly dressed.

The First Lady played piano beautifully and could even play the saxophone, but I never saw her pick up an "axe". She had taught in the public school system after graduating from Salem College where she met Cecil. They married in 1948. Her great causes were Big Brothers Big Sisters of America, the Huntington Museum of Art, Marshall University Artist Series and the Governor's Mansion Preservation Foundation. Cecil lost his most ardent supporter when Hovah died on September 24, 2004. She was a great and eloquent woman.

CHAPTER 92

Party Maven & Great Kidneys

CECIL UNDERWOOD LOVED PARTIES, BUT had an Achilles heel when it came to gatherings; he was not comfortable breaking into conversation with those he did not know, a difficult handicap for a politician.

Regularly he would stand alone in the corner of a room (even at the Governor's Mansion) and we would have to bring people to him. Once the ice was broken, he would talk freely. I often told folks who would sit beside him at a banquet to mention President Eisenhower; if anyone asked him about Dwight Eisenhower he would break into ongoing conversation about the former president and his relationship with him. He *loved* to talk Eisenhower.

He was allergic to garlic and avoided it at all costs. When arranging for a banquet dinner, staff would always caution the presiding chef to avoid the ingredient verboten to Underwood, but loved in every chef's kitchen. One thing to which he was not allergic was his favorite libation—Cecil's choice of drink was vodka on the rocks.

I marveled at the capacity of his kidneys. At 75 he would sit for hours through hundreds of rubber chicken dinner banquets and never take a bathroom break, even though Bill Phillips said Cecil once told him, "I never pass a restroom."

Cecil was on the dais when "Stormin' Norman"—General Norman Schwarzkopf, Jr.—spoke for three hours at the Charleston Chamber of Commerce annual banquet at the Civic Center. The interminable speech was interrupted two hours into it when a fellow near the back of the room stood at his table, clutched his chest, and fell over. A third of the crowd recoiled in horror and rushed for help, while everyone else broke for the bathroom, wishing the fellow well but thankful for the break (he recovered, no heart attack). Cecil never moved. At times I thought perhaps he had attached a "trucker's friend" to his anatomy, such was his containment prowess.

At social gatherings at the Mansion I often worked to get Cecil's ear for one of my clients. If Cecil really didn't want to hear what the person was saying he would fix his gaze on a distant wall and stare at it while sipping his vodka. He was expert at saying nothing to those with whom he cared to say nothing.

After many of those social events Becky and I and other members of the Kitchen Cabinet and their spouses would kick back with the Governor and Hovah in one of the mansion's beautiful parlors and enjoy candid conversation about the night's function. It was a very comfortable and cozy atmosphere.

Sharon and Cecilia Underwood were married daughters at the time. In Cecil's first term they were just little girls in the mansion. Son Craig was born during Underwood's first term and Cecil told folks after the birth that no more children were in sight because "Hovah had a governor on her."

Cecil greatly enjoyed humor. University of Charleston President Edwin Welch introduced him one Friday afternoon as the Charleston Rotary speaker. Welch apprised the Rotarians that he enjoyed living just across the Kanawha River from the Governor's Mansion, with a direct view of the Governor and Hovah's bedroom window. Cecil laughed heartily, and responded that if Ed were indeed looking in the Underwood bedroom, Ed would be observing "Still Life." The Rotarians roared.

Cecil's daughter Sharon worked as my assistant for several years and was a devoted daughter, as was Cecilia. They doted on their mother and father and believed in him each time he ran and lost campaigns. They were in his corner in the 1996 campaign and were ecstatic when he won.

CHAPTER 93

The Underwood Thousand
Yard Stare & Heavy Foot

I ATTENDED A HIGH-LEVEL CONFERENCE at Buck Harless' company two years into Cecil Underwood's term of office. The subject matter was sensitive and small talk consumed the meeting for at least half an hour. Finally, Buck took things by the horns and informed Cecil that we all agreed that he would have to cease and desist in pursuing certain issues that we were aware of and with which we disagreed.

The governor sat and said nothing. He simply stared that "thousand yard stare" at the conference room wall. Minutes passed. The discomfort in the room was so thick it could have only been sliced with a chain saw. Finally someone cleared his throat and said, "Well, what do ya' think the legislature will accomplish this year?" The atmosphere immediately cleared and Cecil quickly joined into the conversation. The matter of great sensitivity was abandoned by all—never to be revisited.

When the meeting dissmissed I followed the governor's limo out of Mingo County and onto Appalachian Corridor G. I was driving a Mercedes 500 sedan that was staying right behind the limo, driven by a state trooper. Cecil loved speed and was often pulled over as he campaigned. He was in a hurry to return to Charleston and I watched my speedometer begin to climb—80, 90, 100, and 105.

"What am I doing?" I asked myself. Even though my license number was 7, I figured I would make headlines if pulled over. Then, I thought that no trooper was going to bother what appeared to be the governor's entourage and I kept it at 105. Cecil must have said something because 105 disappeared and 110 was on the way. I backed off, sweat on my palms.

Later I asked Kitchen Cabinet member Gary White, who commuted from Logan with his number 5 license plate on the rear of his vehicle, if he was ever stopped for speeding. Gary allowed that he was never pulled over although state troopers would pull up behind him from time to time.

"What did they do when they saw number 5, Gary?" I asked. Gary stepped back and said, "They do this,"—and ripped off a smart salute.

One memorable experience with my number 7 occurred while driving home from a round of golf at Edgewood Country Club's course at Sissonville. I was on I-77 when a battered vehicle pulled up behind, riding my bumper. I could sense the driver was focused on the license plate and I wondered what would come next. Would he back off or continue to press? He eased up a bit and then hit the gas, swinging around my car, coming up beside me. I looked over and the guy had a big grin on his face and his middle finger extended toward the roof. He laughed and took off. I told Gary that was the biggest thing number 7 had done for me.

Cecil told me he once was pulled over by a state trooper in Lewis County when he was out campaigning. He gave the officer his license and registration and the fellow spent some time looking at the credentials.

"So—you're Cecil Underwood?"

"Yes, I am."

The trooper paused and said, "Well, being a Republican, I guess you know you're in the wrong county."

Cecil confirmed that he knew Lewis County was registered solidly Democrat.

The trooper handed the license back to Cecil and said, "Yep, you're in the wrong county—but you've got the right trooper."

On another campaign trip the governor told me he was speeding up I-79 toward Morgantown when the red lights came on behind him. "I just hit the gas and outran him for another five miles to where I knew there was a rest stop," he said. He roared into the rest stop, jumped from the car and ran to the restroom. He emerged, zipping up his fly, encountering the trooper who was standing by the candidate's car.

"Sorry! I had to pee!" Underwood said as he approached the trooper. The state policeman laughed and let him go.

One of the troopers that guarded over Hovah and Cecil told me he stopped the governor for speeding once when Underwood was campaigning in Cabell County. "Did you give him a ticket?" I asked. "Nope," was the reply, "he was ahead in the polls at the time."

Cecil Underwood was a storied, loved and respected figure to the astute men in green, and they did all they could to serve and protect him—such was his persona and gift.

CHAPTER 94

Decisions Are Made

My great and good friend Bill Phillips left his position as chief of staff in the first year of Cecil Underwood's term. Bill, the consummate professional, resigned his position without public or private comment as to why. I believe he did so because of differences with Nancy Hobbs, Cecil's scheduling secretary.

Staffers said the day of Bill's resignation was terrible. Nancy was ultra protective of Cecil and did not hesitate to change his schedule if she thought the governor could more productively spend his time elsewhere. Bill and Nancy were at odds and it was Bill who decided to leave. His frustration was palpable. Jim Teets replaced Bill and worked with the same situation but was able to not let it get under his skin—at least not as much. Both Bill and Teets served Cecil admirably.

Cecil increased funding for development and economic infrastructure by 50 percent and invested more than $1 billion in water, wastewater, and development projects, positioning the state to attract billions in new business. He championed new technology and made it the centerpiece of his administration. He brought high-speed broadband communications to the state through a partnership with Bell Atlantic and initiated innovations in government and education. He wired senior centers for Internet connectivity and placed computers in every center.

Fearless, he attempted judicial reform, admirably charging that the tort system was out of control with a handful of plaintiff's attorneys and their clients getting rich while the remainder of West Virginians paid for it through increased insurance rates and decreased economic growth. Years later, governors and legislatures in West Virginia would address the issues Cecil raised and his name was referenced often as tax reform was on the table.

He advocated the nonpartisan election of Supreme Court Justices and suggested the ultimate step would be to install appointment of justices with safeguards to ensure professional standards.

I advocated with him on behalf of *Mountain Stage*, the Public Radio weekly program of music and entertainment that originated in Charleston and was broadcast nationwide on 110 PBS stations in major markets across the nation. I simply believed *Mountain Stage* was a giant tourism billboard for the state that was vastly underfunded and in danger of extinction. Underwood agreed with me that the health of the program was critical and recommended to the legislature that it be given a general revenue line-item appropriation of $200,000. The line-item placement assured that *Mountain Stage's* money would be in the budget annually. The bill passed and *Mountain Stage's* Andy Ridenour gave Underwood credit for saving the program from financial strangulation.

Not to be overlooked in the Underwood list of accomplishments was the governor's *Courtesy Patrol* on interstate highways where stranded motorists regularly thanked him for state assistance in troubled times.

Because I had received extensive publicity as a member of the Kitchen Cabinet, there were individuals and companies that sought CRA's services. I had represented clients before the state legislature and in front of three governors over 20 years and always with integrity. However, I knew having a friend in the governor's chair could create situations that might be borderline as to representations or decisions.

I decided I wanted legal counsel to make certain I made no missteps in this new atmosphere. I retained former United States Attorney Michael Carey of Carey, Scott, Douglas & Kessler, asking Mike to be available to me during Cecil Underwood's term to gauge what business relationships I should or should not enter into. Mike had, during his term as a federal prosecutor, focused on corruption in government and knew right from wrong. So did I, but politics can be a nasty business and I did not want to get blindsided. The week after the election a controversial Charleston businessman called and said he wanted to retain me.

"To do what?" I asked.

"Well, I just want to retain you."

"To do what?"

"Just to be available."

"I'll need to know what that means," I said.

The fellow obfuscated and I told him my services were not available if he could not articulate what it was he wanted me to do. I reported the incident to Mike and he agreed that I had done the right thing.

In that arena and on yet another occasion during another governor's term, I was representing an out-of-state firm that had an issue before the state Public Service Commission. I was asked to find out what the governor's position was on the issue. I asked the question and the answer was, as I expected it would be, that the governor had no position—it was an issue for the PSC.

I made my report and my client's heated response was "What does it take to get to this governor?" The hair on the back of my head stood straight out and I resigned the account, suspecting the client was asking if the governor could be bribed to intervene.

I contacted Mike Carey several times while Cecil was governor. To most of my questions I knew the answer, and Mike usually concurred. It was a great insurance policy and I would recommend anyone involved in politics have a "go-to" person to always make certain a straight and narrow course is charted. For four years Mike (who, ironically, was the federal prosecutor when Arch Moore was indicted) had my back and I emerged from the political swamp unscathed.

Cecil decided, against my advice and, I believe, every other member of the Kitchen Cabinet, to run for re-election. His opponent would be Congressman Bob Wise, a popular Democrat from Kanawha County. We knew the race would be a tough one—Cecil was 78 and age would play a factor.

Bill Phillips, who engineered one of the greatest comebacks in political history, weighed in with the most formidable opposition to another Underwood run for office. He said to me years later, "I recall a meeting at your office that included the Kitchen Cabinet and other individuals at CRA. Cecil looked at me, most upset, saying, 'Are you telling me I should not run?' I said, that is exactly what I am saying. We fixed your life in 1996 and I want you to go out a winner."

With each entreaty to *not* run, Cecil would revert to that long stare at the wall, ignoring us, and we knew he was going to again throw his hat in the ring. Why not? He had a great house in which to live, a driver, a chef, and life was good. He wanted to give it a shot. The Kitchen Cabinet relented and prepared to serve its governor in the coming campaign. Our help this time, however, was not entirely welcomed.

CHAPTER 95

Mike Wallace & 60 Minutes

CECIL UNDERWOOD'S SON, CRAIG, AN entrepreneur in Boston, was not part of the campaign against Charlotte Pritt. Back then, Craig had a business to run and stayed on the sidelines. He sold that business during his father's second term and was free to participate in Cecil's upcoming campaign. He ran the re-election effort with an iron hand and his father's backing. I liked Craig immensely and he certainly had my respect. But, Craig did not know the West Virginia political landscape and we were often frustrated as he took control of all aspects of the campaign.

We had produced two television commercials that the Kitchen Cabinet thought would produce enormous results—one featured the Republican nominee for President, George W. Bush, the other "Rocket Boys" author Homer Hickham. Both Bush and Hickham were eloquent in their endorsement of Underwood for Governor. Craig nixed the ads and they never saw the light of day. It was a major mistake.

Adding to what I believe was a dysfunctional effort, Underwood was stunned when his longtime and great friend Senator

Robert C. Byrd endorsed Bob Wise for governor rather than remain neutral. Underwood had told several people that Byrd had assured him he would remain on the sideline in the gubernatorial campaign.

Underwood's communications director, Dan Page, said later that both broadcast mogul Bray Cary and he were told by Buck Harless that Byrd had told him he would remain neutral. Something changed Byrd's mind and Cecil was deeply hurt by Byrd's action that destroyed a Byrd-Underwood friendship of fifty years.

Adding insult to injury, CBS muckraker Mike Wallace came to town and did an interview with Cecil that left the impression the governor was a doddering old man controlled by king coal. The interview came about as a request from CBS' *60 Minutes*.

The Kitchen Cabinet advised strongly that Cecil not do the interview, but Wallace was persistent. Dan Page says he told the governor he could either do the interview or risk that Wallace, camera crew in tow, would follow him from his office to the mansion and make Cecil look evasive. Page said Cecil said in front of his entire staff that he was confident he could handle an interview with Wallace.

Wallace and his crew swooped into Charleston and registered at the Marriott. The night before the interview was to take place, Becky and I and a few of our friends were having dinner at the Marriott's *Tarragon Room* when Wallace and his entourage arrived for dinner.

Wallace was dressed in a correspondent trench coat and sported his usual deep tan. He surveyed the room, knowing he was center stage. I got up, walked over, introduced myself and stated my connection with the governor, welcoming Wallace to town. He was aloof but cordial and said, "I hear your governor may have some problems because of his ties to big coal." I replied that big coal had ties to everyone in West Virginia. Mike and company sat down at the next table and ordered fine food and what I took to be the best wine in the house.

The following day the *60 Minutes* gang descended on the governor's office and staged a major production. Lights, sound equipment, lighting umbrellas, electrical cords strung across the carpet, a half dozen people with the *Star*—Mike Wallace himself—seated in a chair across from Cecil who waited patiently for the crew to complete its setup as he chatted small talk with Wallace.

"Our error," Page said, "was to set no firm time limits on the interview. That allowed Wallace to ask Underwood the same question over and over about his relationship with the coal industry."

Wallace questioned Underwood about $500,000 in campaign and inaugural contributions from the coal industry and his ties to coal companies. Wallace interrupted the governor time and time again as Cecil attempted to respond to the questions. After the fifth Wallace blast, Cecil, frustrated and a bit angry because Wallace was just plain rude, stumbled through a response.

That allowed Wallace the 'kill shot' he was looking for, showing Underwood faltering as he tried, for the umpteenth time, to answer the oft-repeated question. Page said the *60 Minutes* broadcast (12 minutes long) did not fairly represent the interview. "It was an ambush, pure and simple," Page said.

The Wise campaign, just before the 2000 general election, used a clip from the interview to its advantage and may have violated copyright laws in doing so. The ad implied that in return for coal contributions Underwood chose not to pursue more than $200 million in unpaid worker's compensation premiums owed by contractors.

Page and I and a half dozen other people gathered for a conference call about the Wise ad the morning after it first aired. We felt terrible about it and we learned a lesson. Page said, "I gave Mike Wallace a chance to do what he does best and that will haunt me forever." I felt the same and I called broadcast and communications attorneys who agreed the Wise campaign may have broken copyright laws by unauthorized use of *60 Minutes* broadcast material, but there was no sense chasing our tails; what was done was done. Frustrated, I called CBS to alert them of what I thought was unauthorized use of their copyrighted material. The CBS legal department just shrugged it off.

Underwood responded through media coverage, saying no one should believe that he was in the pocket of coal companies. "I'm not owned by anybody, and not Wallace or anybody else can make that claim," Cecil said.

In subsequent years, as I did media training for companies around the country, I would cite the Underwood ambush by Wallace and advise my clients to always set time limits for interviews. Otherwise, the Wallace technique of asking the same question over and over would invariably be used—and would usually work—deep-sixing the interviewee.

We lost the election to Bob Wise and Cecil moved out of the Mansion. Gaston Caperton's words rang in my ears—*"no one will call"*—and I resolved to do all I could to stay in regular touch with Cecil. He and Hovah moved into a home on Kanawha Boulevard in Charleston and Hovah died in 2004 at age 85. Underwood spent the next few years writing and editing his official papers. He did this mostly by himself. He was an excellent writer and grammarian and he enjoyed the process.

I visited him at his home on the Boulevard in his last years and I also would drive to his residence, pick him up, and take him to our home where old friends would sit around our dinner table. He was gracious and handsome even when Becky and I visited him at his final stop in his room at Charleston Area Medical Center. He died November 24, 2008 at the age of 86. It had been a long, exciting and historical journey from his birth in 1922 at Josephs Mills, West Virginia.

Both Becky and I felt blessed to have had such a close friendship with Cecil and Hovah—two extraordinary and lovable West Virginians.

CHAPTER 96

Manchin & McClendon

MY WIFE BECKY AND I were attending the West Virginia Chamber of Commerce Business Summit at The Greenbrier in August of 1998. I had invited Secretary of State Joe Manchin to our suite for a drink, along with two other couples. There he and his wife Gayle said they would make a run for governor against the incumbent, Bob Wise. Becky and I applauded the decision and afterward one couple expressed doubt that Joe could win. Boy, were they wrong. Joe Manchin had the best political moves I had ever seen. I was a card-carrying Republican, but he had my support in every way.

Joe was born in Farmington in Marion County, where his father and grandfather had been mayor. A star football player, he had a scholarship to play football for WVU but a blown out knee ended his college athletic career in 1965. He graduated in 1970 with a degree in Information Management and then joined his family's carpeting business. The Manchins hired CRA to do advertising work and that was my first relationship with Joe.

In 1982 Joe was elected to the House of Delegates and then the state Senate. He ran for governor in 1996 and lost the primary election to Charlotte Pritt, who was defeated by Cecil Underwood. Manchin then ran for, and was elected, Secretary of State in the year 2000.

Joe again ran for governor in 2004, easily defeating the Republican nominee, Monty Warner. Manchin succeeded Bob Wise. Wise, the most unlikely candidate in the world to be involved in a scandalous affair, had announced he was not going to run for re-election after emails of a relationship with a female statehouse worker surfaced. Joe then smashed through the Democratic primary and general election with landslide victories, easily defeating his opponents.

After Joe entered the governor's office, Chesapeake Energy retained my services as it began expanding its natural gas exploration in four states. Activity with the account increased exponentially as Joe began to lobby Chesapeake CEO Aubrey McClendon to locate the company's eastern headquarters in Charleston.

Aubrey and Tom Price, Chesapeake's vice president of government relations, invited Joe to Oklahoma City and the company's national headquarters for discussions. I flew with Joe and Gayle in a Beechcraft Hawker that took off from Yeager Airport and climbed to 30,000 feet in about ten seconds. Beechcraft was trying to sell the jet to the state and this was a test ride for the governor.

Joe was a pilot and he was delighted with the Hawker. At one point the pilots beckoned for me to come forward to the cockpit and look down toward Earth. There, far below, were three military jets. Pretty cool, we were much higher and seemed to be much faster than the military aircraft.

Upon arrival in windy Oklahoma City we were whisked to Chesapeake's vast campus where Joe was exposed to the company's highly inventive and state-of-the art natural gas extraction and exploration technology. Later, a dinner with McClendon and other Chesapeake executives was on tap. The phone rang in my hotel room.

"Buddy, do you have any cufflinks? I forgot the darn things and all I have are French Cuffs."

"I do have a pair, Governor, but they have the initials "CR" on them. If that's okay, I'll bring them down to you."

"Thanks, buddy, that'd be great," Joe said, and hung up.

I did not see my cuff links again until a state trooper dropped them off at my home after we returned to Charleston. Later in the same day, however, I got a call from Joe who thanked me profusely for the use of the cuff links. I kidded him about his "CR" initials and he said he was proud to wear them.

McClendon came to The Greenbrier at Joe's invitation and I was again charged with making arrangements and guaranteeing a smooth visit. Tom Price and Chesapeake's West Virginia government relations vice president Scott Rotruck, were with McClendon. When our group arrived at the hotel's entrance there was a long line of vehicles and Aubrey's SUV, for which I had arranged, was stuck at the front gates as guests were unloading cars, checking in. Aubrey was not pleased.

I jumped from our SUV and ran across the expanse of green that fronted the magnificent hostelry and found my good friend Dale Mann, lead doorman at the hotel, and explained my predicament. I had always given Dale a $100 tip when leaving The Greenbrier after every visit and he always made certain Becky and I were happy. Dale said, "Follow me, Mr. Ryan," and we ran to Aubrey's car and his entourage. Dale motioned for the driver to pull onto the lawn and escorted us across fabulous turf that had seldom seen the tires of a vehicle—directly to the front entrance of The Greenbrier.

I was impressed, as I always was, with Dale's leadership, instant command of the situation at hand, and poise in resolving an issue. Aubrey was impressed with my performance (made possible by Dale's brilliant "take command" actions) and he let me know it. I was smiling, and Dale, at tip time, also was. Dale Mann is a legend at The Greenbrier and a great friend.

Aubrey was a lover of good wine and had asked Price to make certain appropriate Cabernet was in the private dining room where he, the Governor, the Governor's chief of staff, Larry Puccio, Price, Rotruck and I would dine. Price turned to me for assistance in the wine selection and I promptly summoned The Greenbrier's sommelier and asked for his best wine list.

Price took that to Aubrey and the CEO selected a particular favorite of his. I returned to the sommelier and asked what several bottles of Aubrey's selection would cost. I was aghast at the number quoted and got back to Price, cautioning that we would, under West Virginia law, have to report the cost of the dinner in my lobbying report—along with the pricey wine tab. Price agreed we would have to inform Aubrey we could not order the wine he favored.

I asked for a wine list with numbers attached and hunted for Aubrey, and upon locating him told him the wine he had selected was too expensive to pass muster for the lobbying report. Aubrey did not like the news. He was visibly upset and snatched the wine list from me. He quickly scanned the upscale inventory, pointed to a $175 bottle of wine (Aubrey considered that price rather pedestrian) and said, in a brusque and intimidating voice, "Is that all right!" It was not a question. I meekly said that would be fine and backed away from Oklahoma's billionaire natural gas king.

At dinner, the governor and his chief of staff Puccio, both knowledgeable wine lovers, complimented Aubrey at least a dozen times on the quality of the Cabernet. And the bottles just kept coming. At dinner's close there were several opened, but not empty bottles, that I assume The Greenbrier staff later enjoyed.

Wine and dinner consumed, all was well, and extensive plans were drawn for Chesapeake's eastern campus high above Charleston at John Wellford's Northgate Business Park. It was to be an enormous state-of-the-art building that would feature the best amenities for the Chesapeake employees; Aubrey was known in Oklahoma City for providing working space for the men and women of Chesapeake that was simply stunning—expansive cafeterias, workout centers, gymnasiums and child care.

Alas, the Charleston eastern campus of Chesapeake Energy was not to be. Aubrey became extremely angry when a Roane County jury found his company guilty of allegations it had cheated West Virginia royalty owners, awarding the plaintiffs $404 million. In the aftermath, Aubrey demanded Manchin and the legislature alter laws concerning royalty interests. Manchin did all he could to convince Chesapeake to reconsider and the company eventually located a regional office at Jane Lew in Lewis County, but the big enchilada was gone.

McClendon also launched a campaign in Texas against the coal industry called "Coal Is Filthy." His object was to persuade Texas to favor natural gas over coal when legislation was considered. The campaign gave Manchin heartburn, given the political clout of coal in West Virginia, and it gave me double heartburn in that CRA also represented several coal interests. We did our best to convince Aubrey that he should soft-pedal the coal bashing in the Mountain State and we were successful.

The Chesapeake years were extremely exciting for CRA. The McClendon style was exhilarating and Chesapeake did not hesitate to spend lots of dollars with us. The company quickly became our foremost client as we reported to the peripatetic Tom Price. Tom, and the other men and women at Chesapeake, were solid professionals and we always went the extra mile for them. I regret to this day that the Chesapeake intention to operate its east coast operations from a spacious office complex in Charleston was derailed. West Virginia lost much when Aubrey, totally frustrated, ditched the effort. I really could not blame him.

Chesapeake later came on some hard times and Aubrey was forced out of the company he founded. Aubrey was not daunted, he simply went out and did it all again—forming American Energy Partners and attracting major investors.

On March 1, 2016 the Department of Justice issued a federal indictment charging Aubrey with conspiring to rig bids for the purchase of oil and natural gas acreage in Oklahoma. The announcement stunned Oklahoma City and Aubrey denied the charges, calling them wrong and unprecedented. The following day Aubrey died in a one-vehicle collision when his SUV crashed into a concrete bridge embankment in Oklahoma City.

I consider the work we did for Chesapeake in West Virginia, Kentucky, Pennsylvania and New York to be exemplary and I will always consider it an honor to have personally known one of America's greatest entrepreneurs. Aubrey McClendon was an exciting swashbuckler—a true wildcatter who changed an industry and the lives of thousands he touched in business and philanthropy. "Aubrey always believed he could change the future," Tom Price told the *New York Times*. "He was a guy who was always willing to charge the hill. He believed in himself so thoroughly."

CHAPTER 97

The High Theatre Of Jimmy Manchin

YEARS BEFORE HIS NEPHEW, AND now United States Senator Joe Manchin's name was known statewide, the flamboyant A. James Manchin, a former teacher and wrestling coach, roared across the state. There has never been as colorful a political figure in West Virginia as A. James and he loved the spotlight, speaking in Shakespearean tones that Sir Laurence Olivier would consider worthy of the Old Vic.

Governor Arch Moore recognized Jimmy's talent and political appeal and appointed him the leader of the Moore *Rehabilitation Environmental Action Program* (REAP) to rid the state of junked cars that littered the valleys of the state. Manchin recognized a political gift and took full advantage. He quickly became a household name in West Virginia in a role that bemused and delighted.

Sensing public support of his charge to clean up the state, Manchin quickly commissioned public relations executive John Deitz to design a "suitable for (large) framing" poster that characterized Jimmy's efforts.

Deitz came up with a beauty—a color poster that featured Manchin standing atop a junked car, a giant scythe in hand, resplendent in black fedora and topcoat, gazing sternly out to the distance. Deitz's caption on the poster read, "We Must Purge These Proud Peaks of Their Jumbled Jungles of Junkery." The poster is a collector's item today.

CRA once was retained by Exxon to manage a ribbon cutting for a new bulk terminal plant on Charleston's South Side Expressway, directly across the Kanawha River from downtown. We attempted to persuade the governor to participate, but we were rejected. I then turned to Secretary of State Manchin and our invitation was readily accepted.

Manchin arrived in his fedora and black suit and wowed the crowd with a stem winder speech. The Exxon executives that sat on the stage behind the gesticulating Secretary of State were amazed, enthralled and bemused at Manchin's antics.

A. James had the crowd panting at his conclusion, whereupon he arrived at a crescendo, bellowing, "Thank Gawd for the *United States of America*! Thank Gawd for the *great State of West Virg*inia!" And then, he reached in his pocket and pulled out a plastic card. He raised the card high above his head toward the crowd and shouted, "But, most of all, thank Gawd for my *Exxon credit card*!"

The crowd went silent and the Exxon suits looked at one another, not knowing what to do. There's always a clacker in the crowd (in politics a "clacker" is one who is positioned to start applause as the candidate makes a point) and I assumed the role, applauding loudly—the Exxon officials and the crowd followed, bursting into thunderous approval. It was a smashing success.

Governor Moore and others were startled one day when Manchin, presiding over a groundbreaking, proclaimed at the end of the pro-forma ribbon cutting, "Let the bulldozers roll," while pulling a gun out of his pocket and firing it in the air.

A. James Manchin was prone to visiting all funerals in his home area, garnering appreciation from relatives and friends of the deceased and, not incidentally, their favor at the polls. Manchin told me he had, on one day, a busy agenda.

He rushed from funeral home to funeral home, quickly viewing the dearly departed, uttering the required lamentations to the family, and hurrying to the next stop. At his last viewing he paid his respect to the family at the funeral, glanced into the coffin, and exclaimed loudly, "My Gawd! I *know* this man!"

Jimmy once oversaw the dedication of a sewage treatment plant dedication with typical Manchin creative juice. With flowery body language he waved into the ceremony twelve trumpeters who musically hailed the soon-to-be outstanding facility that would help "Wash West Virginia's pretty face!"

A. James was a solid political animal with a great sense of humor and timing. Senator Joe Manchin loved quoting Jimmy's stump speech where he told voters, "I'm running this campaign on bumper stickers and bullshit—and I'm running low on bumper stickers!"

Jimmy also had a penchant for disliking uptight, stuck-in-the-mud types. I was with him one day when he showered praise upon a rather conservative fellow only to look at me as he walked away from the conversation and say, "He's so uptight I'll bet he's never peed in the shower!"

Then there were the events where clients asked to see the secretary of state and CRA dutifully arranged the meeting. We did not inform them as to how they would be introduced to A. James.

We would escort our clients into the secretary of state's reception office where we sat until we were asked to move to an adjacent room. Our clients were then seated before a black curtain. Within a few moments Manchin's top aide would walk to the side of the curtain, face the clients, pull a cord that opened the curtains, and shout in a stentorian voice, "Ladies and Gentlemen, the Secretary of State of the Great State of West Virginia, the Honorable A. James Manchin!"

As the curtain swept open, a smiling A. James would bound forth and begin shaking hands, his voice booming flowery welcomes. He would end these forays by saying, "May God save the precious state of West Virginia and may God bless the United States of America."

Our clients were always speechless and we never tired of the theatre provided by the man from Marion County. A. James went on to become state treasurer, a move he would always regret. He and his deputy made some serious monetary mistakes and, as a result, the state lost $279 million in bad investments. Manchin was charged with negligence in delegating and supervising the state's investment fund and faced impeachment. Hearings in the House of Delegates made it clear that Jimmy was out of his league when it came to understanding the financial investments in the Treasurer's office.

I sat in the House gallery when Jimmy was directed by attorney Jim Lees to view numbers on a large screen at the front of the House chamber. The numbers had brackets around them. Lees asked the state treasurer what those brackets signified. Jimmy was clueless, not knowing they designated a loss.

Manchin vowed he would stay in office, but if the Senate had convicted him he could have lost his state pension and would have been banned from again running for public office. He resigned before his trial was completed and won election in 1998 to the House of Delegates where he had served a term at the age of 21. He died of a heart attack in 2003, while in office. The House honored him in a resolution following his death.

He will always have a special place in my heart. The first week I was in business I heard a loud voice down the hall demanding to know in which office he would find Charles Ryan. I knew the voice and stepped out of my office to greet West Virginia's LaGuardia. The black mane of hair and the stentorian voice came toward me, waving a plaque in the air. It featured a black fedora at the top with A. James Manchin's name emblazoned on the hat. Below that was an inscription to me, wishing me well in my new endeavor. Jimmy's message, written on the plaque, was, "The best way to succeed is to begin." It was an incredibly meaningful gesture as I ventured forth on the high seas of entrepreneurialism.

CHAPTER 98

McGraw, Roark & The Jones Boys

WEST VIRGINIA POLITICS FEATURED ROUGH antics. Accusations and innuendo were commonplace in campaigns. One candidate was harassed with billboards claiming that he was a "Neophyte" (he was!) and another saying he had "Matriculated" (he did!)—hoping to take advantage of voters who were not well-educated—"My Gawd, Maude, he's a neophyte!"

Politics was ready money and I took to it well, given my interest in politics and politicians. Some of my conservative friends will find it surprising that I once did political work for ultra-liberal Darrell Vivian McGraw, who served as an administrative assistant to Governor Hulett Smith and then spent several terms as West Virginia's frequently controversial and media-magnet attorney general. Darrell engaged our services in one of his early campaigns and I was mighty glad to have him.

After a meeting in our offices one fall day, Darrell grabbed his suit jacket after we had made a decision (I'm not sure what it was) and bounded from the room, entering his car, and dashing away.

From my second story office (a really fine venue that featured a bay window and three times the space 1 had enjoyed in the Barber Shop) I watched Darrell drive off and turned to grab my jacket, a dark blue one similar to Darrell's. I put it on and realized the sleeves practically dragged the floor. I will always remember that "jacket switch" as Darrell proceeded throughout his career as a liberal while I became a staunch conservative; I can truthfully say, however, that I once wore a liberal's clothes.

Darrell and his brother Warren McGraw were flamboyant and fun. I had many great moments with both of them as a reporter and as an entrepreneur working with them in campaigns. Darrell won the attorney general's office and Warren went on to become a Senate president, a Supreme Court justice and finally circuit court judge in Wyoming County. In a film documentary about the McGraws, one of the brothers turns to the other and says, "Let's go see Charlie about it." I cherished the mention.

Another political client was Kanawha County Prosecuting Attorney Mike Roark. He hired CRA when he ran for re-election as mayor of Charleston in 1987. Roark was a crusader known for his zeal in fighting drug abuse, earning him the nickname "Mad Dog". A former Marine, Mike often wore an Army jacket and fatigues to the office.

We worked closely with Mike, municipal judge, and esteemed lawyer John Charnock (who served as Mike's campaign manager) and Mike's second in command, Ed Esposito, a former broadcaster who was perhaps Mike's closest friend. Esposito was a professional and adept city leader.

Mike was a native of Nitro, graduate of the University of Virginia and the West Virginia University College of Law. He served in in Vietnam and was an assistant United States attorney in Pittsburgh before his successful run for prosecutor in Kanawha County.

He was smart and an incredibly capable mayor. We were successful in the campaign—Mike won and had a bright future ahead of him—all the talk said he would run for governor in the next election. It was not to be. On November 17, 1987, the *New York Times* reported the following:

"Mayor James E. (Mike) Roark, on the morning his drug trial was to begin, pleaded guilty today to six misdemeanor counts of cocaine possession and agreed to resign."

Mike was sentenced to 179 days in prison and fined $5,000. He entered prison on February 12, 1988—seven months after his re-election—and served just over five months at the Federal Correctional Institute in Petersburg, VA. While there, he worked as a clerk in the prison's education department. Called a model prisoner, he was released 18 days early. He walked out of prison with his former aide, Ed Esposito, always faithful, by his side. John Charnock said Mike's mood was good and he'd like to get back to Charleston.

Mike died of leukemia at age 53. The *Charleston Gazette* said:

Former Mayor James Edward "Mike" Roark was one of the region's most flamboyant and controversial political figures. During his stormy life he had been a teen-age radio announcer, a vice-raiding prosecutor (dubbed "Mad Dog" by some), a professional actor, a runner and a promising Republican politician, until his career was derailed by a cocaine conviction."

John Charnock was quoted in the same article as saying, "He was an extremely talented individual with a brilliant mind."

The campaign time with Mike revealed to me an intense young man with all the right political moves. He had good looks, style, and the ability to give the right sound bite and flair and flash that made him irresistible. If drugs had not entered his life I am convinced he would have been elected governor or United States Senator.

CRA was the agency of record for two of the most expensive (at the time) state senate races in West Virginia—for the Jones Boys. One won, the other lost. The winning candidate was Ned Jones of Cabell County. Ned was the son of prominent Mason County landowner Bartow Jones, a noted political mover and shaker in the area. Ned, a graduate of the University of Virginia and standout golfer, ran for the State Senate in 1986 against heavy odds. Ned won the race and we added another "win" to our list of successful campaigns.

Ned's brother, Brereton Jones, was elected to the West Virginia House of Delegates and became the Republican minority leader in the lower chamber. "Brery" liked politics, moved to Kentucky and ran for and was elected lieutenant governor in 1987. Liking that, in 1991 he ran for and was elected Kentucky governor—by the biggest majority ever recorded. I liked both

Brery and Ned immensely and got to know them and their parents well. They were handsome, wealthy people with absolutely no airs.

We were not as successful in our "Jones" senatorial race in Kanawha County when Charlie Jones, no relation to the Mason County Jones', threw his hat in the ring. Charlie, known far and wide in the senatorial district as the CEO of storied towing company Amherst Industries, was a John Wayne type and was sure to be a great candidate. As of this writing he is 99 and still going strong. Charlie lost his bid for the Senate even as he spent more money in a senatorial race than any other candidate in state history.

I always felt another $50,000 in television advertising would have put us over the top. Easy for me to say, I wasn't writing the checks. It was a race I heavily regretted losing. Charlie would have been one of the best men to ever be elected to public office. But, we failed—and I taste that failure to this day.

CHAPTER 99

Kelly Castleberry & Richard Neely

CRA ALSO DID COUNTY POLITICS and accepted a job with a Kanawha County Commission candidate who stood little chance against the long-time and entrenched incumbent Kelly Castleberry. It was one of our first campaigns. Harry Peck and I decided we would utilize only television commercials in the quest to upset the apple cart. Our strategy was to suggest the incumbent commissioner was part of a political machine.

We bought an Erector set and built a moving machine of some sort that cranked away in front of the film camera we utilized. I then did voice-over for the commercial. The copy went something like this (with a sneer in my voice):

"The Kanawha County Courthouse—a *machine* cranking away with *sordid* politicians at the controls. It's time for a change, Kanawha County—time to stop the oily politics spreading through your courthouse let's clean it up—elect (our candidate) to the Kanawha County Commission and grind the machine to a halt!"

We did a second commercial, this one equally high tech—we filled an empty paint bucket with about a pound of night crawlers and affixed a picture of the Kanawha County Courthouse on the outside. We then placed the bucket on a turntable and slowly turned it to show the other side of the bucket. As the bucket turned the camera lens moved to the top of the container and peered into the mass of twisting, entangled earth worms. A hand reached into the bucket, pulling up a fistful of slithering earthworms.

I then read the copy with the same sneer:

"The Kanawha County Courthouse—on the outside (picture of courthouse as bucket slowly turns) it's a picturesque, historic building—but—inside (camera moves up and peers into bucket)—it's a tangled mess of political infighting. It's time to put a lid on (lid slams loudly onto bucket) this mess Kanawha County! Let's elect (our candidate) our County Commissioner!" The candidate's picture then appeared atop the paint can lid.

Well, our campaign worked and our candidate won the election. But, in the next election cycle, Castleberry again ran against our client, who allowed as how he did not need us, since he was now the incumbent. He then lost the race.

Then there was *Billboard Man*, a nickname I used for Richard Neely, grandson of the storied governor and United States Senator Matthew M. Neely. Richard Neely was a brilliant young attorney who graduated from Yale Law and served as a captain in the U.S. Army during the Vietnam conflict, organizing the economic development plan for much of South

Vietnam. Neely had run for and was elected to the West Virginia House of Delegates and then became a candidate for the state Supreme Court—to which he was elected in 1973, the year before I went into business.

Richard's second run for the court came 12 years later when he was up for re-election. He called me and engaged CRA as his campaign agency. I pushed hard for television and radio. Richard countered—"Billboards!"—he said.

I hated billboards as part of a campaign. They helped establish name recognition, but, I argued, Neely's name was well known throughout the state, and he needed television commercials to define his case for re-election.

"Nonsense," Richard said. So, we bought billboards and the majority of the money spent on media went to—billboards. Richard, I knew, was wrong and would lose. When the polls closed and the votes were counted, Richard won handily. He was right and *I* was wrong. What the heck, he was *brilliant* and I was just a flack.

Truth is, Richard and I had hit it off since I was a reporter and he was in the legislature. After I went into business, he and I would regularly have lunch or I would visit him in his Supreme Court office where he would wax eloquently about issues and pols of the day. Always adept with salty language and complete candor, he would colorfully describe friend and foe, giving me grand theatre as he expounded—always dressed to the nines in his vested Savile Row suits and Turnbull & Asser shirts that sported huge cuffs and dramatic cufflinks. He seemed to always be puffing on a Dunhill pipe and, at times, he would leave his office wearing a cape similar to that made famous by the character Sherlock Holmes.

In 1976, CRA engaged in yet another West Virginia Supreme Court race as a result of Governor Arch Moore filling a vacancy on the court by appointing Charleston attorney and Jackson County native Don Wilson to the bench. Don ran for re-election later that year, hiring CRA on a shoestring budget.

Don, a cultured gentleman, sported immaculate French cuffs and gold cuff links that set off beautifully tailored suits. His loafers were English and of the finest leather. He smoked cigarettes in a long gold holder. He was simply elegant.

CRA's Carolyn Perry and I handled his campaign. We would sit in Don's office as he expounded on the legal system. We often had glazed looks on our faces as the sessions ran into hours.

We traveled around the state with Don in his Lincoln Continental, meeting with media, exposing them to the erudite Jackson County lawyer. Don drove and continued to educate Carolyn and me. Occasionally, we drifted off. Don didn't mind.

Don, not your average Joe, fought an uphill battle, running against a guy who had no problem connecting with every West Virginian—Darrell Vivian McGraw.

We used billboards that presented the name "Wilson" in a manner similar to the Wilson Sporting Goods logo. It was instantly recognizable and gave our candidate some "every-man" element.

We were thrilled with the result but Wilson Sporting Goods Company attorneys advised us to cease and desist or face legal action. We did not hesitate to do so.

McGraw won going away and Don went back to private law practice. His short tenure on the court, however, was indeed stellar, and Don gave us an insight into a brilliant legal mind.

CHAPTER 100

McHugh, Murphine & Sprouse

I BEGAN MY POLITICAL CONSULTING work in the early seventies when we (or, rather, "I"—at the time I was a one-man shop) became the agency for Tom McHugh, who ran for circuit court judge in Kanawha County. Tom was my first political client and the nicest political figure I would ever meet. We were successful in the campaign and Tom went on to become a Supreme Court justice, charting a course that saw him become one of the most respected jurists in state history.

In his second quest for the governor's office, attorney and mega Democratic Party stalwart Jim Sprouse hired CRA and the Arnold Lazarus Agency of Wheeling as his campaign agents. Our work for Jim was in the Democratic primary election against John D. Rockefeller IV. Needless to say, my success in politics was about to come to an end—Rockefeller had deep pockets and Jim had mostly empty ones.

CRA and the Lazarus Agency were each given an initial $5,000 to cover our consulting hours in launching and running the marketing effort. When that sum was expended, Laz and I would track Jim down, wherever he was, and demand another $5,000, without which, Laz and I threatened, we would leave the campaign.

Jim always delivered, but it was a chore wringing the money from him; he was running on a shoestring. Jim proved to be a difficult person to work with as a candidate. The moment the campaign ended, however, he became the same sweet and considerate person he had been prior to the campaign. The stress of politics changes the people who run and those who work in the campaign. I saw it time and time again.

One of my co-workers when I was in media was a very talented fellow by the name of Ralph Murphine. Ralph migrated from media to national and international political consulting and confided to me that "to know the candidate is to loathe him." Ralph simply meant that the campaign causes normally mild-mannered men and women to become raging bulls. Sprouse was one of those folks, questioning on a daily basis the consultant's decisions, asking, "Are we doing the right thing?"

Murphine's response to such insecurities was to place a billboard as near the candidate's home as possible so that the office seeker would see it each morning while driving to campaign headquarters and would think to him or herself, "My campaign's working."

Sprouse may have been difficult to work with as he ran for office, but he was a totally honest man who played by the rules. He expressed dire concern when he would return to his hotel room after campaign appearances and find cash stuffed in his jacket pockets. Most pols would not have given that a second thought, but Jim truly agonized over it.

Sprouse, who was not destined to become governor despite excellent credentials, later won a bigger prize—he became a federal judge.

CHAPTER 101

Babies Need Feeding

THE AGENCY BUSINESS WAS TOUGH and not for the faint hearted. Supreme Court justice Richard Neely once remarked to me at one of our regular lunches that it must be a difficult business—always going back to the well. His comment unnerved me a bit, but Richard was correct. However, I learned not to panic. I walked through the front doors of the Charleston National Bank in 1975, six months after establishing my fledgling public relations firm. The gleaming new bank at the corner of Virginia and Capitol Street had just moved from its decades old location at Capitol and Quarrier Streets.

In my briefcase were my financials. The receivables were small, but good. Trouble was, my cash flow was poor. I needed bank financing to float the business until the money came in.

The banker was young—younger than I. I made my case. I needed, I said, a $5,000 line of credit a sum that seemed huge to me. After a short review of my financials and a question to re-affirm the amount I needed, the banker looked up from the papers I had placed on his desk, furrowed his brow, and said, "Well, I'd like to have $5,000, too."

I was embarrassed, my face turned red, and I began to gather my papers.

"Hold on, I didn't say no," the young bank official protested.

"No, no, that's okay, I really don't need your help," I said, as I hastily made my escape, feeling as though a hundred eyes were watching me grovel for help. I decided I could cope; I simply would not pay myself that month.

But, babies need feeding, and I soon found myself across the street at Kanawha Banking and Trust, the bank that had cashed my $10 check when I arrived in Charleston in 1962. There, I encountered a very smart young banker. His name was Rick Whisner. He listened, understood, and made me feel I was making a smart decision to partner with KB&T. The relationship lasted for many years, until KB&T was sold and Rick went on to other financial institutions—and I followed him.

I learned that 33 years of creating and running four successful businesses encompasses a lot of lives; the men and women I hired had children and those children then had babies of their own. I take great pride in having taken the risks that created jobs out of whole cloth. CRA was a an entrepreneurial startup that created hundreds of high-paying jobs—and, I'm proud to say, that economic engine continues to produce today, decades after it first chugged to a start in 1974.

CHAPTER 102

Courtrooms & Crisis Management

In the early 80s, Monsanto hired CRA to provide public relations regarding allegations of pollution by its plant in Nitro in the Kanawha Valley. Seven former workers brought suit against the chemical giant in federal court. The trial would be a long one, everyone knew. CRA's job was to attend each day of the trial, listen to the testimony of the day, and frame media messages to make certain Monsanto's side of the story was always told.

Newspapers, and particularly radio and TV, would not always send a reporter to cover every moment of the trial, so a CRA staffer was always present to take up the slack; when a member of the media showed up we filled him or her in on proceedings. In those days before the Internet, we called Monsanto headquarters in St. Louis on a daily basis to give the PR folks there a complete rundown on the day's trial events.

We also, as lay people, gave the Monsanto attorneys our perspective on points they had made with the jury—and our opinion as to where they had fallen short in arguments or approach. They accepted our comments sincerely, wanting different eyes on the trial. Before each trial we media-trained the attorneys who would be interviewed on camera—they were to make three salient points no matter what questions were asked.

The Monsanto years were the birth years for our national media training and crisis management practice; these activities were the backbone of our PR business for many years to come. I worked directly with Dan Bishop, vice president of Monsanto public relations services worldwide. Bishop was a man's man. A former Navy pilot, he loved to zoom in and bomb the enemy. Bishop considered me his Mike Wallace surrogate and loved to have me skewer Monsanto executives in media training. "Give 'em the Mike Wallace treatment," he would instruct me.

I studied Wallace's style and did my best to please Dan—he loved it. I was at The Greenbrier attending the annual state Chamber of Commerce meeting when Bishop called and asked me to hurry to St. Louis to media train a Monsanto physician who was going to be interviewed by—guess who— Mike Wallace. The physician, a female, was to go head-to-head with Wallace regarding growth bovine hormone, a Monsanto development to produce more milk from cows. Our lady did very well in the interview for *60 Minutes* and Bishop called upon me many times to repeat my performance with other Monsanto executives that were being led to the TV gallows.

CHAPTER 103

Body Builders & Babies

—⌒

In 1978 I acquired the advertising and public relations business of Midwest Corporation, based in Charleston and Nitro. Midwest supplied the burgeoning cable television eruption with the hardware it needed and manufactured steel products for the national railroad and coal industries. Midwest CEO Jerry Thompson selected us as agency of record. Jerry was an accountant and had been the chief financial officer for the City of Charleston before taking the CEO chair at Midwest.

Midwest's corporate offices were in the Heck's building where our agency was headquartered. Jerry and I were friends—a friendship formed when he was city treasurer at city hall and I was a reporter there. He was a sweet man who loved people.

We produced great material for Midwest under the direction of Tad Walden, a genius in the advertising field. Tad's mantra, and that of CRA's brilliant Rick Mogielski, was if one wanted a successful campaign, put a baby in it. Their baby campaigns for various clients featured adorable babies crawling across the floor, being fed, etc.—followed by a universal, "Awwww!"

Tad took a look at the railroad media in which Midwest had to advertise its wares and came up with a unique idea to sweep away the clutter and cause readers to pick up the magazine and say, "Wow! Look at this!" This time, however—not a baby—a bodybuilder.

Our success was reported in the *Wall Street Journal* and related in the *Charleston Gazette*:

Saturday, May 16, 1987, *The Charleston Gazette*:

Charleston based Midwest Corp. set out to garner publicity for its steel railroad track products, but got more than it planned for Friday when The Wall Street Journal reported on its use of a female bodybuilder in magazine advertisements promoting the company.

Midwest President Jerry Thompson said he was delighted with the reaction to the advertisements, which have appeared in Railway Track and Structures, Coal Age, Modern Railroads and Progressive Railroads magazines.

"It's an excellent reaction. It's working for us," he said.

"We were looking for a new and fresh idea to raise awareness of Midwest Corporation." Thompson said the company contracted the Charleston public relations firm Charles Ryan Associates last summer to think of an advertising campaign for the company.

The result has been a series of advertisements showing world-class bodybuilder Marjo Selin clad in a bathing suit and flexing her muscles next to three steel rails.

"Midwest rail. The beauty is in the strength," and, "Better lines with Midwest," said the captions of the ads.

Thompson said the ads succeed in being interesting while pointing out the company's emphasis on the strength of its products, but representatives of the National Organization for Women criticized the ads for exploiting the female form. "Clearly, they're selling the woman's body, not the product," the Journal quoted Kathy Bonk, who heads a NOW research project seeking to improve the media's portrayal of women.

"At least in a Maidenform bra ad, you have a connection between a seminude figure and a woman buying a bra," she said

Florette Angel, of NOW's West Virginia Chapter, had a similar reaction. "I would suggest the company's public relations department look at some of the excellent materials available on how women feel about their body," she said.

Thompson said the ads are tastefully done. Tad Walden, a senior account executive with Ryan Associates, said he and other ad executives thought of the idea to use a bodybuilder to promote Midwest products. They next thought of using a female bodybuilder. "We wanted to do it in a classy manner," Walden said. "The message was we wanted to communicate strength, and a female would help us cut through the clutter of mundane industrial ads placed in railroad industry magazines." Two of the people creating the ad were women, he said.

The ad series created controversy—and sold lots of product. Jerry was very pleased and Marjo carried the ads on her website for many years.

Jerry was *not* so pleased one day when I, with my office located in the exact location of Jerry's office two stories down, exited my private lavatory and heard the phone ringing and, upon answering it, found Jerry on the line.

"Charlie, did you just flush your toilet?" he asked.

Wondering how Jerry could have known I had just finished my morning constitutional, I replied that I had, indeed, just flushed the toilet.

"Charlie—don't do that," Jerry said, and proceeded to explain that there must be some plumbing problem in the building because everything I had flushed down had come up through Jerry's toilet and was now on the floor of his private lavatory.

It became a running joke—Ryan had literally s—t on his client. After he recovered from his shock, Jerry thought the incident was incredibly funny, to my extreme embarrassment.

After many years at the helm of this growing company Jerry was ultimately forced out at Midwest. It was a nasty deal by those in charge.

Jerry Thompson was a great friend and wonderful client. He died too early. He will always have a special place in my heart.

CHAPTER 104

Union Carbide & MIC

IN 1984 I ENCOUNTERED HISTORY when a chemical known as MIC escaped from Union Carbide facilities in Bhopal, India. I represented Union Carbide in the Kanawha Valley, the birthplace of the petrochemical industry.

I first listened to the breaking story on National Public Radio as I was shaving early one weekday morning. India was remote in my view of the Carbide world, and I did not immediately realize the number of lives lost and the size of the story in which I would soon be immersed as events began to roll out in that distant location, rumbling straight toward the Kanawha Valley.

I listened throughout the day to news reports that began to reveal many had died in the chemical emission. A call to Thad Epps, who managed Union Carbide's communications in West Virginia, brought a startling revelation: the chemical known as MIC was stored in only two places in the world—Bhopal, India, and Institute, West Virginia, in the Kanawha Valley.

"The media's not aware that MIC is stored here domestically, but as soon as they find out, we're gonna' have to make certain they understand it's safely stored and that the situation in India is not the situation here," Thad told me.

Thad Epps was the quintessential community relations person. He was honest, sincere, forthcoming and liked by anyone with whom he came in contact. He wasn't given to over-reaction, and I could tell Thad was concerned.

I kept in contact with the various media reports that were surfacing. When it became apparent that the loss of life in Bhopal was going to be staggering, some local media inquiries were made. By that time I had made it to the Institute plant where a ruggedly handsome plant manager was in charge.

Hank Karawan resembled Robert Mitchum, the Hollywood star of the 40s and 50s. Karawan was a chemical engineer who knew his plant and knew his stuff. He was not, however, given to worrying about public relations or community involvement. He was a swashbuckling star at Carbide.

A "war room" was created and Hank, Thad, numerous production supervisors, and I, gathered there. The conference room walls were beautiful—wood paneled—and the communications equipment was 1984 state of the art. That is to say, we sat around the table looking at a speakerphone as we dialed Basking Ridge, New Jersey—Carbide's corporate headquarters.

The two weeks I spent in our makeshift war room was a classroom experience. Bhopal was a major news story that became a sensation within days. We were immersed in multiple strategy sessions with Basking Ridge and CEO Warren Anderson—and we collectively watched as revelation after revelation from India smashed directly into the company's central nervous system—its stock price.

The folks at corporate were increasingly nervous as they watched the stock gyrate. They urged us to keep uppermost in mind that the situation in India was an anomaly and we needed to manage the domestic story in a manner that would emphasize Carbide's commitment to safe operations—and in a way that would not cause its stock to tank.

Meanwhile, in the war room, we were trying to get a handle on the developing media mindset that said Institute might not be India, but it has the same chemical stored in India, and therefore Institute *is* the story. Never mind that there had never been an incident with MIC at Institute. Never mind that the Institute plant and the domestic chemical industry were historically much safer than almost any other area of manufacturing; all that was of little interest to the media.

What *really* interested them? It was the skull and crossbones displayed in a large orange icon on the exterior fence that surrounded the MIC unit. There, by golly, was a visual that greeted media desperate for a handle on the story. The skull and crossbones image was quickly broadcast on all the major networks and to worldwide audiences.

Hank Karawan walked confidently to the podium we had placed at the top of the steps leading to the plant's office building. He considered the necessity of responding to the media as so much BS, but he had acquiesced to our insistence that he be media trained and be our spokesperson. I, and an account executive from Carbide's national public relations firm, Burson Marsteller, had coached Hank for several days, giving him pointers on how to answer and deflect questions from reporters. Hank performed well in practice as we shot hundreds of questions to him that we thought the media might ask.

As he approached a bank of microphones that resembled a hornet's nest, he looked out on a sea of roughly 100 media representatives from throughout the world who had descended upon Institute where they could put the Bhopal story into words, people, and no language barrier.

Hank's plant functioned marvelously well, and he had few if any safety problems at his facility, considered a shining example of the chemical industry. But, the media seemed to have decided Hank was guilty, as was Carbide, because MIC was stored at Institute.

Among crisis management people, there exists the "chaos cluster." That theory says that a major incident, such as Bhopal, almost always births another crisis. And so it was at Institute in the wake of the India disaster.

The Institute plant, in addition to MIC, stored aldicarb oxime, a chemical used in making insecticides. At 9:24 a.m. the morning of August 11, 1985, while 100 or so media folks were in town, the aldicarb unit had an emission.

Five miles from the plant, as the crow flies, was a strip shopping center that was located roughly eight miles from the state capital of West Virginia. A heavy haze of aldicarb slowly drifted across the large parking lot at K-Mart and Big Bear stores. Evacuation or shelter-in-place orders were issued and much of the community surrounding the plant was marooned and panicked, thinking MIC was seeping into their homes and places of business.

Network news jumped on the story like a starved dog. MIC was stored at Carbide. A cloud was stealing across one of the city's strip shopping areas. Was it MIC? More than a hundred people headed for hospitals.

The war room crackled with the sound of the speakerphone. "What, for God's sake, is going on down there?" said the disembodied voice from Basking Ridge, in a tone more frightened than threatening.

Then began a series of efforts with media to explain that the chemical was aldicarb, not MIC. That was the plus side. The minus side was that a leak *had* occurred and aldicarb was indeed something that could and did cause respiratory problems. But it was not deadly.

The media continued to claw wildly at the story. Karawan was again in the spotlight. Congressional representatives who wanted some of the media spotlight ordered an investigation. Henry Waxman, the California Democrat who chaired the House subcommittee on health and environment, came to town to begin a congressional look-see that generated yet another round of sensationalism. Waxman was vicious in his condemnation and national news was made.

It was the beginning of the end for Union Carbide, which no longer exists. Dow Chemical owns the Carbide properties in West Virginia and the operations there are miniscule compared to their previous size.

Hank's experience in the MIC maelstrom caused him to come full circle. He had learned how necessary it is to build strong community and media relationships when running a business. He left Carbide in early retirement, given the bum's rush because of the tragedy that originated in India.

Hank's departure from Carbide presented him, and me, with opportunity. I asked Hank to join our firm as a vice president of government relations. He came on board and served with distinction for ten years, before his death.

CHAPTER 105

Dr. Bob D'Alessandri

IN THE 1980S, THE WEST Virginia University Health Sciences Center was at a critical junction. The Health Sciences buildings (which encompassed an area the size of a football field on the Evansdale Campus) needed major upgrading. Health Sciences President Dr. John Jones hired me to assist in lobbying the West Virginia Legislature, seeking millions of dollars to upgrade the facilities. At the time, Marshall University was getting increased support for its medical school and southern state politics seemed to favor Marshall green.

Dr. Jones also asked that I make Dr. Robert D'Alessandri, the med school's young and handsome dean, a household name to help drive the funding for the school. I was in Morgantown almost every week from that time forward for nearly five years—with the exception of when the legislature was in session.

Assisting me in lobbying for the school was account executive Raymond Joseph, one of the wittiest hires CRA ever made. When asked in an intra-office poll of employees what one change he would make at the agency, Raymond's answer was, "The carpet in my office." Raymond was a favorite of mine and of West Virginia University's lead lobbyist, former West Virginia Welfare Commissioner, Edwin Flowers.

Prior to the first legislative session of my school of medicine representation, I asked Senate president Dan Tonkovich if he would fly to Morgantown with me on the university's plane to tour the school to see first-hand the repairs and renovations that were needed. Tonkovich agreed and I was off to a flying start, so to speak. I then arranged a tour by the finance committees of both houses and a realization set in with both the Senate and House that the medical center with the state's name on it was indeed in critical need of major additional funding.

I sat in the Senate gallery as debate flowed through the chamber regarding the funding needed. Finance Committee Senator William Sharpe of Lewis County waxed eloquently as he supported the upgrade. He said he did, however, have concerns about the amount of the requested allocation. "Big Bill", known for his outbursts, stopped abruptly in his speech and pointed to Dr. Jones and me in the gallery and said, "There's Charlie Ryan and Dr. Jones sitting up there watching what we do." He then told his fellow senators that Dr. Jones and I were elite lobbyists and the bill certainly would pass. We were taken aback, but when the dust settled we had the millions needed to upgrade the Health Sciences Center. Bill Sharpe was a unique politician and got things done in a robust manner. Today the state's mental health facility at Weston is named after him.

After winning the funding, our effort continued unabated to make certain legislators and the executive branch retained awareness that the WVU School of Medicine was integral to the state's good health. We emphasized in our messaging that WVU was graduating doctors that would stay in the state and adopted a mantra that we were the core of Appalachian medical education. I proposed we create an annual Rural Health Care Summit. We did so—attracting First Lady Hillary Clinton to our initial conference in Morgantown.

During non-legislative months I was busy creating the persona for Bob D'Alessandri, following Dr. Jones' instructions that I was to make him a household name.

But—how could I do that—D'Alessandri? It was pronounced "Del uh san dree" and the name didn't exactly trickle off the tongue.

I created and executed a strategy to convince WCHS-TV in Charleston, WTRF-TV in Wheeling and WHAR-TV in Clarksburg to incorporate into their newscasts a weekly three minute segment produced in the Health Sciences Center video studios called "Dr. Bob"—wherein Dr. Bob would address a health issue and explain in layman style how to diagnose and treat a malady. Dr. Bob would also comment on news of the moment in health care and occasionally would appear live on the stations to have repartee with the TV anchors.

This was before the advent of shows such as Dr. Phil, Dr. Oz and the mainstream docs that now appear on TV with regularity. Back then Dr. Bob was a novel idea and his good looks and personality quickly made him that household name that was desired. Bob and I became good friends in the course of all this as I did with President Jones and Dean Rich DeVaul who succeeded Bob. I was in the corridors of the medical school so often I used a payphone booth (cell phones were not common back then) as my satellite office to keep up with things down in Charleston.

Bob and I drove and flew all over the state as he spread the word about WVU's medical prowess. We flew into Martinsburg one hot summer day for a speech and TV interviews and I picked up our rental car. The rental agency was a shed with several used cars on the lot. I was given an ancient Mercury behemoth and found to my dismay that there was no power steering fluid and no air conditioning. It was like steering a tank and half-way to town the car gave out and Dr. Bob and I rolled up our sleeves and loosened our ties as we waved down passing cars, hoping for a ride—saddlebags of sweat forming under our armpits. It was some way to treat a client. Somehow we made it to our appointments and Bob good-naturedly said to me, "Ryan, you've rented your last car for Bob D'Alessandri."

I believe the years CRA served the Health Sciences Center were integral to its economic and scholastic health, and I will always be grateful for playing a role with the gifted physicians and educators who brought prominence to our state's major contribution to rural health care.

CHAPTER 106

The Lottery and Jack Whittaker

WHEN LEGISLATION WAS PASSED CREATING the West Virginia State Lottery, CRA was hired as its public relations agency. We contributed greatly to the initiative's great success and then also acquired the Lottery advertising account.

CRA talent and creativity helped increase the state's lottery dollars to record numbers with innovative and unique campaigns designed by CRA vice presidents John Auge and Rick Mogielski. Contributing greatly to the Lottery's success was vice president Caryn Durham's media-buying genius. Executive vice president and COO Harry Peck's sharp pencil was a key to CRA's success in coming in, year after year, as the low bidder for state contracts.

The Lottery was a fascinating client. Not only did we have to create "scratch off" games on a regular basis, we dealt with publicizing lottery winners, assisting both the Lottery and the winner in handling media announcements and subsequent news conferences and media interviews.

I was at our mountain home in the Canaan Valley on Christmas vacation in 2002 when I had a call from my office.

A West Virginian, Jack Whittaker of Putnam County, had just won what was then the largest jackpot in Powerball history—$314.9 million. Whittaker was a West Virginian with a cowboy hat and a winning smile—a multi-million dollar smile as it turned out.

I was out-of-pocket or I would have grabbed at the chance to accompany Whittaker, his wife and daughter, on a chartered NBC jet to New York for a *Today Show* interview the morning after the announcement that he had won the stunning jackpot. Further, *all* our public relations pros were at various distant points for the holidays. Who could we send to escort Whittaker into the jaws of New York City publicity—chatting with the nation and the world?

As it turned out, only our creative director, John Auge, who dealt with the Lottery on a daily basis, churning out stunning campaigns for the client, was available. John did not work in the PR sector within our agency, but he had, in his twenty-plus years in the business, soaked up plenty of PR prowess. Our man Auge jetted with Whittaker and his family to the Big Apple, chatted it up with former *Today Show* host and former Huntington newscaster Matt Lauer, and did a magnificent job of projecting a great and gratifying profile of a mountain man winning untold fortunes.

A year after his big win, Whittaker's car was broken into as it was parked in a strip club lot in Cross Lanes—thieves made off with a half-million in cash that was stashed in a suitcase in the car. The media came to call. We called Jack and he agreed he needed PR help. We assigned Bill Bissett to handle the fallout.

Bissett began to weave his magic and the media liked Jack. When Whittaker was asked why he would carry over $500,000 in cash around in a suitcase. Jack replied, "Because I can." Bissett grinned—good copy. But, unknown to Bissett, the rest of the story revealed that apparently drugs might have been placed in Jack's drinks before he had been robbed. Jack was then hit once again by thieves in 2004 when assailants broke into his car and took what was estimated to be about $200,000.

Bissett and I counseled Jack to stem the tide of stories about his personal life by establishing a Whittaker fund to benefit churches and he responded by giving 10% of his winnings to Christian charities. I advised him to lose the cowboy hat he wore at all times. He dissuaded me from that by removing his hat, grinning, displaying several missing teeth under a few strands of distressed hair.

"Keep the hat, Jack," was all I said.

Tragedy struck Jack as his granddaughter Brandi's boyfriend was found dead of a drug overdose in Whittaker's home and a year later Brandi was found dead after having been missing for days. Her body was found wrapped inside a plastic tarpaulin and left beside a junked car. No one was ever charged with the crime. In 2009 Brandi's mother, Ginger, was found dead at 42. Jack Whittaker won fortunes, but many tragedies overshadowed the winnings.

CHAPTER 107

Tom Craig & Bob Goodman

OUR FIRST CAMPAIGN WORK FOR Arch Moore was in the public relations arena, and I worked regularly with Tom Craig, Moore's campaign manager. Tom was a dynamic young attorney from Huntington with credentials from Yale and the University of Virginia. He was urbane, handsome and simply brilliant. We became good friends.

Tom met and married, while assisting Moore, a young and beautiful member of the West Virginia House of Delegates from Cabell County, Michele Prestera, whose father had died in 1979 in the plane crash that killed the Marshall football team and several prominent Huntington residents who had attended the team's game at East Carolina University. Michele had government and political experience, and she and Tom hit it off from the beginning.

During the Moore campaign Tom and I were at Moore headquarters in the former Frankenberger's Men's Store on Capitol Street when Tom pleaded for campaign assistance of some sort from a Huntington reporter. Not one to waste words, Tom began his telephone call with the reporter with the words, "This is Tom Craig—I'm on a mission of mercy." Tom achieved his goal with those words.

Following the election, we bid the state advertising business. As agencies gathered to make their pitches, Bob Goodman, whose Baltimore agency had provided the advertising skills for the Moore campaign, approached me and boasted he had been fully paid for his campaign work. "Have you been paid?" he asked me. I replied that the campaign still owed us money, whereupon Goodman threw back his head and scoffed as he strode briskly away, saying, "Then, what in the hell am I doing here?"

Regardless of Goodman's contention that we had an upper hand because of Moore's campaign debt to us—and later criticism from the *Charleston Gazette* that we won state contracts because of political relationships—we pitched great material and excellent price points for our service and won the advertising business fair and square. The tourism work we did was exemplary, as attested to by the fact that we were the travel and tourism agency of record for far more than a decade as governors came and went—something no other agency has achieved. We also were later paid, in full, by the Moore campaign for our public relations services.

Caryn Durham carried the major load during most of the tourism years as the account rep for the tourism commission. Working with Tourism Commissioner Betty Carver, Durham initiated the first travel advertising on the web, sneaking it into *washingtonpost.com* because the commission members would have freaked out if they knew we were trying something that was unheard of at the time. The Internet was a fad back then, but Caryn was prescient.

After doing public opinion research with Repass Partners out of Cincinnati, CRA was persistent that the state bring back the *Wild & Wonderful* tagline for our advertising. We also developed a lead tracking system, working with tourism's research & call center. It enabled us to provide cost-per-lead and cost-per-inquiry data to better manage and target the ad budget.

Caryn, Rick Mogielski and John Auge developed and launched a scavenger hunt with a national publication and negotiated a deal to do a West Virginia event at the Forbes Gallery, attracting elite travel writers by the dozens. Durham was a brilliant innovator and leveraged media spending to create an event for Canadian travel writers in Toronto. She took along National Public Radio's Mountain Stage, lock, stock and barrel.

The ever funny and fun-to-be-with Caryn grabbed a *Time Inc.* writer who was visiting, stuffed her in a whitewater raft and took her down the rapids, both women screaming above the roar. The *Time* writer survived and wrote a smashing story that praised the whitewater industry—she talked about the trip for years. Caryn just smiled that smile of hers.

Her genius also led to the first-ever state advertising on the Washington Metro system and in Cleveland's massive train station, capturing on a daily basis thousands of commuters who would all be taking vacations. Because of that campaign many of those commuters came to West Virginia at the gentle (well, maybe not *so* gentle) urging of Caryn's ideas.

CHAPTER 108

Gaming

IN 1986, RESORTS INTERNATIONAL, A large gambling organization out of New Jersey, targeted Charleston as a river city prime for riverboat gaming. Rudy DiTrapano's law firm was hired to represent the company and lobbyists were retained to push the needed legislation through the West Virginia Legislature.

CRA was hired as the public relations firm to acquire positive media for the effort. I purposefully abstained from seeking a role for CRA as a lobbyist. We had not dealt with the gambling industry before and I wanted to make certain all we would be doing was media, not legislative, interface.

It was a decision I have always appreciated, given the way it worked out. Here are some excerpts from a *Charleston Gazette* report that tells part of the story:

Former Sen. Si Boettner, DKanawha, testified Friday that former state Senate President Dan Tonkovich "exploded" when he learned that a gambling company did not hire his public relations firm in 1986 to work for a bill to legalize casino gambling.

One of the charges against Tonkovich alleges he tried to win a contract for his public relations firm from Resorts International, a New Jersey company seeking to have gambling legalized in 1986.

Boettner said that when Tonkovich learned the public relations firm Charles Ryan & Associates had been hired by Rudolph DiTrapano, a representative of Resorts, "Tonkovich exploded," Boettner said.

"He was very angry. He began cursing out DiTrapano's firm," Boettner said. "He said they should have hired his firm or Willard & Arnold Associates, where he would get a fee if he referred work to them." Later, Boettner met in his Senate office with representatives of Resorts and told them of Tonkovich's reaction.

During that meeting, Tonkovich called Boettner. After the call, "I told them Tonkovich said he was angry they hadn't come to him first and he asked me to tell them they should hire him or Willard & Arnold. He got some sort of fee from them," Boettner said.

One of them said that hiring Tonkovich would not be legal," Boettner said. "I said I didn't know if it was legal or not but it was unethical." Boettner's testimony corresponded to that of two of Resorts' representatives who were meeting with Boettner when Tonkovich called Rebecca Baitty and Joe Buffa. Both testified they were shocked by Tonkovich's reaction to news they had hired Charles Ryan to perform public relations.

CHAPTER 109

Constitutional Amendments

BY DESIGN, OUR AGENCY BECAME an integral part of a number of constitutional amendments and bond issues over 33 years. One such issue was the Freeport Amendment, which exempted property from the state ad valorem property tax. Tom Burns, CEO of Chesapeake & Potomac Telephone, came to my office and asked me to commit my firm to the effort. We decided to make it simple. We would use the number of the amendment and give it a "Yes"—such as "Yes on 5"—a gentle push for voters who often did not know what the amendment was all about. Tied to that was a statewide PR campaign where we spread out well-known business people to visit every newspaper and television in the state with message points that were identical.

The approach seemed solid and the pay would be good, but both Tom and I knew the amendment had zero chance of passing. Our strategy succeeded beyond our possible dreams however, and the amendment we pushed won going away—guaranteeing us more "issue" work.

The successful Freeport effort spawned a number of additional campaigns and road trips throughout the state. David

Hardesty of the Bowles Rice law firm and I went from town to town to meet with West Virginia media to push one amendment we were working on together. David and I, and the ad campaign we produced on a shoestring budget, were highly successful. Our issue passed handily, this time leading a list of amendments that were on the ballot.

Hardesty, a tax commissioner in the Rockefeller administration, would later become president of West Virginia University, where he once was president of the student body. He would kid me for years about our excursions in my Mercedes, which he called the "Yes Mobile." David and I formed a friendship bond that carried through his years at WVU when he employed our agency to do work for the University.

As usual, the media gave extensive coverage, most of it critical that CRA would go so low as to accept money in pursuit of approval of constitutional amendments.

CHAPTER 110

Steve Gens & John Cabot

AGENCIES GROW ON THE BACKS of long-time, steady clients and Cabot Corporation was one of those. Godfrey Cabot founded Cabot Corporation in Boston in1882. He needed natural gas to produce carbon black and West Virginia had the natural resource he needed.

Cabot Corporation was a big operation in West Virginia in the 70s, and my benefactor at Jackson & Kelly, Paul Chambers, was their attorney. He recommended me to the vice president who ran Cabot in West Virginia, Henry Gruver.

Henry was 5-7 and of slender build. He was in his early 40s and I was 34. He wore horn-rimmed glasses and was a true intellect—but his favorite TV shows were Chuck Barris' "Gong Show" and "The $1.98 Beauty Show". I learned the natural gas business at Henry's eclectic knee and developed great respect for his nurturing managerial style.

Retained as Cabot's public relations/government affairs counsel in West Virginia, I reported to Vice-President of Public Relations in Boston, Steve Gens. Steve and I traveled the back roads of West Virginia, into every nook and cranny where Cabot Corporation had holdings. We were at lunch at the Glenn Ferris Inn in the upper Kanawha Valley when the husband of the local postmaster opened a pouch of chewing tobacco and, before plopping the tobacco in his mouth, politely asked his wife, the postmaster, if she wanted a chew.

I came very close to laughing out loud and saying to the husband, "I don't think so," just as the postmaster, in her best feminine manner, said, "Don't mind if I do," and reached into the pouch, withdrawing a wad of tobacco, which she put in her mouth. Well, I was speechless and Steve and I did all we could to contain our reaction. Needless to say, the witty Mr. Gens was very fond of relating that story to his buddies back in Boston.

Steve gave speech after speech in the tiny hollows where Cabot extracted gas reserves and served as the primary gas supplier for the rural population that, we felt, could help us achieve a needed increase in rates. These speeches were often held in the only meeting place in the area—the local church.

Steve laced his remarks with humor and the locals readily accepted the Yankee in their midst who said, "pock the caw," instead of "park the car"—signaling their approval of his remarks with boisterous shouts of "Amen!" Steve, an urban Jewish boy intrigued with Appalachian religion, was fascinated, and began to judge his effectiveness by counting the "Amens!" he received.

On one occasion, upon completing his speaking engagement, he was in extremely high spirits. Once we were in the "caw", pulling away from the church, Steve turned to me and said, "Whoooeeee, Ryan! *Three* "Amens!"

One evening before yet another scheduled Cabot dinner, Steve and I were engaged in a strategy session in my office on the second floor of the old mansion in which my firm was located. We were to be joined once again by John G. L. Cabot—who was late. Strange "pings" began to resound through the room and Steve and I looked at each other, wondering what the pings were.

Finally, we realized pebbles were being tossed against the window. We walked to the bay window, looked down, and saw Boston Braham John Cabot, grinning beneath a shock of white hair cascading over his forehead, shouting, "The door's locked—let me in!"

If only the Lodges of Boston could have seen Mr. Cabot picking up stones and throwing them up, up, at the bay window.

In 1985 Steve and his wife Freddy and their family moved from their native Boston to Amarillo, Texas as Steve followed Cabot's Energy Group. Steve was Boston to his very being and he crossed a cultural divide with the move to Amarillo, but he said he fell quickly for his new hometown, its causes and its western way of life.

Following retirement from Cabot, Steve became, in 1988, president of Harrington Regional Medical Center in Amarillo, a post he held until his second retirement in 2002. He was an inquisitive and brilliant person and a leader in the Amarillo community. He was chairman of the Amarillo College Foundation Board and a founding member of the Amarillo Opera. Along the way he became an accomplished horseman at his ranch, the "Rocking G"—characteristically, he referred to himself as "the last Jewish-American cowboy." When his favorite horse died, Steve was heartbroken.

Steve and I were close. We remained in contact throughout his retirement until his death in 2013 at age 77. Without fail we would send each other a gift on our respective birthdays. Steve's wife Freddy and his son Mark and I remain in touch and treasure the memory of our Boston Jewish cowboy who embraced the culture of the west and loved the people there.

His was a "Three Amens" life.

CHAPTER 111

Louie Cabot & Curtis Cook

AT ONE TIME, CABOT'S GRANTSVILLE, West Virginia carbon black plant was the largest in the world. To move natural gas to Grantsville, Cabot established a pipeline network of hundreds of miles—from Grant County to southern West Virginia.

I traveled to Boston several times to sit down with Cabot executives to discuss their holdings in West Virginia. My first visit there saw Steve Gens introducing me to Chairman Louie Cabot. Louie was 5-6, at best, with white hair and an aristocratic demeanor. Upon learning I was from West Virginia, Louie practically jumped for joy, smiled broadly, shook my hand and exclaimed, "West Virginia! West Virginia! I was conceived in West Virginia!" He then paused, backed up, raised a finger in the air and said quite pointedly, "But—born in Boston!"

John Cabot spent quite a bit of time in West Virginia and Charleston. He was quite a handsome fellow with that shock of white hair and tortoise-shell glasses and a wonderful smile. He was always interested in what I had to say and marveled at my explanation of state government and politics.

Cabot changed its West Virginia vice president several times during my decade with the company. One such fellow ruled with a heavy hand and the employees he lorded over would duck into closed offices when they saw him coming down the hall. Rod Gerik, Cabot general counsel in West Virginia, warned me to be on my guard in my first meeting with the new boss.

Our meeting began with small talk but eventually turned to the *Charleston Gazette* and this fellow's distaste for the liberal voice it espoused. As the conversation ensued, I was directed by the new executive to prepare to attack the *Gazette*, demanding it back off its position on various issues that affected extractive industries. I listened to him with concern; he was about to upset the inroads we had made with the *Gazette*—its editorial staff was listening to our voice as we attempted to explain an environmentally sound approach to exploration and drilling for natural gas in West Virginia.

My new client knew nothing about the *Gazette* or its legendary publisher Ned Chilton—a publisher so devoted to the news side of the business that he eschewed the typical office in the executive suite for digs adjacent to the newsroom floor—demanding investigative reporting and damning his fellow newspaper owners as the "Insipid Press". All these thoughts went through my mind as I was ordered to attack the *Gazette*.

Once the new man in town's diatribe had been completed, I swallowed hard and laid it on the line, putting at great risk my future with my biggest client. I said something like, "That would be a disastrous approach. The *Gazette* will take great offense and we will lose the credibility we've earned over the last four years. If this is a mandate, you'll have to find someone else to do your public relations."

Silence.

Cabot's new man on the West Virginia scene grunted after a few minutes and said, if that was the case, I should give him an updated media strategy and he would consider it. From that moment forth I was golden with him—he was one of those guys who simply wanted those he accosted to show some backbone. For those who did not, he mowed them down.

Then, Cabot transferred a Texan by the name of Curtis Cook to oversee its West Virginia operations. He had gravitas spiced with humor. Curtis and his wife Joy and I became close. He and I played golf, and Joy shared with me her research on Civil War relatives and a vast collection of truly historical papers.

One summer evening Steve Gens and I arranged for dinner at Tidewater Grill with Curtis and John Cabot. Early in the afternoon, Curtis, an engineer by education, called me to ask what time we would meet at Tidewater for dinner.

"How about between 6:15 and 6:30?" I replied.

There was a pause on the other end of the line and Curtis said, "Well, which is it?"

I paused and said, "Make that 6:18, Curtis."

Curtis said, "Okay," and rang off. Yes, yes, indeed—Curtis, a Texas A&M graduate (*Q: "What do you call an Aggie after you've worked with him for a year? A: "Boss.")* was an engineer. He was born in March, 1940 and died in his home state of Texas, in Huntsville, January 12, 2015.

He was a true friend with a quick smile, eloquent mustache and delightful sense of humor. He and I played many rounds of golf together and he once bought both of us antique golf clubs. He wanted to see if we could score as well with them as with modern equipment.

We played at Edgewood Country Club and may have performed better with the old clubs. We often enthusiastically repeated the "old clubs" fun and did so one winter's day. Curtis and I were kicked off the Edgewood course that day—the Edgewood pro did not appreciate our fervor for the links as a winter sports palace featuring orange golf balls.

One of the best things about my consulting career was the opportunity to meet people who made a difference in my life. Curtis and Joy Cook personified that perk. Joy and I have stayed in touch and I cherish the times I spent with the tall mustachioed Texan.

CHAPTER 112

Jack Fairchild

IN THE EARLY EIGHTIES CRA captured a major client in the coal business, Fairchild International, a maker of longwall mining machines and equipment for the coal industry. Fairchild was sold in 2012 to General Electric, but we had the good fortune of working with and for the founder, Jack Fairchild. Jack was a wildcatter who bet it all to follow his dream. Harry Peck and I wooed Fairchild and landed the account in a red-letter day for CRA. Jack and his lifelong partner, Myrleen, contributed mightily to our growth—I believe we did the same for them.

Harry and I were regularly called to Fairchild offices in Beckley on snowy Fridays to review advertising materials we had produced for the major coal publications of the time. We sat at a large round conference table as Jack looked over the ads.

He would say at almost every meeting, scrutinizing the material, "Who authorized this?" To which Myrleen would respond, each time, "You did, Jack." Harry said, while driving back to Charleston one day, that he wanted *Who Authorized This?* on his tombstone.

Following the meetings Jack would follow us to the parking lot where my Mercedes 300 Diesel awaited, parked next to Jack's custom-made stretch Cadillac. Jack would point to the Diesel and say, "How do you like your truck?" and laugh. He would shake his head in a "tsk, tsk," fashion, look skyward to the snow that was coming down fast and furious, covering the interstate leading back to Charleston, and say, "Y'all drive careful now!"

Jack Fairchild was a genius and a determined entrepreneur. He was a giant of a guy who resembled Conway Twitty—a man's man that had equal appeal to all with whom he came in touch. Harry and I will always be grateful to the Fairchilds—Jack, Myrleen and their sons (one of whom, Jack would say, was enrolled at West Virginia University, majoring in "Girlology"). Jack died in the 1990s but his memory is etched in my mind.

Ironically, in a state dominated by the coal industry, one of the toughest things to accomplish for CRA was acquisition of accounts with large coal-producing companies. Yes, we had Fairchild Industries, a supplier of heavy machinery to mine coal, but we struggled to sell our public relations services beyond suppliers. We broke through that ceiling when Massey Energy hired us in 1985. At the helm was Morgan Massey. The company was headquartered in Richmond.

CHAPTER 113

Massey Energy & Don Blankenship

IN 1985, UNITED MINE WORKERS of America struck Massey, and firearms rang in the hills. Jack rocks were tossed on highways to puncture tires. Lives were threatened. We were hired by Morgan Massey himself to handle media relations for his subsidiaries during the strike. A young executive with Massey at that time was Don Blankenship, a name that would go down in history following miner deaths at the Upper Big Branch mine in southern West Virginia in April of 2010.

Massey's offices in Richmond were handsome; black waiters in white jackets served us lunch in a large and eloquent dining room that was complemented by a massive wooden bar featuring only the finest of liquor and wine. However, spirits were consumed only at dinner, a rule that was strictly enforced.

Morgan Massey was a very unassuming CEO. He dressed in what appeared to be off-the-rack suits, was soft spoken, patrician in nature, and exceedingly kind to us. He demonstrated none of the bravado so common among the big coal crowd. He asked we call him by his first name. After meetings in his office, he would insist he personally drive our crew to the

Richmond airport in his small BMW to catch our flight to Charleston. Morgan was a pilot but was barred from flying by himself after he had gone to sleep while alone in the plane and at the controls—awakening miles off the coast—thankfully with enough fuel to return to his base of operations.

Don Blankenship was a most unique fellow who spoke in a monotone and treated his employees, some said, as though they were serfs. We media trained and speech trained Blankenship. Professor Dottie Johnson, wife of Bos Johnson, and chair of the speech department at Marshall University, trained Don in our offices on Kanawha Boulevard. It was tough because of the dispassionate monotone. About his job, however, Blankenship was extremely passionate.

During one large Massey meeting, CRA receptionist Shirley Bullard kept running from her post in the reception area to our conference room, delivering messages to a beleaguered operator as his mine was under siege. Shirley was a totally confident lady who was at the top of the ladder when it came to managing what I called one of the most important jobs in any company, welcoming the public—she fielded every call and request with aplomb. She never forgot a voice, and upon receiving a call from a client she had not spoken with for five years, immediately called him or her by their first name. The Massey executive she cared for that day cornered me in the hall later and thanked me for her attention, saying, "That woman could run one of our companies."

During one strike, our Dan McGinn was scheduled to fly to Blankenship's headquarters in Williamson. Before Dan boarded the chopper he was asked to put on a flak jacket. Massey helicopters were regularly receiving incoming fire from rifles in the mountains. Dan knew he was putting his well being in danger but he bravely got aboard. Dan's chopper flew low over the mining site and landed without incident. Dan later related that, during the visit, Blankenship called a miner into his office and told the fellow to tell Dan how much money he made in the prior year mining Massey coal. The figure was impressive—around $80,000. Blankenship had made his point; miners were not low-level earners. Dan charmed Don, I think, as he did most of his clients, laying out strategy and tactics that were always impressive.

Blankenship himself became extremely wealthy once Massey became a publicly-listed company. However, wealth did not prevent a federal grand jury indictment of him in November 2014. He was charged with conspiracy to violate safety laws, defrauding the federal government, securities fraud, and making false statements to the Securities and Exchange Commission following the Upper Big Branch mine disaster. Blankenship pleaded not guilty, denying any wrongdoing.

ABC News said Blankenship was despised and feared. Kris Maher wrote in the *Wall Street Journal* as Blankenship's trial began that, as chief executive of Massey Energy, Blankenship would hand out cans of Dad's Root Beer to employees he was unhappy with and explain that D-A-D-S stood for "Do As Don Says."

Blankenship was convicted of only one of the charges against him—conspiracy to violate mine health and safety standards—a misdemeanor. He was acquitted on the three felony charges that could have led to a prison term of 30 years. He was sentenced to a year in prison and fined $250,000. Blankenship said he would appeal but entered prison before the appeal was heard. After serving his time, Blankenship continued his protest, seeking to clear his name. The U.S. Supreme Court, in October 2017, refused to hear his appeal. Blankenship then announced he was running for the U.S. Senate seat as a Republican.

Blankenship seemed to always be a major player in his years at Massey. He certainly was during the 1985 UMWA strike against subsidiaries of Massey Energy. The strike was almost a year long and violent. CRA's folks in the field were Carter McDavid and Greg Houston.

The strike focused on the union's desire to secure a UMWA umbrella contract with Massey, rather than separate agreements with each Massey subsidiary. Massey fought the effort, preferring to negotiate at each mining site. UMWA President Rich Trumka called the Massey approach a shell game that allowed Massey to close mines and reopen them with non-union workers.

Striking miners staged sit-ins reminiscent of the 60s. They orchestrated church services at mine sites and fielded huge parades. Circuit Judge Elliot "Spike" Maynard said the parades violated his order limiting the number of striking miners at each mine site to 10 (Maynard was to become a State Supreme Court Justice and remained a close friend of Don Blankenship until the Judge's death in 2013).

Massey armed guards patrolled mine sites with attack dogs and miners were arrested for various activities, including blocking state roads, causing Governor Arch Moore to call in the state police. I was holed up in Charleston with other CRA folks as we handled statements to worldwide media.

Out in the coalfields a Massey coal truck crashed through striker's cars on West Virginia Route 49 and miners retaliated by burning a companion Massey truck. Blankenship was president of Rawl Sales and Processing (one of the Massey subsidiaries) and Don added fuel to the fire, saying he predicted snipers in the hills, harkening back to the mine wars and Mother Jones.

He was correct in his forecast. Bullets, rocks, paint bombs and jack rocks damaged hundreds of vehicles, shots were fired and a thousand miners were on strike. We entered the world of a coal industry forged anew in strikes and violence. But, our convincing performance at that turbulent time established our reputation as an agency that could deliver professional services to help King Coal tell the positive side of its story.

CHAPTER 114

"Bring Me A Hospital, Bring Me A Bank!"

I CONTINUED TO TRY ENLARGING CRA's footprint and market size by concentrating on banks and hospitals. I railed at our folks, "Bring me a hospital! Bring me a bank!" These were excellent accounts, but it took a great number of them to make us profitable

A big break arrived when we landed Camcare, a hospital holding company venturing into managed care that took us into several markets. In 1995 we scored big with Camcare when we won several national awards for advertising campaigns we had produced for the company. In 1999 CRA was named by *PR Week* as the nation's 18th fastest growing public relations agency in health care.

Yet another major step in health care was when we signed Charleston Area Medical Center as a client—it was a large account that took our health care business to a new level. We did both PR and advertising with CAMC, working with administrators over several decades, beginning with Jim Crews, then Phil Goodwin and, finally, Dave Ramsey.

CAMC and CRA were very connected during a twenty-year period as John Brown, and then Jack Canfield, both vice presidents of marketing for CAMC (at different times), joined CRA. Later, CRA's Elizabeth Pellegrin moved from her position as vice president of advertising to become CAMC's vice president of marketing.

CAMC's Phil Goodwin was a fireball and frenetic in style. Jack Canfield said Phil talked at 300 words a minute with gusts up to 525—maybe faster. When Cecil Underwood was governor I arranged for Phil to meet with him regarding an issue of great concern for CAMC. Cecil, never one to give assurances, gave Phil the "quiet" response—meaning he listened and said nothing.

After the meeting we waited for Phil's report. Goodwin said he had, at the end of the meeting, taken the Governor's hand and said, "Governor, if you can hear me—squeeze my hand." Phil had a keen sense of humor..

When David Ramsey came along as the CAMC CEO, our working relationship blossomed into a great friendship. Dave and I connected and each of us had great admiration for one another. Dave, at the helm at CAMC, built it to be one of the nation's great teaching medical centers with more than 7,000 employees and a world-class cancer center.

CHAPTER 115

CRA's Lexington Office

FOLLOWING THE HOSPITALS AND BANKS trail, I decided to go beyond the state's borders and establish an office in Lexington, Kentucky, partnering with a Lexington firm. We hired a Lexington advertising executive to run the office. She was a veteran of the scene and had great inroads to the "horse community" of Lexington. She was a character, wearing ankle length mink, laughing as though she loved the world—immensely likable. At our get-together function that brought Charleston staffers to Lexington to see the offices we shared with the Lexington firm, our new VP took a liking to CRA's Matt Sheppard.

The meeting moved from discussions of strategies designed to make us a force in the Lexington market to after-hours wine and liquor. After a few drinks the Lexington leader we had chosen was overheard advising Sheppard she wanted to take him to a horse farm. "Have you evuh' seen a steed "covuh" a mare," she asked, in her best breathy southern voice, looking up at Sheppard. Sheppard allowed as how he had not, and slipped away from the inquisitive and throaty breath in the floor-length mink.

Well, our strategy in Lexington worked—somewhat. Not because we conquered the market, and not because of any horse farm visit. We had an advocate at the University of Kentucky hospital system. Her name was Mary Ware, marketing director for the system. Mary, who had started her PR career at CRA, worked hard to get us a small piece of the UK public relations work that was outsourced. Along the way we came to the attention of Mark Birdwhistell, CEO of CHA Health in Lexington. Birdwhistell needed to establish a brand for CHA in Kentucky.

We assigned our "go to" guy to CHA with orders to quickly ingratiate CHA to the Kentucky media. Matt Sheppard quickly found himself in Lexington for most of every week. Birdwhistell loved Sheppard, as did all his clients. Sheppard, a former television sports anchor at WGAZ-TV, had the gift of gab and he was a marvelously entertaining guy. Birdwhistell was an easy executive with whom to work and the team of Mark and Matt became incredibly effective.

Matt was fascinated by Mark's penchant for collecting ties. I shared the same quirk, and Mark always noticed the ties I wore. Sheppard was downright hilarious when he would do an impersonation of Mark wondering just how many ties Charlie actually had in his closet. When Mark was a bit down in the dumps he would say to Matt, "I need to go buy a tie, come on." Out they would go, tie hunting.

The dynamic duo was sort of an "Odd Couple" in that Birdwhistell was sartorially resplendent at all times while Sheppard cared little for suits and ties. He was the guy who would loosen his tie at the first opportunity while his shirttail drifted above his belt line. His was an office full of papers on the floor, papers on the desk, briefcases atop filing cabinets, and a wallet that was always missing, causing him to search the office, car, restaurants, and men's rooms, to retrieve it.

But Sheppard was marvelously brilliant in the agency business, clicking every time with his clients. Birdwhistell was delighted we had assigned Matt to handle his account. Sheppard did a gangbusters job with free media placement, and our advertising side produced superlative creative for paid newspaper and television messaging. We held Mark's account for several years until he moved on to become Vice President for Administration and External Affairs for University of Kentucky (UK) HealthCare.

CHAPTER 116

Mike Perry & Marshall Reynolds

BACK IN WEST VIRGINIA, BANKING'S face in the Mountain State had begun to change with the arrival in the 1980s of a young Kanawha Banking and Trust executive by the name of Bill Shearer. Bill was a native of Virginia and introduced branch banking to West Virginia. He was aggressive in lobbying for banking change and planted the seeds that eventually allowed bank holding companies in the state. From that point forward, West Virginia's largest banks began rolling up smaller financial institutions.

As bank holding companies materialized in the state, CRA was fortunate enough to land as a client Huntington National Bank. Huntington National became the first bank in a holding company known as Key Centurion Bancshares. Its CEO was a lawyer turned banker—Mike Perry was five feet, six inches tall and a human dynamo. He had been lured away from his law practice and hired by the bank's largest stockholder, Marshall Reynolds. Reynolds had embraced branch banking in a major way and wanted to grow a dominant banking group by convincing the CEOs of smaller banks throughout the state to throw in with Key Centurion—and get rich.

It was a hard sell—the smaller banks were owned by folks who were so conservative they had a difficult time trading shoelaces for tassels. Mike Perry, the Cadillac Banker, was the man for the job. He incorporated CRA into the effort as the agency for advertising and public relations—and Mike picked me to travel with him on his sales pitches to the men (there were no female executives save Mike's strong, essential and powerful right arm, Beverly McKinney) who respected him and his effort, but who were independent thinkers and professionals comfortable in their own skin.

Mike drove the largest Cadillac that had ever come off a Detroit assembly line and it served as his office as he crisscrossed the state. People loved the Cadillac Banker; Mike had a big smile, the right amount of praise and eloquent small talk for the folks he met. He had a genuine love of the business of acquisition. He was the quintessential gentleman and he systematically convinced his banking peers to join him in his quest. Mike made history and all of us at CRA were fortunate to be there with him.

We met regularly in Mike's offices in Huntington as he reviewed our creative for ad campaigns and annual reports. Back then the annual report was a huge undertaking with financials and the chairman's report paramount in the full color, high priced brochure. Each year we had to come up with a name that personified the year Key Centurion had experienced. It was a gut wrenching experience with ideas shot down like a duck hunt.

Then, once Mike signed off on the theme, John Auge went to work on layout ideas. We would sit in Mike's office as John gave the prelude to the storyboards we had slaved over and Mike would become impatient. Early on he had taken to calling John "Icon" after John had made a presentation with a number of iconic symbols.

Mike squirmed in his seat as John waxed on about his creative idea and, when the Cadillac banker could stand it no longer, he would say with a wag of his fingers, "Just, just, just get on with it, Icon, just get on with it!" Whereupon John would jump to the chase, revealing the storyboards.

Mike would study the creative, begin a sentence that trailed off as he sought a word to finish his thought, and Beverly McKinney would supply the final word. As in:

Mike: "That's very good, Icon, but it lacks, uh, uh…"

Beverly: "Spontaneity, Mr. Perry."

Mike: "Yeah, yeah, spontaneity!"

When we were a "go" on theme, design, etc., we began production under Beverly's close eye. Harry Peck, John, and Tad Walden were always at Beverly's beck and call. Beverly was a woman in a man's world back then. Some of the bank presidents who agreed to join Key Centurion were aghast that she had such power within the organization she was, after all—a female! For her part Beverly took no prisoners. She was a leader and solid professional and cared not whose feet she stomped upon. And she had Mike's full blessing because he knew she had his back and got the job done. She and I had a good relationship through mutual respect and humor—a necessary ingredient to keep us sane in those "go-go" days.

In the background of the Key Centurion picture was always a giant figure—chairman of the board Marshall Reynolds. Marshall, CEO and founder of Chapman Printing, had in his youth applied for a loan at a small Huntington area bank and been refused. He *also* forgave but did not forget—he began buying stock and one day walked in as the largest stockholder and boss of the bank that had summarily refused to make him a loan. From that banking beginning, he bought more stock in more banks and then hired Mike Perry to put the pedal to the metal—aggressively rolling up banks in West Virginia.

Marshall was the kind of guy who did not care for frills. One day after Harry and I had made a trip to Huntington to meet with Marshall in his small Chapman office filled with piles of papers and annual reports strewn about the cubicle's floor, he asked if he could hitch a ride to Charleston with Harry and me. "Sure," we said, and Marshall sat in the back seat of my car as we drove to Charleston, all the while giving us a tutorial on ways to grow our business.

Marshall Reynolds was a genius and those bankers who threw in with him became rich indeed.

CHAPTER 117

Washington

IN 1987, WE SET OUR SIGHTS on Washington, DC. Harry Peck and I were quite naïve in our thinking that we could make a go of it in the nation's capital. Harry and I rode the Metro as we began our Washington journey. On one occasion I looked across the car we were in and a decidedly bored looking gentleman was hanging onto a strap with one hand, reading the *Washington Post* that he held in his free hand. He looked familiar and then I recognized the face—it was Dick Cheney, a congressman from Wyoming.

Harry and I sought out and met with Matt Reese, the storied West Virginia politician who, along with Bob McDonough, was a large reason John F. Kennedy won a presidential primary in West Virginia in 1960. We had lunch with Matt in an upscale restaurant in downtown D.C.

Matt weighed about 350 pounds. He had founded and grown a nationally-known political research firm in Washington and he knew what it took to succeed there. He squinted at us through large black-framed glasses

"Why do you fellows want to do this?" he asked.

It was a good question, and we came away from the Reese lunch sobered in our vision, knowing there was very little chance of success if we opened a D.C. shop. But, we convinced ourselves that we could succeed, and succeed we did—with the right fellow to open and grow the office and our willingness to provide him funding for two years as our DC office ran negative numbers into the hundreds of thousands of dollars.

On the Hill was Dan McGinn from Nitro—who had spent a decade in Washington, working first for Representative John Slack, and then Representative Bob Wise. I knew Dan from his forays into Charleston on behalf of Wise. We struck up a relationship and Dan greatly admired what CRA had done in West Virginia. I recognized him as smart and aggressive, and there was some factor about him that made me think he would be great in my business, and I set out to hire him to open the Washington arm of my firm.

After some hesitation—was it the right thing to do?—McGinn agreed to make the jump from government safety and a lifetime of benefits, into the unknown—a place I had been for some time. We leased one room over Dunkin Donuts at 1015 18th Street, NW. I bought a phone, a card table and a chair and we were in business. We were near K Street, where all the major lobbyists hung their shutters. Impressive!

Well, not quite so impressive, perhaps—but, by that time, there was never a doubt in my mind—failure was not in the picture. McGinn was special; he worked long hours, had a great Rolodex and came up with an idea a day. Some were great, others not so much. For me, the relationship with Dan was father and son, and I never said no to any idea he proposed, believing he could produce.

Our first hire was a young WVU grad by the name of Mike Fulton who had been on the Hill for several years as an aide in Senator Robert Byrd's office. Fulton's hiring was a stroke of genius on McGinn's part.

It is said that one cannot travel for 15 minutes in the Mountain State before encountering a road, bridge, courthouse, dam, airport, library, school, or medical center named for Senator Byrd—and that's not far from the truth. He was a beloved figure that West Virginians placed just after the Deity on their scale of reverence—and we had Mike Fulton, whom Byrd loved.

CHAPTER 118

Dan McGinn's West Virginia Day

DAN MCGINN WAS BRILLIANT AT creating events leading to income. He initiated *West Virginia Day in Washington* and invited Senators Byrd and Rockefeller to our offices in Arlington, Virginia to help us kick off the celebration. The staged media event was designed to garner publicity for an office that had originally been opened to give CRA a piece of the Washington, D.C. market. We reached out to West Virginia businesses that donated funds for the event.

We repeated the event for several years, enlarging it in 1992 with a reception at the Hart Senate Office Building with "Special Mountaineer Culinary Treats" and wine from state vineyards. We coaxed West Virginia University's Jazz Ensemble to come and play. A special feature of the reception was a twenty-minute play title "Between Two Worlds", a presentation by the Pearl Buck Museum on Ms. Bucks's life.

McGinn was certain Senators Byrd and Rockefeller would not ignore these continuing Washington outreaches to the Mountain State. They attended our events, were gregarious, offered eloquent remarks on various occasions, and demanded no special treatment.

Jimmy Huggins, the little dynamo from Byrd's staff, worked diligently on those first West Virginia Day events. He observed West Virginia Day 2017 on Facebook and harkened back to those nascent days, saying, "All West Virginians on 'the Hill' and D.C. were invited for great mountain entertainment, superb food from the state, and—of course—many speeches."

Senator Byrd chaired the Senate Appropriations Committee and Mike Fulton knew in intimate detail how appropriations were sought and meted out. Our first appropriations target was institutions of higher education that needed federal assistance. We rolled up an impressive number of clients in the field, beginning with WVU and the University's Health Sciences Center. Mike was ethical and followed all the rules—he simply knew the playing field.

In 1988 McGinn made a major catch—the CRA Washington office was hired by the London Stock Exchange to monitor activities in Congress and the Administration relating to the stock market crash in October of 1987. Our press release said the client wanted to monitor the U.S. to plan and adjust for their own markets.

We then acquired a $200,000 contract with the *Washington Post* for creative services for the newspaper for a 15-month campaign to promote the *Post* to prospective subscribers. John Auge developed stunning creative that did the job. We were on our way in D.C.

CHAPTER 119

D.C. Red Ink

OUR D.C. OFFICE BLED MONEY for two years. At the end of that time my associates at CRA were fearful I was going to cause irreparable harm to our base business as I added heavy debt to our shoulders. I resolved the issue by going to Doug Leech at our bank, asking for a separate line of credit for a new company, Ryan-McGinn. Both McGinn and I signed the note, McGinn as a 40% owner and I with 60%.

I pushed all my worth (CRA, home and all) out on the table. I am not a gambler, but I am a risk taker. And, as Gene Hoyer had said, risk is mitigated by average intelligence and the willingness to work very, very hard. Again, I hoped Dan and I were above average, but there were lots of folks who thought we both fell far short in taking the D.C. bet.

Fortuitously, the business turned profitable shortly after we took the plunge. McGinn was outstanding, working even harder. I always think of McGinn when I hear Billy Joel sing "The Entertainer". The song conveys a kinetic singer who moves from stage to stage, never knowing what town he is in. McGinn's existence was similar. At one point he was holed up in a hotel room with a telephone receiver glued to each ear, counseling two clients at the same time.

McGinn, as he grew the Washington business, was the best salesman I ever saw. He was highly effective with what I called the "McGinn Lean". He would, when making a pitch, lean forward, his elbows on his knees, and stare intently at the prospective client, mesmerizing the individual with some detail of Washington politics. McGinn was a storyteller—and storytelling sells.

McGinn's efforts and strategic utilization of CRA personnel enabled us to hire 3M lobbyist, AJ Donelson. Then, the dam broke and the business rushed in. AJ delivered 3M as a major client in the area of public relations support in class action lawsuits that had been filed against the huge company. We worked for seven years on one case that was being tried throughout the United States, providing media training, public opinion polling, and media relations on a national scale.

The 3M business evolved into work with 3M Media—its billboard company—and then led to engagements with Fortune 10 clients; extensive work with GM, Texaco, and many other household names.

McGinn's wife, Deb, was on First Lady Hillary Clinton's staff and apprised Dan the White House was seeking an agency to which it would give the honor of designing and producing the 1998 White House Christmas card—pro bono. Dan thought it would be a tremendous publicity coup if we designed the card. I agreed and the pitch was made to the White House.

We were given the green light—and CRA's John Auge produced a stunning card. We were invited to the White House on the evening of the lighting of the nation's Christmas tree where the card was introduced. CRA staffers rubbed shoulders with Tony Bennett and many other celebrities. We shook hands and chatted with President Clinton and Hillary. It was a grand night.

CHAPTER 120

Rubbing Shoulders

IN 1996, DAN MCGINN DECIDED THAT he and I should attend the Democratic National Convention in New York. Bill Clinton was seeking re-election as president. We scored credentials through Deb McGinn who pulled strings as a Hillary staffer. McGinn and I flew into LaGuardia and checked into a hotel downtown near Madison Square Garden.

I unpacked in my hotel room and tuned in a local TV channel while getting ready to leave for the Garden. A talk show host was taking calls from visitors who were in the Big Apple to attend the convention. As a lark, I called the number posted on the TV screen. Unbelievably, I got straight through to the host. He asked me some questions and then inquired as to what airport I had flown into. I hesitated, not really knowing at which airport we had landed. This delighted the host—the rube did not have a clue! He said of me—the rube—"He's just here for the beer," and hung up. Within minutes McGinn was on the phone to me—he had been viewing the same show in his room and was laughing to beat the band.

We had a fabulous time at the convention and indeed showed our chops to potential clients who were impressed we were credentialed and in the hall. We also ran out to Pocantico Hills, the vast estate of John D. Rockefeller, the patriarch, for a reception sponsored by Jay Rockefeller. The party was held at the Playhouse, the enormous game and recreation center used by Rockefeller and his relatives on grounds originally owned by the original John D. We rolled through 3,410 acres that featured a nine-hole reversible golf course and numerous private roads, most of which were designed by Rockefeller and his sons. It was said that Pocantico Hills was "What God would have built if only He had the money."

Many homes dotted the property, all built for various generations of Rockefellers. Our event was held in a large banquet hall at the Playhouse. The structure included indoor and outdoor swimming pools and tennis courts, basketball courts, squash courts, a billiard room and bowling alleys.

Inside the Playhouse were the political glitterati of the Democratic Party. I drank fine wine, made chitchat and wandered through the extravagant setting. At one point I excused myself and found a huge locker room. There, I stood urinal to urinal with United States Senator Chuck Robb, former governor of Virginia and husband of Lynda Bird Johnson. The senator and I both marveled at the excess of the entire estate, the Playhouse, and the enormous locker room and ornate plumbing.

McGinn's genius finagled many such political venues. We found ourselves one evening in the Northern Virginia home of a major political fundraiser, Bahman Batmanghelidj, an Iranian known as "The Batman". Present were foreign dignitaries, lobbyists, and a guy by the name of Alexander Haig. After dinner we chatted quite amiably in the drawing room with Ollie North as he waxed on about his new business—bulletproof vests. You can't make this stuff up.

Dan also used his political connections to round up annual convention speakers for the West Virginia Chamber of Commerce. He brought the "Rajin Cajun", political consultant James Carville, to one meeting. McGinn accompanied Carville on the charter flight from Washington and told me Carville had neither notes nor any idea what he would say to the Chamber attendees. His speech was a rambling one and he said football games at his alma mater, LSU, featured a stadium filled with folks who could not spell LSU. He went on, saying a successful date in Louisiana was when a boy would turn to a girl and say, "That's a real nice tooth you got there!" The crowd loved it.

McGinn had a knack for attracting big names to the agency. He formed a bond with Geraldine Ferraro, the first woman to run for Vice President (with running mate Walter Mondale). Ferraro was at The Greenbrier for a McGinn arranged appearance and Becky and I were to have dinner with her one evening in the hotel dining room. She did not show at the appointed time and I went to her room and knocked on the door. She came to the door adjusting an earring, apologizing for her tardiness. We sauntered back to the dining room, chatting amiably. Both Becky and I thought she was a delightful lady.

CHAPTER 121

Washington Travels

OUR CLIENTS IN THE WASHINGTON market were varied. A firm that supplied jet fuel had a public relations problem when their underground storage unit developed a plume that threatened the value of million-dollar homes in an upscale development near Dulles International Airport. Ryan-McGinn was hired to make the problem go away. We worked with local realtors, resolving the public relations fallout through community outreach as the company fixed their storage problem.

During the initial days of the campaign, McGinn and I walked through the affected neighborhood that was replete with construction equipment needed to correct the seepage of jet fuel into backyards. Dan spread his arms as we walked and said something like, "What could cause the devaluing of these exquisite homes?" He then paused, looked at me, grinned, and said, "Could it be the end loader in the front yard?"

Ryan-McGinn's business grew and we signed a lease for 5,000 square feet at Arlington Courthouse for $2 million for five years. Again, everything was pushed out on the table. By the end of that five years we had 40 professionals working at Ryan-McGinn with $10 million in billings—making us, at that time, one of the top ten PR firms in the DC market.

For seven years I spent a lot of time on airplanes. I flew to Washington so regularly that the flight crews at Kanawha Airport would hold the morning flight for me if I were a few minutes late. This was, of course, before September 11 and the attack on the Twin Towers and air travel was much easier, allowing me to always arrive just a few minutes before takeoff. I traveled throughout the country as the office grew in size and billings.

My wife was left to fend for herself for weeks at a time. Becky and I did, however, punctuate those difficult times with some fun travel. We were in Washington so often that we would catch the shuttle to New York and spend the day shopping, sightseeing and enjoying a world-class lunch. We would hop the shuttle back to D.C. and be in our apartment at the Charleston House in Arlington in time for dinner. Washington was a fun and eventful time filled with adventure as we plowed new ground for an entrepreneurial company that made a difference.

Following acquisition of the London Stock Exchange as a client, we began partnering with a London firm. McGinn called one day and asked if I could go to London. Our partner there was seeking business with the Falkland Islands government and I was to help create a joint pitch.

We quickly made arrangements for the trip. During our week in Britain Becky toured London and took in all the sights. I was largely confined to a conference room where I found the

Brits I was working with were pretty much in awe of public relations firms in the United States. They constantly looked to me for direction and I did my best to assist, but at times they suggested approaches to the client that I thought made little sense.

The Brits were, however, nice blokes, as the English say, and I think we made an excellent presentation. During those days of intensive strategy sessions I was able to get free in the evenings and escaped early one afternoon to ride the triple-decker buses with Becky and visit St. Paul's Cathedral where we decided to take communion with about twenty other folks. Only when we were in a semi-circle at the front of the sanctuary, with Becky and I on one end of the group, did we realize the priest was going to pass *one* cup of wine for *all* to use.

I whispered to Becky that I thought it was okay—we would be the first to get the cup. Wrong—we were the *last* two folks to receive the cup from the priest. We drank. Becky said the good Lord would protect us and she was correct—we experienced no ill results. We then visited the "Whispering Gallery" at St. Paul's. The gallery was a large circular room beneath the cathedral dome, accessed by climbing 257 steps.

Becky sat directly across from me, high above the sanctuary and we could see one another across the expanse of the church. She whispered, "I love you," and the sound was carried around the circle to the other side of the cathedral where I heard her words as though she were sitting next to me. I repeated, "I love you," and she instantly heard my whisper on the other side of the dome. Amazing. A whispering gallery, we learned, is a circular wall that allows whispered communication from any part of the internal side of the circumference to any other part.

In the evenings we visited Piccadilly Circus and took in the musicals *Miss Saigon, Sunset Boulevard* and *Phantom of the Opera*.

For days after returning to Charleston, I called the Falkland government representative we were pitching, only to learn no decision had been made. Finally, two weeks later, came the word. Another firm had been chosen. We had made a failed pitch—but it was a great venue in which to fail—and learn.

CHAPTER 122

Europe

MY WIFE BECKY AND I HAD MADE our first trip to Europe in 1992. We traveled to Brussels, Belgium where we attended a meeting of the *Worldcom* public relations group. Following that three-day meeting we took a train through miles of tulips and picturesque windmills, arriving in France within the day. We rented a car and began our tour of the French countryside, visiting Giverny and Claude Monet's home and gardens, Normandy, the breathtaking Mont St Michel, and numerous small French villages.

And then—our first visit to Paris. We drove into the city in 90-degree heat and rush hour traffic. I wielded a stick shift Peugeot with no air conditioning as Becky acted as navigator, warning me of approaching motorcycles and ambulances with sirens screaming. We survived and had a basket lunch and wine on the Eiffel Tower. In the days that followed we toured the Tuileries Garden and the Louvre and mixed with locals, as they shared a bottle of wine.

Fast-forward to 1997, and Becky and I were again in Paris. It was shortly after Princess Diana, whom Becky adored, was tragically killed in a car crash in the "City of Light" and a French memorial service was to be held at the Eglise de la

Madeleine Cathedral. Becky was reading the English edition of the *New York Herald Tribune* while having breakfast and the article announcing the service caught her eye.

"Let's go!" she said.

"No! We'll never get within three blocks of the place, besides, we've got all these shopping bags," I said, pointing to our treasures from a morning of visiting boutiques.

"We won't know unless we try," she said, and we were off. We walked several blocks to the Cathedral and found a large crowd sequestered off from the church by barricades and stern police protection. Still, every once in a while the gendarmes would move a barricade aside and allow some folks in. I nervously looked around for terrorists and found none, thank goodness, but the fact that this was a large public event kind of spooked me—Becky was not fazed.

"We're almost to the front of the crowd!" Becky exclaimed. I responded that the folks being allowed in must be dignitaries of some kind. Just then a policeman looked directly at the beautiful woman accompanying me, pointed to us, and waved us toward him. Minutes later we were climbing the steps to the historic cathedral and entering the sanctuary. The church was huge—we walked down the center aisle, shopping bags in hand, and found seats on the aisle almost in front of the sanctuary. Unbelievable. "You go, Beck," I thought.

The service, of course, was completely in French except for a welcome in English and comments from the British Ambassador to France. However, even with the language barrier, it was extremely beautiful. We were assisted with an English translation of the hymns and had an extraordinary experience that we would never have enjoyed had it not been for Becky's great admiration of Diana and her determination to attend her memorial service.

Then, yet another call from Dan McGinn who asked if I could travel to The Hague, the seat of government in the Netherlands, to conduct Ryan-McGinn spokesperson training for a company that was splitting from its parent firm. Becky and I again traveled together. We stayed in a Golden Tulip hotel—the chain featured premiere hostelries throughout Europe. We found that our room was extremely small. Upon our complaint, apologies were received and we were told the room was for one person only, rather than two. We then asked for a two-person room and were told the hotel was full.

We made do. It was not easy. The television set was mounted on the wall behind our heads as we lay on the bed. In order to watch CNN and English newscasts I took a large mirror off the wall and placed it at the foot of the bed. I discovered another problem the next morning as I showered to get ready for the day's work. There was no shower door or curtain and the water from the shower splashed freely upon our bed as Becky covered her head with a blanket.

In the evenings I dined with the clients and they did *not* invite Becky—the meeting and training were to assist the client in legal proceedings and the strategy being discussed was to be protected under attorney-client privilege. Ergo, Becky was included out. The hotel was most gracious and made certain Becky was under protective eyes as she dined alone.

We worked with another agency in the Hague effort and the firm's president was a good-looking guy who was quite dashing. He wore velvet loafers with a golden crest and was with us quite a lot as we explored. He told me he had returned to New York from one European trip and, upon exiting the aircraft, was accosted by a German shepherd dog trained to sniff for marijuana. The dog cornered him and placed his paws upon the shoulders of the man with golden crests as a security officer approached. My friend carried no pot, but he had been in enough nightclubs in the Netherlands to ensure that his clothes reeked of marijuana.

When the work was completed in The Hague, Becky and I traveled to Amsterdam to see that historic city. We took in Anne Frank's home and museum and delighted in the city's waterways. Alas, I did not get to visit the famous red light district.

When it was time to leave the Netherlands, we had to take a train to Rotterdam to make connections. We caught a cab at 4:30 in the morning and it dropped us at the station. There we waited in isolation except for characters of the night that frequented the station platform where we were to board the train. Both Becky and I were certain we would be attacked as we stood there with expensive luggage and quality wardrobe—we were obviously American tourists and carried cash.

When the train arrived we hurried aboard, glad to be in safety. The train was clogged with teenagers and college students who had spent the night in drunken revelry. We were mighty happy to be in the midst of the odor of beer and pot and made it safely to the airport and back to West Virginia.

CHAPTER 123

Ryan-McGinn Is Sold

THIRTEEN YEARS AFTER CRA HAD naively entered the nation's capital, Interpublic, a publicly-listed worldwide communications firm, approached Dan McGinn and me; they wanted to buy us. We agreed to do the deal in 2000.

In the process, I sat in my office in Charleston, participating in a conference call. The Interpublic deal was great news; trouble was, we needed a million dollars to erase line-of-credit debt from our D.C. bank before the sale was made. The million dollars would eliminate the debt, pay for outstanding receivables, and give us an excellent purchase price at a significant ratio to earnings.

But—where could we come up with a quick $1 million?

I told the conference call group I would make a call. It went to Doug Leech, CEO of the bank I had engaged when Rick Whisner had moved cross-town to the National Bank of Commerce. Rick had since moved on, and Doug, an astute entrepreneur, was my banking partner.

Doug listened to my need and our great opportunity. He said to call back in an hour. When I did, the money was in Ryan-McGinn's account.

To make that call and ask for a million dollars was a long way from that day I sat perspiring at the Charleston National Bank, asking for a $5,000 line of credit. The positive and amazingly rapid response from Doug, who went out on his own to form Centra Bancshares (a bank that was consistently on the *Inc. 100* list and later merged with United Bank) was not a simple act. It was the result of having an outstanding banker as a partner, and the years of growing a significant bond with his financial institution.

With that we were able to complete the sale of Ryan-McGinn. We accepted a two-year transition that gave us less money upfront, but a bonus based on earnings during those two years of time. McGinn worked incredibly hard for an extra 24 months to make that deal a huge plus for us. Dan, a star in our industry, went on to form two other companies and is a major success in the public relations world. He is one of a kind and he brought a special dimension to our business and lives.

CHAPTER 124

CRA's Richmond Office

I CAME TO KNOW DAVID LOWE, CEO of C&P Telephone, when he was chairman of the West Virginia Roundtable. We worked together for years and became friends. When David retired from C&P he became the chief executive for West Virginia operations of the Clinton Forge-Waynesboro Telephone Company (CFW) of Waynesboro, Virginia, a traditional rural local exchange landline company, which later became nTelos wireless.

David left CFW to join CRA as a vice president and brought CFW on board as a client. That work became huge when nTelos was formed and made us a large regional advertising agency. nTelos became the 9th largest provider of mobile broadband in the United States. We worked with Carl Rosberg, Rob Cale and Mike Minnis, giving nTelos a boost as it spread its wings in advertising and public relations.

Several years into the arrangement nTelos took Chapter 11 bankruptcy while owing CRA $2 million. The bankruptcy court froze nTelos' funds and our $2 million was solidly encased in ice. We did not panic; we buckled down to help. I worked with

CEO Jim Quarforth in preparation of bankruptcy documents, preparing press releases and readying him for media interviews.

In 1990 Becky and I built a mountain home in the Canaan Valley in Tucker County, and much of the work I did during the bankruptcy was there in the mountains at my computer—looking out on a beautiful setting that was perfect for preparation of arcane court and public documents.

Out of bankruptcy nTelos became a privately-held company with former senior note holders retaining almost all the common stock. We went through a year of no cash flow from nTelos, betting on the come we would be made whole when the company emerged from the process. We rode the tiger, but we were paid every dollar owed when the legal process ended. If we had not been paid, it might have been CRA's turn for Chapter 11—a $2 million hit at that time could have been devastating.

nTelos' Rob Cale and Mike Minnis became friends to us. They were taskmasters but wonderful and fair folks with whom to work. The nTelos account required a three hour drive from Charleston to nTelos corporate offices in Waynesboro—several times a month. After a year of commuting, Rob Cale said we needed to open an office in Waynesboro. Harry Peck and I countered that we'd like to open an office in Richmond instead, an hour from Waynesboro. Rob agreed.

The rationale was that we knew it would be difficult for CRA to grow if we were confined to the West Virginia market—we needed access to bigger clients. Yes, we had been in the Washington market with Ryan-McGinn. But, it was complicated; CRA had been a lifeline for Ryan-McGinn for two years as the Washington firm steadily utilized CRA folks, allowing it to service national clients with our personnel. That helped Ryan-McGinn grow exponentially with personnel not on its payroll. CRA loved the income and relationship with Fortune 500 and even Fortune 10 companies, but the arrangement left CRA dependent upon Ryan-McGinn for more than 50% of its income. The situation was untenable if CRA was to grow.

An answer to the predicament was to open the office in Richmond and grow CRA there. The startup was not easy. We leased space downtown, in Shockoe Bottom, the historic area of old Richmond, in a building with rustic exposed brick walls and wide plank floors.

We hired Willoughby Adams, a veteran advertising executive, to run the office. A former client at AT&T, and great friend of CRA, Lowell Connor, came on board to run the Virginia public relations unit. Lowell was retired after heading up AT&T's operations in West Virginia and a thirty-year career with AT&T. Upon retirement he was in Richmond, and the marriage between Lowell and CRA was again made.

Willoughby left us after a year and we transferred Caryn Durham, vice president of Advertising in Charleston, to Richmond—with hopes she would grow the satellite operation—and boy, did she. We moved offices to the suburbs after Caryn arrived and then, several years later, moved back downtown.

I was in Richmond at least monthly, facing an uphill battle. No one had ever heard of us in Virginia's capital city and we existed solely on nTelos dollars for almost a year. Caryn, however, gritted her teeth and made things happen. Her bright personality and determination impressed people and she snagged clients that had heft. Before long we were sustaining the overhead there and, after a grinding five years, found Richmond approaching sales that rivaled the Charleston operation.

Becky would drive to Richmond, giving me the opportunity to work the cell phone while in the car and utilize my laptop to catch up on correspondence. We stayed downtown in Richmond's Berkeley Hotel, an historic hostelry. The folks there came to know us and we were treated as though we were family.

We ferried Charleston account executives in and out of Richmond, helping to build accounts there as we had at Ryan-McGinn—with people already on the payroll. This time, however, they were building CRA accounts. The cost of hotel rooms caused us to lease an apartment in upscale renovated lofts in the old Tobacco Row district of the city. Becky was called upon to find furniture and decorate. The result was stunning. When the office moved again we had to once more find a nearby apartment. We moved all the furniture and Becky again decorated.

During the toughest part of the Richmond growth I would walk over to the Martin Agency, a 400-person firm, and gaze at their large building as I drank a latte. The CEO of the firm was John Adams, a native of Charleston, West Virginia. I always said to myself on those sojourns that CRA would be that big. That did not happen (at least not yet), but 15 years later CRA is an established and well-known firm in Richmond and Virginia. I know that because I will regularly meet people in such places as St. John in the Virgin Islands and when names are exchanged someone will ask if I might be the Charles Ryan of Charles Ryan Associates in Richmond. "Yes, I am," I would proudly say—gratifying indeed!

For Becky and me, the Richmond years were both stressful and highly enjoyable. We turned what could have been tough years of travel and being apart into an adventure of travel and exploration of an historic southern city. We ate at fine restaurants and shopped in the burgeoning retail malls of the area. We remember the Richmond years with great fondness.

CHAPTER 125

David Rollins

DAVID ROLLINS IS THE LEADER of the Charleston accounting firm Rollins, Cleavenger & Rollins. In its nearly 90-year existence it has counseled thousands of firms. Its value is that it knows and follows all the rules, attracts loyal people, and serves as an arms-length partner to its clients to help them sustain and build a business.

My first mentor, Dean Lewis, advised me to engage Rollins Cleavenger & Rollins when I founded my business. No way, I thought—how could I afford an accounting firm? But—I hurried off to see the firm's main man, David Rollins.

The first time I saw David he was seated in his office chair, surrounded by stacks of files and voluminous annual reports from publicly-listed companies at his feet. The walls of his office were papered with photographs of Old Charleston. He lovingly nursed a calculator with at least twenty feet of paper roll oozing out of it. He constantly accessed and quickly devoured numbers and expertly managed multi-million dollar portfolios.

His hair was gray, and his smile and laugh contagious. His tie was looped over without a final knot, giving it a flat look. It was his trademark. No one wore a tie that way other than David Rollins. He was a storyteller who had seen it all. It was obvious the Almighty broke the mold when he created David, a Wikipedia of Charleston's history. David knew all details regarding every major mover and shaker, past and present, in the capital city.

I began my pitch to David by saying, "I've been told by Dean Lewis that I really need you as my accountant, Mr. Rollins. But, like I told Dean, I can't afford your services." David just laughed and said he would know, as he ran the quarterly numbers, what I could afford—and that he would charge me accordingly.

"Deal," I said.

True to his word, David charged me little, if anything, that first year and then gradually began to bill me sums I could afford as my business grew. Thirty years later I was one of his largest clients. What David did not tell me was that his secondary role as my accountant was to be my therapist. Countless were the times I would drag myself to his office, practically in tears, to bemoan my quarterlies; I thought I was making money, but, no, the tax man took a large chunk of the numbers and I was back where I began—barely breaking even.

"It's all on paper!" David chortled, "You drive a nice car, you live in a beautiful home, you regularly travel to great places, you eat well, and, most important, you have your health and a community that supports what you are doing." I went into Rollin's therapy in quiet despair. I emerged full of piss and vinegar, energized and ready to meet all challenges, ready to soar to the moon. David's support was so important—creating a business is tough, and countless were the times I thought I might forfeit my home or face overwhelming odds of making a payroll.

Simply put, I would not have succeeded in business without David Rollins. He was not just my accountant; he was a transformer. His magic was applied many, many times, as we developed a friendship through thirty-three years. "D" Rollins, as he often called himself, was and remains a super hero to me.

David's father, Roy B. Rollins, was a founding member of Rollins, Clevenger & Rollins, established in 1921. He bought a house on Kanawha Boulevard as his business grew— with a pool in the back yard. "My brother Haven and I were mighty excited about that pool and couldn't wait to move into the house. The day of the move we ran through the new quarters to the backyard to go swimming and there was the old man with a backhoe operator who had just filled in the pool. The old man wasn't having any of that pool nonsense," David laughed.

David's brother Haven was the CFO for Lawson Hamilton's coal empire, headquartered in the very small town of Handley in eastern Kanawha County. Regularly I would seek donations for fundraisers of good cause and David advised me that the route to Lawson's largesse was through Haven. I called Haven at his Handley office one summer day and went to great length about the current cause to which I had pledged and Haven said to mail the details to his office and he would take the request to Lawson. This was in the early days of the Internet and I responded that I could email the material to him at his office in the tiny town of Handley, that very afternoon, if he would give me his email address.

There was silence on the other end of the line.

"Would that be okay, Haven? I'll just use the Internet rather than the mail.

Haven's reply was, "The Internet don't come into Handley.

I responded that my letter would go out that day.

CHAPTER 126

Rex Burford, KPCC & Dana Waldo

DAVID ROLLINS INSTILLED IN ME the fact that the engine that propelled my business was networking—getting to know as many people as possible. On his advice, I joined the Rotary Club and Edgewood Country Club, essential memberships back in 1974, if one were to become a card carrying "Businessman".

Rotary did not accept women when I joined, and it was delightful to see our club open debate on the subject of female membership. I shall never forget when the extraordinary lawyer Bill Mohler took the floor to argue against admitting women. Bill was a wonderful man and gifted orator who truly believed Rotary should be male only.

His argument was certainly heeded by us Rotarians, but we voted to open our doors to the ladies. It seems odd now that women were not always Rotarians, but the issue was a big deal at the time. However, the women members would soon find that Rotary, which I loved, could sometimes be a dull process—I often told folks the definition of a Rotary speech was, "A 200 pound sleeping pill in a blue suit."

I was a Rotarian for 35 years, ultimately becoming president of my Club and a Paul Harris Fellow. I wanted to serve, but I also wanted to contact and ingratiate. I make no apologies for that, nor should today's budding entrepreneur.

Rex Burford, president of the West Virginia Oil & Gas Association, was a mentor and great friend and had also encouraged me to join Rotary, where he was my sponsor. I had acquired Rex's great friendship when, in the early days of CRA, I lobbied the West Virginia Legislature. In so doing I was constantly running to and from the Capitol, balancing agency business and management with the long hours required at the legislature. I had several clients, but the bulk of my time on the marble floors was spent working for Cabot Corporation, trying to keep up with the trials and travails of natural gas legislation Rex's specialty.

Without fail Rex, a lawyer, would brief me on the natural gas action while I was absent from the legislative halls and update me on arcane bills affecting natural gas and my client. I owe Rex a tremendous debt because, without his help, I would not have been able to adequately serve my biggest client. Rex was yet another example of the fact that no one succeeds alone—success comes with the help, assistance and friendship of many. My friendship with Rex was strong and I served as his best man when he married Judy, a great lady who brought sunshine into Rex's life.

Civic clubs and board service, chambers of commerce, business roundtables, professional groups, all enabling contact and dialogue between people who want to establish, grow, or perpetuate a business and serve the community. It was and is the perfect way to grow a business—and to give back.

Over thirty-six years I served on more than 25 boards. I would not have succeeded without the relationships these boards provided. I worked at it; I would seek as much information as I could about individual likes, dislikes, family, hobbies, favorite movies, sports, religion, you name it. How did I remember those names? Simply by remembering that I'd *better* remember. All those people were important to my success.

I volunteered for many causes, one of the best being the Kanawha Pastoral Counseling Center (KPCC), a non-profit interfaith counseling center staffed partly by ministers representing a variety of nominations. KPCC's mission was to make counseling affordable to all who came to them. As a result it often found itself in monetary need. One evening the board of the counseling center met to seek a way to shore up funding. We gathered in the living room of the Charleston home of Angus and Nina Peyton. Nina was a board member who served KPCC for many years. I was a creative person and looked for ways outside the box to help support the very worthy cause of KPCC.

I suggested we think long-term and develop something that would have legs—something we could look to year after year to funnel dollars to KPCC. What could it be? I knew that one of the former members of the Washington, D.C. political parody group, the *Capitol Steps*, had gone out on his own to do stand-up comedy. I said we should bring him to town and offer a night of comedy as a fundraiser for KPCC. Further, I suggested we name the event the *Jim Dent Dinner* in honor of the late *Gazette* humor writer. That, I said, was a worthwhile effort because it would honor Dent's memory annually while providing a platform for giving to KPCC (I also said honoring Jim might afford us *Gazette* support and feature articles each year prior to the dinner—and it did).

KPCC's executive director, Sky Kershner, took the ball and ran with it. The *Jim Dent Dinner* was a huge success and, to this day, is the major fund provider that benefits hundreds of people and keeps alive the memory of the brilliant Jim Dent. Volunteering helped me make my contribution to KPCC.

Board work also brought me lifelong friendships. In 1996 the West Virginia Roundtable Board of Directors was conducting its summer meeting. Among those present were Roundtable President and C&P Telephone Vice President David Lowe, attorney David Hardesty of Bowles Rice McDavid Graff & Love, and a young man named Dana Waldo, state president of West Virginia American Electric Power.

I had not met Dana and I reached across the table to shake the hand of this handsome and articulate fellow. Little did I know I was shaking the hand of a guy who would become my best friend.

Dana and I worked together for many years. He nominated me as a candidate for the West Virginia University School of

Business Hall of Fame and I was elected in the second year of that prestigious award. Dana left Appalachian Power and its parent, American Electric Power, and became president and CEO of the West Virginia Business Roundtable where he led efforts to better the state's business climate. He held that post for three years and returned to American Electric Power to become president and CEO of AEP subsidiary Appalachian Power, and its holdings in West Virginia, Virginia, and Tennessee.

Upon retirement from AEP he accepted the post of senior vice president and general manager of Frontier Communications in West Virginia, continuing a distinguished career. Five years later he retired to Hilton Head Island and Sea Pines where the Waldos and Ryans became neighbors. The Waldos then moved to Scottsdale, Arizona to be close to their grandchildren.

Dana, his wife Cheryl, their children Jennifer, Kevin and Chris, are family to us. In retirement Dana and I are golf partners, bourbon drinkers, and lovers of Coen Brothers movies. Cheryl and Becky are like sisters and share a love of Sauvignon Blanc. We share travel, laughter, and warm family relationships.

CHAPTER 127

Harry Peck

HARRY PECK, PRESIDENT AND CHIEF operating officer of
Charles Ryan Associates, defined the "Art of the Sale" for me.
Harry was my friend, partner and confidante throughout my
business career. He served in the United States Army in the
1960s and was stationed in Germany. He traveled throughout Europe and skied the Alps. When he returned to West
Virginia he obtained a journalism degree from West Virginia
University, and then worked in Charleston for Phil DuPont's
direct mail firm and Fred Haddad's Heck's discount chain.

Harry married Draza, daughter of Max Koff, a Jewish merchant who owned a jewelry store and loan company on
Summers Street. Harry became the best son-in-law Max and
Frankie Koff could ever have hoped for. He doted on Max, as
he has on Draza and his children and grandchildren.

Harry converted to Judaism several years after his marriage
to Draza. No one was prouder of him than Max Koff. As was
typical of Harry, he became more Jewish than those born to
the religion. That was Harry, devoted and dedicated. In retirement Harry not only volunteered for many charitable and

humanitarian efforts, he wrote his memoir, *Who Authorized This?*

He then produced Volume II of the memoir, after thoroughly researching, writing, and publishing, in 2014, a complete history of Charleston's oldest country club, titled, *Edgewood Country Club—Our Heritage.*

Harry knew advertising inside and out. He suffered no fools and he was solid as a rock—he practiced and preached integrity. And he was the guy who made certain we were on solid footing as we grew. I was the guy who said, "Let's do this!" or, "Let's do that!" Harry would listen and then shake his head, saying, "No way!" I would continue to push and push to convince him I was right and I was determined to put my plan in action, but regardless of how strongly I felt about it, if Harry drew a line in the sand, I relented. I respected his intellect, his knowledge, and his awareness of what was financially possible.

He was tough on his exterior, but deep inside he was a creampuff—especially when it came to the people with whom he worked. When then-media buyer Caryn Durham was on maternity leave he called her every day to find out how she was doing. Caryn will never forget that.

Harry and Draza have two children, Alexa and Ben. Alexa was drawn to a career in health and wellness, and Ben became a pharmacist. When Harry's grandchildren were born to Ben and his wife, Harry was ecstatic. It was great to see Harry in his grandfatherly glow.

Harry loved his cat, even though he was allergic to her. The cat came by Harry's house one day and it never left because Harry started feeding his friend, whom he named, "Lovey", and the bond was established.

Harry was born to advertising and the sales game; he often related his interview with Smoot Fahlgren, the legendary founder of Fahlgren Advertising, as instructive of *Rule Number One* in the agency business. Harry had just graduated Journalism School and waited nervously for his appointment with Smoot. Harry imagined the questions this giant of the ad biz would ask.

Would Smoot immediately leap to market research? Would he query the new graduate on creativity, media buying, copywriting, or ask an esoteric question about the origins of marketing and branding?

Smoot's office doors opened and Harry advanced cautiously, waiting for the great man to speak. Smoot sat at his desk, and quickly scanned Harry's resume. He tossed the resume on his desk, kicked back in his chair, looked intently at Harry, and asked the burning question uppermost in his mind: *"Can you peddle?"*

"Huh?" Harry said.

"Can you peddle?"

"What do you mean?"

"You know—*can you sell?*"

Smoot asked the right question. Selling had never been mentioned in WVU Journalism School advertising, marketing or public relations curriculum; yet, it was the heart of the business. Smoot, a serial entrepreneur, understood that.

While waiting to make a pitch to a new prospective client I would always remember Smoot's question—"Can you peddle?" I would spend my time in the reception area raising my level of excitement about the product I was about to pitch. "This is a terrific idea, an incredible approach! Our agency has found the answer! When our creative hits the street, heads will turn! Home Run! Out of the Ball Park! Amazing Stuff!"—I murmured all this to myself as I sat and waited.

"Mr. Ryan? The Marketing Committee will see you now," the receptionist would say, shaking me from my Superman reverie of leaping the tall building in which we sat. I jumped from my seat with stored up adrenaline and bounded toward the conference room and the pitch, ready to show the suits sitting there that my ideas were the greatest things since a pocket-on-a-shirt. And, more often than not, as the Eagles once sang, "By God, they bought it."

Sales also were, of course, a matter of persistence and numbers. I constantly preached in pre-email days that our folks had to "pick up the phone and make the call!" I labeled the action the "Thousand Pound Phone" and put signs to that effect on receivers in every office because it seemed to be incredibly hard for people to ask for the work. When John Isaacs took over the

Heck's discount chain, I called him every day for 48 days. We got the account.

My partner Harry Peck had a great sense of humor known only to those who knew him well. One day he was following media buyer Caryn Durham down the hall, asking endless questions about a "buy" she was making for an ad client. Harry was not satisfied with the buy. Caryn ignored him, entered her office and began fiddling with a printer that would print out the buy.

Harry moved on down the hallway. A few minutes later Caryn was down under her desk, adjusting the paper feed to the printer when she heard someone rush into her office. She raised her head above the desk and saw a red-faced Harry, who said, in rather a loud voice, "And you need to get your time sheets to me, now!"

Caryn responded by saying, in a calm voice, "Harry, you simply cannot come in my office and shout at me."

Harry said nothing, turned around, and walked out of the office and down the hall.

A few minutes later Caryn's intercom rang and she picked up the phone. It was Harry.

He said, "Caryn, please come to my office."

Caryn walked to Harry's office with growing concern—she said later it was a long, long walk down the hall.

She opened the door and walked in. Harry was sitting in his chair, looking out the office window. He turned to Caryn and motioned for her to sit. She grabbed a chair, swallowed hard, and waited for Harry to shout.

Harry said, very, very, softly, "Caryn, I need your time sheets."

"Yes, sir," she said, and quietly left the office.

CHAPTER 128

The Friends Of Coal

IN 2001 THE WEST VIRGINIA coal industry was under a barrage of accusations by environmentalist groups. The industry commissioned a public opinion poll to determine what state residents thought about coal mining and its practices. Only 45 percent of those surveyed had a favorable image of the industry.

The very next year, in 2002, legislative debate began to build about coal truck weight limits on state roads. The West Virginia Coal Association, under the leadership of its president, Gary White, decided to take action. The Association members agreed to impose a "per ton fee" on themselves to "move the needle" of public opinion regarding the industry.

The Association put out a call to three state public relations/advertising agencies, asking them what approaches they would suggest to blunt unprecedented criticism of the mining of coal—criticism that said coal was a "filthy" fuel source—a persistent message from liberal groups such as Mountain Justice.

We made our pitch and Ralph Ballard, a CRA gold star friend who was greatly respected within the industry, championed

CRA as the firm that could be most effective in addressing the issues at hand, and we were hired.

Ralph agreed with me that his industry was simply sitting quietly—almost numb—as environmentalists lambasted it. Some of the critique was fair, but much of it was exaggerated, and the fact that there was no counter to any charge, fair or not, was damaging as legislators and government regulators heard only one side of the story. Both Ralph and I knew the other side needed to be heard—and in a meaningful way.

Once we were on board we assigned CRA account executive Susan Lavenski to the account and we began working with coal operator Warren Hylton who envisioned a widespread grassroots campaign that would recruit members who were both directly and indirectly affected by the positive economic return from mining coal. "We have lots of friends out there," Hylton said. "If we ask them for their help, they'll help us." With that, the *Friends of Coal* (FoC) campaign was born.

I came to the battle with one message: West Virginians who supported the coal industry vastly outnumbered those who lashed harsh criticism of coal, but their voice had no chance against the organized effort of the anti-coal activists. I urged a strategic and organized approach to give coal's supporters a voice of their own and a platform to project *their* voice in a loud and articulate manner—enabling them, in Warren Hylton's words—to help us.

However, I strongly cautioned that *any* grassroots campaign required an intensive effort and the valuable time of men and women employed in the coal industry—plus a tireless ideologue to doggedly nurture the movement once it was underway. I told the Association board members each of them would need to wade into the coalfields and spread the message.

Warren Hylton was the perfect pro-coal ideologue that devoted enormous time and energy to not only form the grassroots, but also make the grassroots erupt. He was relentless in his attention to the FoC, recruiting far and wide. In his wake, CRA's John Auge created the FoC logo that can to this day be seen on vehicles nationwide, and Susan Lavenski, a CRA star, orchestrated strategic approaches for our effort as she launched an incredibly effective campaign.

When Susan was promoted to senior vice president of public relations at CRA, we assigned vice president Bill Bissett to run the FoC account—and Hylton and Bissett became a dream team. Bissett organized events that drew thousands of fans of coal, and Hylton ran the roads and ridges of the state, spreading the word to coal companies that a movement had begun. I knew we were on to something special.

Bissett, a graduate of Marshall University, was an incredible force, embracing the FoC effort with enthusiasm, dedication, strict attention to detail, and the ability to communicate directly with the media who respected him and loved his humor. His network of associates and antenna for opportunity were without equal. He was yet another CRA star; a star that squeezed every vital juice from the FoC campaign.

Bissett was all over the state in FoC venues, assisting and advising Hylton, orchestrating FoC gatherings. I could not help but be fascinated by Bissett—one of the most unique and talented public relations professionals we had ever hired. In various meetings with our coal clients, Bill and I would listen intently as PR strategies were presented that were not only not practical, but also at times bizarre. We used our code word— "powerful!"—to silently indicate to one another that the idea proffered was ludicrous.

In a short time, FoC grew into thousands of members in West Virginia and became a force with which to be reckoned. Aiding that growth was CRA's insistence that we needed a spokesperson to be front and center to deliver the word. I counseled that our spokesperson would have to be trusted—revered—in order to draw crowds to events in support of coal.

We met with and pitched to former and beloved West Virginia University football coach Don Nehlen that *he* become the face of FoC. Don hesitated only momentarily, knowing the role could be controversial—but he had deep belief that coal was the backbone of West Virginia's economy and he accepted our offer. He then traveled throughout the state to meet FoC and WVU fans.

It was obvious that Don reveled in his role, as he was greeted warmly everywhere we went. Having served as WVU's football coach for two decades, he enjoyed being treated well without the pressure of leading a college football team. "I haven't lost a game this year," Nehlen would laugh. "Heck, they haven't even scored on me." Later we added retired Marshall

University football coach Bob Pruett as a second spokesperson and captured fans of both of West Virginia's major universities.

Our first real test to determine the effectiveness of our campaign was a *Friends of Coal* Day at the West Virginia state capitol during the legislative session. Although a lot of effort and planning went into the event in advance, none of us were certain about what level of success we might achieve. Would people show up? Would the media cover the event? Would hordes of environmental activists pelt us with Birkenstock sandals? We had absolutely no idea. What we did know was that West Virginia's elected officials were eager to attend—even those office-holders whose voting record on coal issues was less than stellar.

To our relief, thousands showed up in support of coal. Some were coal company employees who were given the day off, but the largest contingent represented mainstream West Virginians who felt a connection to coal, realizing the enormous impact the industry had on each of them in tiny towns across the state.

Standing in the crowd, watching Warren Hylton and Bill Bissett work their grassroots magic, I knew we had hit a viable chord—the enthusiasm was palpable and contagious to everyone in attendance, including the legislators who would from that day forward think twice as they voted on coal issues. Their voting equation would now include thousands of mainstream voters who *favored* coal, not just those who objected to the industry.

The news coverage the next day served as a clear indicator that FoC was here to stay. We had at least two dozen environmental activists at that first event and they also received a fair portion of media coverage. They did little, however, to help their anti-coal agenda in the face of thousands who waved the banner of FoC.

The *Charleston Gazette* was quick to criticize FoC, as were the state's environmental groups, but our organization was a juggernaut that pierced the sheet of contempt that had enveloped the coal industry.

The strategic campaign we developed stands today as one of the great grassroots movements in the nation's history of public relations. I am proud of CRA's integral part in a movement that helped the public understand the benefits of coal and the economic backbone it provided the state; a backbone severely weakened in later years as the Obama administration targeted coal.

The FoC campaign became a multi-state effort and it grew tentacles throughout the country. *Friends of Coal-Kentucky* quickly boasted 100,000 license plates on personal vehicles across the Commonwealth. The logo is as ubiquitous there as it is in West Virginia. Bill Bissett continued the campaign through the *Friends of Coal-Kentucky* as he became, less than ten years after he oversaw the FoC movement in the Mountain State, president of the Kentucky Coal Association.

Coal was in Bissett's blood and his imprint on the industry is huge.

CHAPTER 129

The Coal Princess

ONE MORNING AT THE GREENBRIER during the annual meeting of the West Virginia Coal Association, I called Bill Bissett at 5 a.m. and explained that Becky and I were leaving with our daughter Jennifer and her husband Chad because Jennifer's water had just broken and a baby was on the way—five weeks early. I was to deliver a speech to the Association members at 10 a.m. that would detail our first year of work for the *Friends of Coal* and the subsequent success we had with the FoC campaign. Bissett mumbled okay and, as he told me later, went back to bed to awaken around 8:00, brush his teeth, look in the mirror and say to himself, "Oh, God! Did Charlie call and ask me to deliver a speech?"

Bill did deliver the remarks and was, as always, spectacular. Granddaughter Lily Caroline arrived in fine shape at Charleston Area Medical Center later in the morning. West Virginia Coal Association President Bill Rancy announced her arrival to the Association attendees at The Greenbrier and dubbed her "The Coal Princess."

We were later told that if she had been born at The Greenbrier she would have had free visits for the rest of her life. I don't think that was correct, but it was a great story to treasure and tell over the years. A Greenbrier birth probably would not have occurred if we had decided to ask the doctor in residence to do the honors. The doctor on call that rushed to the room after our alarm was a cardiologist from The Greenbrier Clinic. He looked ashen when he thought he might have to deliver a baby—something he said he had not done for thirty years.

The Coal Association folks were excited about the FoC campaign. President Bill Raney, a skilled professional, recognized the initiative was of great benefit and he conveyed that to his membership. Raney was respected and trusted throughout the state by friend and foe alike and always acted with the utmost integrity—his imprimatur on any coal activity lent enormous credence to it. Anyone who came in contact with Raney valued his friendship and his status as a gentleman. His was a job that became inordinately difficult in the face of ever increasing governmental regulation.

Unlike Bill Raney, some of the FoC group could be pretty rough at times—great guys, but often with a lack of finesse. We labeled that element of the FoC group the "Coal Boys". In one "Coal Boys" meeting at our office, a fellow espoused his theory on a PR approach—Bissett and I silently disagreed with him as we glanced at each other across a conference room table and said in unison, "Powerful!" Our coal guy was frustrated with our hesitancy and one-upped us, arguing that his position was obvious, saying, "It's as plain as a goat's ass!" It was hard to argue with the logic.

But that wasn't all. Standing in the hallway waiting for the elevator after a Coal Boys' meeting, a discussion occurred about an issue at hand and one of the coal guys offered a solution, capping it off by saying, "It's like a monkey f----g a skunk—it ain't pretty, but it gets the job done."

In yet another meeting, the rough and rowdy of the group expressed great frustration with what they considered unfounded criticism from environmentalists. Seizing the moment, one fellow let loose in front of the only female in the room—account executive Caryn Durham. He pounded the conference room table, and screamed, "Those mother f----s!" and instantly looked at Caryn. With red face, he began to apologize. Caryn just laughed it off, assuring the fellow she'd heard it all before. But, she took delight in asking before each subsequent coal meeting, and to the delight of all, "Will mother f---r (insert the fellow's full name) be there?"

Working with FoC we were regularly visited by providers of trinkets we could give away at coal shows. One salesman was quite excited by his new product, *Coal Bubble Gum*. It was black. We asked obvious questions, such as, "Would this turn your tongue black?" No real answer, just another blast of support for the incredibly innovative product. Powerful.

CHAPTER 130

High Rent District

FOLLOWING OUR MIGRATION FROM THE "Barber Shop" on Capitol Street Charles Ryan Associates was housed in the Heck's building on Kanawha Boulevard for 18 years. We occupied most of the second floor, all of the third floor, and the penthouse. In 1992, we made the decision to once again push our resources out on the table and take another calculated risk—signing a ten-year lease on 15,000 square feet—all of the 11th floor—in One Valley Square, later to become the BB&T Tower, on Summers Street; it was the most expensive real estate in town. After two years we leased another 2,500 square feet on the 12th floor to house our subsidiary, REV Interactive—17,500 square feet, in all, and a multi-million dollar commitment.

The build-out we did of the 11th floor was exquisite; Becky managed the effort, bringing in Janet Clayman from Capitol Business Interiors to design the space. They collaborated with our brilliant creative vice president John Auge to fashion beauty from a blank canvas—resulting in an artistic rendering of spacious, colorful offices and floor-to-ceiling windows that formed a 360-degree panorama that gave visitors a sensational view of Charleston.

A CRA logo was embedded in the glass in the reception area and logos framed the elevators that opened onto shining marble floors. Twelve-foot high ceilings and doors accented hallways and common areas.

The reception area and halls featured paintings by West Virginia artists, selected by art consultant Morgan Peyton. Four conference rooms were utilized, the largest contiguous with our media training center so that doors could be opened to present an imposing space for large meetings.

The offices shouted "success" and contributed to our bringing on board multi-million dollar clients. Dow Chemical came to town to interview agencies to assist them in the transition planned during their acquisition of Union Carbide. Dow representatives told me later the offices of Charles Ryan Associates sealed the deal between us the minute they walked off the elevator. "Stunning," was their comment.

Becky designed for me a large office that included oriental rugs, custom bookcases, built- in TV, plush sofas and chairs, and exquisite "layering" of memorabilia, pillows, window treatments, and a bed for our Maltese Amalfi—all back-grounded by spectacular views of downtown from the 11th floor. Adjacent to the office was my personal conference room, a workout center, bathroom and shower. It was top notch—Fortune 100 executive space.

We staged a spectacular grand opening for 300 people with Governor and Mrs. Underwood in attendance. John Auge had designed a large and impressive reception desk that welcomed visitors to the floor.

The *Charleston Daily Mail* featured our new offices in an article on April 8, 1998:

The floor-to-ceiling windows in the boardroom at Charles Ryan Associates offer a sweeping view of the interstate highway that loops around Charleston, and Charlie Ryan says that's no mere matter of geography.

The room was designed so that staff and clients of the advertising and public relations firm can take advantage of the "energy" of the busy road as they brainstorm around the large conference table.

Indeed, Ryan's new 15,000-square-foot offices in One Valley Square were built with all kinds of creative forces in mind.

That's appropriate planning for an advertising and public relations firm that hopes to continue its growth.

Charles Ryan Associate's four-dozen employees moved into their new home along with half a dozen employees of Ryan-McGinn-Samples Research, Inc., a separate company Ryan founded. Last summer tight quarters at 1012 Kanawha Boulevard found new hires being stationed in the hallways— forcing the move.

The move not only gives Ryan the room to grow, but allows form to follow function at the agency. Ryan wants the firm to be known as "a total communications agency," with a range of advertising, public relations and other services.

The new setup is designed to ease communication between workers with glass-walled offices and conference rooms along the exterior and cubicles with half-walls in the middle of the floor.

Offices are decorated in the style chosen by their inhabitants. Ryan's own suite is done in rich hues of red and brown; a treadmill sits in the corner of a private conference room.

By contrast, Creative Director John Auge chose sleek black and white furnishings and whimsical touches such as toys piled on top of a bookshelf. Cabinetmaker Bob Jarboe's work is placed throughout the offices.

With more breathing room, Ryan said he has space for more employees, which he may hire this year. If necessary, Ryan-McGinn-Samples can move out of its quarters to another floor in the One Valley building. Ryan has signed on at One Valley Square for at least a decade.

An open house is planned for May 7.

After we moved into One Valley Bank I became aware that its CEO, Bob Baronner, was tremendously proud of *Cabriole*, the sculpture fronting BB&T Tower (formerly One Valley Bank) that features three male figures performing a cariole, an advanced ballet jump. The male dancers, dressed in little other than loin cloths, face away from the bank with their buttocks presented to anyone gazing from the bank's lobby.

There, one day, CEO Baronner walked through One Valley's lobby to cash a check. He presented his check and turned toward

Cabriole, asking the teller, who did not know the man cashing the check was the bank's CEO, "What do you think of *Cabriole?*

The cashier's response was, "Listen, mister, I have to look at enough a— h---s here every day, I don't need three more." Baronner was not pleased, but managed a smile.

CHAPTER 131

Accusations In A Ring Of Fire

DURING THE 1997-2001 ADMINISTRATION OF Governor Cecil Underwood, Charles Ryan Associates held several state contracts. We bid on them fair and square, but the *Charleston Gazette's* Dan Radmacher and Fanny Seiler wrote articles that questioned my veracity and WCHS radio's Stephen Reed castigated me daily in his talk show, playing Johnny Cash's *Ring of Fire* as he did so.

I felt I had no choice but to respond to the *Gazette* attack and additional onerous columns that followed the article—and I did so with this op-ed:

The Charleston Gazette, in the past seven days has, 1) reported in its news columns that Charles Ryan Associates has received almost $3 million in state government work and has implied it is because of a friendship between Charles Ryan and Cecil Underwood; 2) commented in a column that "Ryan has gotten a lot of mileage out of the Underwood administration"; and 3) finished off its grand slam with an editorial that says Ryan is a Republican press agent.

Obviously, the political season is upon us.

Let me set the record straight. Charles Ryan Associates is an out-standing business with a stellar reputation. We are very proud of the extremely talented men and women at our agency who produce quality, world-class, award-winning materials to help our clients achieve their goals. We are an ethical firm and operate with complete integrity.

The Gazette's Dan Radmacher, in his July 28 column, implies it is purely by political association with the Underwood administration that Charles Ryan Associates receives work from the State of West Virginia.

First, I would point out that any state work we have received is legally bid or legally contracted to us. Our firm has stressed integrity above all else in its 25 years and we have turned away business if we felt it was in any way questionable or unethical.

The Gazette also reported under Fanny Seiler's byline on July 25 that Charles Ryan Associates had received millions in state contracts for services provided. Seiler's article then tied to that fact my friendship with Cecil Underwood and my association with his campaign and inaugural. The clear implication was that Charles Ryan was awarded state work because of political connections, and nothing else.

Lightly brushed over in the article was the fact that the huge bulk of those dollars was pass-through money that Charles Ryan Associates paid out to media for advertising placement for the state. A quick check of the files shows Seiler reported May 28, 1998, that Charles Ryan Associates had won the state tourism contract. "The Division of Tourism's advertising budget is about

$2 million. Ryan bid $242,125 as its cost, meaning that will be the amount the firm receives for its work," Seiler reported two years ago.

Now, two years later, we find roughly 89 percent of the $2.8 million tourism advertising dollars received between July 1, 1999, and June 30, 2000, was paid out by Charles Ryan Associates to media and for production services. Charles Ryan Associates retained $318,553.

Additional income was generated for Charles Ryan Associates for non-advertising activities, including seminars on media relations and public outreach activities for other state agencies.

Readers of Seiler's most recent column, I assume, believed Charles Ryan Associates kept $2.8 million in its entirety. Not so. We are paid an equitable amount for services rendered and performed a huge amount of work in our effort.

Charles Ryan Associates is 25 years old this year. During that time, it has grown into a large regional advertising/public relations firm that employs almost 60 West Virginians. Private and public clients that need to communicate through advertising, Web site strategy, collateral materials, public relations and government relations services seek us out. These are needed tools in today's high-tech world.

It is accurate to say Cecil Underwood is a friend of mine. He has been a friend for 40 years. But to imply to the public in any way that my firm receives work based on political connections is to ignore what Charles Ryan Associates has achieved: creation of good-paying jobs in an area where that is not easy; creation of a firm that has grown to such size and respect it brings employment to West Virginia by attracting clients regionally and nationally; and a stellar record of giving back to the state and the city of Charleston through hundreds of hours of community service and tens of thousands of dollars of contributions to civic and charitable causes.

Charles Ryan Associates is a great business success story for West Virginia. State government work is but one client area we serve. We are successful there, as we are elsewhere, because of professionalism, not politics, and would have it no other way.

CHAPTER 132

The Blows Keep Coming

THEN CAME ADDITIONAL CRITICISM BY the *Gazette* regarding contracts awarded to CRA from the State Department of Highways. I wrote another op-ed. In this one I pulled out all the stops. Here's my response:

The Gazette said in a Nov. 21 editorial: "The public relations firm owned by a political supporter of Gov. Cecil Underwood received illegal preferential treatment, according to an audit released by a legislative interim committee." This conclusion and accusation by the Gazette is patently false.

The Gazette based its statement on the content of a legislative interim committee audit of a subcontract by Michael Baker Jr. Inc. with Charles Ryan Associates to provide public involvement services for the West Virginia Division of Highways. The audit said that "the use of a subcontract to procure public relations services is not specifically authorized" under state code.

The language did not say such subcontracts are illegal. The audit said they are not specifically authorized, and said the effect was that "The Division has procured services using noncompetitive selection that are not allowed to be procured in this manner by the West Virginia State Code and the Code of State Rules." The DOH and the State Purchasing Division disagreed with the interim committee report, saying the procedures used were entirely proper and legal. In this regard, rule 15717 of the West Virginia Code of State Regulations allows the DOH to negotiate direct contracts relating to road projects, with consultants to provide management and related services. Nothing prevents a consultant hired by DOH to subcontract a portion of those services to another firm with particular expertise.

That is exactly what transpired here at the request of and with the specific approval of the DOH. I agree there may well be a difference of opinion on how subcontracts are to be awarded. But for the Gazette to state "We have long suspected that Underwood has been repaying this loyalty with lucrative state contracts, given under suspicious circumstances," is to use this disagreement between state entities to smear the good name of my company and me. The Gazette accusation is absolutely false.

Charles Ryan Associates has, for 26 years, bid on state contracts and performed state work for both Republican and Democratic administrations. Our firm has always strictly abided by the rules in obtaining state contracts and has strictly followed the letter of the law in performing any state work.

Charles Ryan Associates' work with the West Virginia Lottery and the West Virginia Department of Tourism was won in competitive bids. The work is exemplary and has brought business, praise and awards to the state of West Virginia. The work we have performed in conducting public involvement for DOH was acquired legally and under the rules and guidelines that have been used for years, through many administrations, when DOH contractors hire subcontractors.

Michael Baker Jr. Inc. was asked by DOH to contact public relations firms and recommend the firm most qualified to conduct public involvement. As in all major transportation projects nationwide, particularly those supported by federal funds, public involvement is an integral part of the process of managing construction projects. To this end, the Federal Highway Administration has published a manual outlining various methods to involve the public in such construction projects.

Michael Baker Inc. contacted Charles Ryan Associates as a possible subcontractor for the public involvement work. Their call was the first we knew about the need to sublet such a service, and it certainly did not result from any request by our firm to the Underwood administration for work. In fact, James B. Richards, vice president and southeast regional manager for Michael Baker Inc., said publicly in December: "Neither Gov. Underwood or members of the DOH in any way mandated or influenced this selection, but rather the credentials of Charles Ryan Associates made this selection easy."

Michael Baker Inc. chose Charles Ryan Associates to do the work based on our extensive experience and demonstrated ability. In regard to credentials, Charles Ryan Associates is the fourth largest public relations firm in the southeastern United States, as ranked by the O'Dwyer's Directory of Public Relations firms, May 2000 edition. Our firm has 26 years of experience in public involvement work in West Virginia and regionally.

Our men and women are professionals who have provided a quality product for Michael Baker and the state of West Virginia. To charge that the professional public involvement activity provided was merely a venue for a political payoff is a gross miscarriage of journalistic responsibility, proper research and good homework on the part of the Gazette.

The Gazette also cited in its editorial a protest by another advertising agency to our bid in response to a request for proposal from the Department of Health and Human Services. The protest suggested the bid was written to favor our firm because we have a relationship with Ryan-McGinn-Samples Research. What the Gazette did not inform its readers of is that Ryan-McGinn-Samples made that bid with another Charleston advertising agency.

I am a 10 percent minority owner of RyanMcGinnSamples Research. Robert Samples owns 90 percent and exercises total control over his business. In other words, Charles Ryan Associates held no advantage in the way the bid request was worded, nor did we request nor would we want any such advantage.

CHAPTER 133

Tom Miller

FINALLY, THE GAZETTE CHOSE TO print a Nov. 27 column by Tom Miller that stated, *"Charles Ryan Associates has lost its meal ticket as a result of Underwood's loss."* The *Gazette* printed my reply: *Miller wildly and recklessly, and with total disregard for the truth, said that the loss "has prompted speculation that the business is up for sale." Miller drew this ridiculous conclusion without even a telephone call to me, and the Gazette printed his fiction, ignoring our 26 years in business and broad client base.*

I am not concerned about or opposed to fair comment by the Gazette.

But in drawing its conclusion that my company and I have acted illegally, in printing Miller's statements that Charles Ryan Associates has "lost its meal ticket" and that the Underwood loss "has prompted speculation that the business is up for sale," the Gazette unfairly and seriously damages my company and me. I resent the implications by the Gazette and deplore its lack of homework in rushing to smear a responsible and honest business that has followed all the rules.

Following my op-ed, there were no more *Gazette* jabs at CRA or me.

I always believed any firm accepting public dollars should be fully vetted and transparent to the public. I also believed in total, truthful transparency, even as I realized our success might be unfairly pilloried.

As a footnote: Talk show host Stephen Reed, who regularly criticized my friendship with Cecil Underwood, called me after he left WCHS radio to inquire about a job at CRA. I declined.

CHAPTER 134

CRA Is Sold

IN AUGUST OF 2007 I was sitting in my office when I received a call from Henry Harmon, owner and CEO of Triana Energy. Harmon was a wunderkind in the exploration and production of natural gas. He had timely formed Triana as an exploration company in the nascent development of innovative techniques that offered the ability to discover and reach new deposits of natural gas. With that development, the Marcellus Shale and other natural gas deposits could be explored and developed.

Harmon asked if he could come by my office—he had something he wanted to discuss. I was glad to welcome him, assuming he might be interested in engaging CRA to represent Triana for publicity, media relations or creative production of print or new media.

Harmon was a handsome individual who reminded me of Lincoln—reserved yet powerful, of high intellect and revered by all who knew him. He had given heavily to charity and was actively involved in improving the state's economy. As a board member of the University of Charleston he had participated in the school's development of its business curriculum and engaged in conversation with UC's President, Edwin Welch, about the possibility of a Graduate School of Business at the University.

Henry had more than 20 years' experience in natural gas exploration and had served as president of Columbia Natural Resources. When CNR was sold Harmon was said to have garnered hundreds of millions. Henry had a Bachelor of Science Degree in accounting from West Virginia University Institute of Technology, a Master of Science Degree in Management from The American College and a Ph.D. in Economics from the Union Institute in Cincinnati. He eschewed being called "Doctor" Harmon but used the title in his biography on the Triana website.

Harmon had purchased the old Boll Furniture building in downtown Charleston, gutted it, and built out the five-story building in exquisite style. Triana's offices were on the fifth floor and the building was connected to a parking garage by an attractive walkover that stretched across Dickinson Street at the foot of the South Side Bridge.

My Maltese, Amalfi, was in my office when Harmon stopped by. Only later did I learn Harmon did not care for dogs. The natural gas tycoon exchanged some small talk and got down to business: he wanted to buy CRA.

I was shocked—what would Henry Harmon want with an agency? I said, "You're a commodities guy, and used to a big margin of profit. Agencies, this one included, do well to make a 4% margin of profit and some years we just break even—why would you want to buy CRA?"

He replied that Triana had acquired twenty-some companies and needed marketing for them. He said his folks had talked about creating an agency or buying a smaller one when one of his executives suggested Triana might want to seek to purchase the state's largest agency.

Henry said if we were to do a deal we would need to close by the end of September.

"That's not possible—you can't do due diligence in 30 days," I said. Thirty days later I was in the offices of the Jackson Kelly law firm, signing the papers that sold CRA. It was an excellent deal for CRA and it was 2007—the year before the beginning of the Great Recession. Timing, as they say, is everything.

CHAPTER 135

Henry Harmon & I Disagree

THEN—I EXPERIENCED GREAT DISAPPOINTMENT. HENRY HARMON elected to let Harry Peck and me go, disagreeing with my sentiment that he should keep both of us for two years for an orderly transition. Instead, he bought yet another PR firm, a small agency whose CEO had previously been a vice president for CRA. I told Henry I thought that was a mistake, that the individual was an excellent public relations professional who served clients brilliantly, but I said, it was my opinion he was not a manager and would not keep and develop clients. I told Henry his choice would last in the CEO slot for two years. I was wrong—he retired in less time than that.

Henry, I believe, was told that the new, smaller, firm had a connection to the international PR powerhouse Interpublic following the sale of Ryan-McGinn, and national business could be achieved through the connection. I believe Henry bought that pitch—hook, line and sinker—convinced that the connection would quickly build extensive business for CRA.

My understanding is that very little, if any, of the promised business was realized. I am convinced to this day that had

Harry and I stayed CRA would have flourished. I also believe that if I Harry *alone* had remained, CRA would not have lost all its state accounts—Harry of the sharp pencil.

I think Henry also had great hope for our REV Interactive group that we had launched five years before—it was part of the deal. An engaging and brilliant young man by the name of Kevin Hall from Left Hand, West Virginia, was the guy who had the idea that we could interface with Fortune 100 companies to provide instant and multi-faceted information internally and externally should they experience a crisis that threatened a company. The theory also was that insurance the companies owned could underwrite the cost of employing REV. All this was at the beginning of the Internet explosion.

I will give Henry credit. When the CEO of the small agency he had brought in to run CRA was out of the picture, Henry sat in his office and said to me, "I know you won't say it, but *I* will—you told me so." Henry treated us well and believed in our agency. He unknowingly stepped into a business totally different from the commodity enterprise in which he excelled.

The agency business is a different animal; intellectual capacity is the stock and trade and when the people leave the building the capacity leaves with them. It is like herding cats—the people are brilliant and you have to keep them satisfied as to challenges and yet direct and guide them. It is a creative effort in every area and that's what makes it special.

CHAPTER 136

Susan Lavenski & Caryn Durham

CARYN DURHAM AND SUSAN LAVENSKI were passed over as leaders when Henry Harmon's first choice as CEO was appointed—but they were asked to head the agency when he departed. The two women inherited an enormous task, one that required the ingredients of tenacity and belief—and Durham and Lavenski had that in spades. Henry, beneficent as always, backed the firm with the rescue dollars needed and it once again prospered under the direction of two extremely talented leaders who could service, sell and manage—not an easy case of multi-tasking.

Lavenski and Durham then bought CRA from Harmon. Lavenski was the public relations guru and Durham headed advertising. They grabbed the agency before it went down the tubes and brought it back to viability. Lavenski directed operations in Charleston and West Virginia and Durham in Richmond and Virginia. One would think, in the traditional agency sense, such a split hierarchy would not work, but it did—Lavenski and Durham melded together like sisters. They are tough, dedicated and extremely talented. My hat is off to both Caryn and Susan for succeeding in running and growing an agency—one of the toughest jobs in this world.

The two women are roughly the same age and are good friends; they operate almost of a single mind. I am proud of what they have achieved and I have a loving relationship with both of them because I consider them almost daughters of mine (indeed, Caryn was born the same year as my daughter Amy and their mothers were in the same room at Charleston Area Medical Center).

In 2014, CRA celebrated its 40th anniversary and staged a large reception at its headquarters in Charleston, in luxury office space at Appalachian Power Park, the home of the West Virginia Power. Caryn and Susan initiated a special surprise award—*The Charlie*—a beautiful microphone carved out of the finest West Virginia hardwood. The award was presented to me as the first recipient of the annual recognition of excellence in the field of communications. Needless to say, I was humbled.

The *Charleston Daily Mail* quoted me as saying at that event, "We've always had fantastic people and a fantastic product. I'm very proud the agency continues today under great, dynamic leadership and continues to produce stunning work." When asked by the *Mail* reporter what it was that I was most proud of after 40 years I replied, "Staying power. We're still here after all these years when many others have not lasted. You have to attract the best and brightest to produce the best and brightest." I told the *Mail* I hoped to see a 50th and 75th anniversary.

The *Charlie* I received is a great legacy and the 40th anniversary celebration served to complete a circle; when I left CRA after the sale of the company, there was no goodbye event, no "gold watch", no retirement party. I am indebted to Susan and Caryn. I believe they came to appreciate Harry Peck and me even more as they took over the reigns of the agency and realized it was an even tougher ride than they thought.

Susan, interviewed in 2016 by the great Sandy Wells in the *Charleston Gazette*, gave me a wonderful tribute when she said, "Charlie has always been there for us if we needed advice. He always just said, 'I don't want this firm to be about Charlie Ryan. I want it to be about the largest communications firm in the state. Keep that vision and don't let it die because I'm not here.'"

Susan also said in the interview, "We grew up under Charlie. He taught us the basics of the business. Don't ever lose sight of the business that is the business. You always have to have sales in the pipeline. You can't just work on the accounts you have. You have to plan a year or two in advance. We use the techniques today that Charlie taught us."

Her words on business decisions resonated with Harry Peck and me. She said, "We would get aggravated and say Charlie doesn't know what he's talking about. Sometimes we called to say we were sorry. He'd say, 'What are you sorry about now?' We'd tell him it was because he was right. When you get in the position of running the company, you understand why things are done the way they are done."

It is gratifying to know one's ethics are remembered. Susan said, "We learned a huge work ethic from Charlie. Agency life is hard." Also gratifying was Susan's remembrance of my first question to her when she interviewed for a job at CRA. "I was introduced to Charlie and his first words were, 'Can you sell?'

I told him I had five clients already, and he said 'Great!' Six weeks later, 18 years ago, I started at CRA."

Caryn Durham was the quintessential agency advertising star. She created a remarkable media-buying department and was essential to our success in our work with state government contracts.

When she moved from directing media purchases into the position of vice president of advertising, her contribution to the agency's well-being intensified.

Caryn was indefatigable, her energy level soaring off the charts. When our Richmond vice president left us, Caryn came to Harry Peck and me and said she wanted to move to Richmond and take over the reigns there. We did not want to lose her in Charleston, but we knew we had to succeed in Virginia and we knew Caryn was the person that could make that happen.

Caryn never looked back. She and her family made the big move, and our human dynamo charged forth to capture Richmond. She built an incredible staff, she joined many business organizations, and she did world-class networking. Caryn blew us away—Richmond was going to be a success, without doubt.

Both Susan and Caryn are women of tremendous talent. They are a meaningful force in strategic communications to achieve competitive advantage in business in the Mid-Atlantic region of the United States.

CHAPTER 137

Bittersweet

I SHALL NEVER FORGET THE day we called the firm's men and women together to tell them CRA was sold. It was a day of joy and regret. Joy to be leaving the firm in the hands of a multi-millionaire who could keep it vibrant, and regret to leave a labor of love of 33 years. Regret that my "baby" was passing to another. I spoke and then Henry Harmon spoke. It all came crashing home to me when Henry shook my hand and said, "Welcome to retirement!"

George Hohmann, business editor of the *Charleston Daily Mail*, wrote the following in his column—a lovely and spot-on commentary for which I will always be grateful:

If you're a West Virginia business person, the sale of Charles Ryan Associates to a group of local investors led by Henry Harmon has to make you feel good.

Charlie Ryan persevered—even prospered—for 33 years in West Virginia's business climate. That's a monumental achievement. He survived economic downturns too numerous to list. Think of the double-digit inflation of the late 1970s and early 1980s, when the bottom fell out of West Virginia's economy. It was so bad the state quit paving roads.

No doubt Ryan spent countless sleepless nights thinking of new opportunities and developing strategies for exploiting them.

Think of the late-night calls from clients seeking a friendly sounding board and a viable public relations strategy.

Consider the welter of competition, most offering the same services at an attractive, lower price.

Think of the political thickets to be analyzed and negotiated in a town where political hardball can be an art form.

And then there's the constant pressure to meet the payroll. To employees, payday seems like a distant dream. To employers, payday always seems like yesterday and tomorrow.

Ryan took big risks years ago when he left a steady job with a regular, guaranteed, paycheck to try his hand at public relations and advertising. And he's had to take risks, large and small, ever since. Neither Ryan nor Harmon will divulge the sale price for Charles Ryan Associates, but Ryan is a savvy guy and the agency is a $35-million-a-year business.

Harmon is savvy, too. He's the fellow who bought Columbia Natural Resources for $330 million and sold it two years later for $2.2 billion. He knows a good deal when he sees it and he knows the value of buying quality.

In the absence of a disclosure of the sale price, what we have is the deal itself—which is proof that both of these businessmen arrived at a number they liked.

Ryan deserves that number.

Many small business owners are successful right up until it's time to leave. They don't sell their companies because they can't find a buyer. They simply close.

Sometimes the market has moved elsewhere. Think of the hundreds of businesses that flourished in the southern West Virginia coalfields for decades, only to see their hometowns shrivel up and die.

There are a thousand reasons things don't work out.

Every business owner's dream is to build a thriving business and, either through family or sale, pass it on to the next generation.

Charlie Ryan succeeded. It worked out the way it was supposed to. And that has to make you feel good.

Well, the column certainly made *me* feel good, and George nailed it—the risk, the sleepless nights, the deal, the result. George Hohmann is a respected and extremely talented journalist, and I treasure his observations and his friendship.

CHAPTER 138

Academe

ONE THING I WAS NOT ready for was *retirement*. I winced when the word was spoken, feeling as though my productive years may have come to an end. I joked that I knew I was in trouble when I turned to our Maltese, Amalfi, and asked him if it was time for Oprah.

Thank God for Ed Welch, president of the University of Charleston.

Ed called me when he learned Henry Harmon had purchased CRA and asked me to stop by his office—he had something he'd like to discuss. I met with him and Provost Charlie Stebbins. To my surprise they wanted me to come on board at the University of Charleston to do a start-up as Dean of the University of Charleston Graduate School of Business. It was quintessential Ed Welch; the odds of succeeding were slim indeed—and yet I knew Ed was cut of the same cloth as I—we would not fail because failure was out of the question.

Nevertheless, I assured Ed I knew nothing about academe. I had an undergraduate degree in journalism from West Virginia

University—but no master's degree, let alone a doctorate. I was, I said, totally without qualification to enter the world of higher education. Nonsense, he said, I had successfully started and sold four businesses and knew the power structure in state business from top to bottom. He assured me I was eminently qualified for the job they offered and I said I'd give it some serious consideration.

Oh yes, Ed sent Charlie Stebbins to stress I would always be remembered as the *Founding Dean*, no less—attempting to appeal to my vanity.

I met later with Bob Bliss, Dean of the Business School for undergraduates and the director of the program for Executive Master's Degrees (EMBA) for business leaders who wished to earn the degree on a part-time basis. Bliss and I would work together under the Graduate School of Business umbrella, should I take the job.

Long story short, the challenge was something I rather liked. I said I'd come on board if I could work ten months (taking less money) and receive two months off for R&R. Welch agreed to the deal and I added one more thing without which I would *not* take the job. That ultimatum was that I needed Cheryl Fout, my assistant at CRA, to move with me to UC. Again, Welch agreed and we began the journey in December of 2007. To entice Cheryl and make her whole income-wise, I shared a portion of my salary with her.

The school was to be located in Henry Harmon's Equity House—the old Boll Furniture Store he had bought, gutted and was building out in a world-class fashion. The second floor was to house the graduate school. When Cheryl and I came on board the school-to-be was an empty floor and we were temporarily housed on the UC campus in the School of Pharmacy. It was there that we staged our approach.

CHAPTER 139

Dr. Ryan

DURING MY TIME ON CAMPUS I regularly ran into a security officer who had been at the University of Charelston for many years. Each time I encountered him he would hail me as "Dr. Ryan". It made me uncomfortable and I felt I needed to correct him. One morning as I hustled up the stairs to Riggleman Hall to one of Dr. Welch's meetings, the guard was coming down the steps and said, "Mornin', Dr. Ryan!" I stopped in my tracks and said, "Thanks for giving me the title 'Dr.', but I have to tell you I do not have a doctorate."

The guard looked at me, shrugged his shoulders, smiled, and said, "They're all 'Drs.' to me, Dr. Ryan." It was the last time I corrected anyone who gave me the title—from that point forward I considered it honorary.

Starting a business requires an enormous amount of time, energy, commitment, hard work and endless meetings. We needed to be functional eight months hence—by August 2008—with faculty hired, curriculum created, and plans laid to recruit 30 graduate students. On the surface, it sounded easy, but obtaining that number of students to an untested program would be very difficult.

We sought to develop a *problem based learning (PBL)* curriculum. The PBL approach required cooperation of businesses in the Kanawha Valley who would be asked to accept our students into their place of work to observe and interact with their employees where our students would learn in real time. This was a major reason my services were greatly valued by Ed Welch—I knew business owners and could open those doors.

I was to oversee the program; report to and coordinate with the provost; coordinate faculty and staff duties and responsibilities; assist an experiential director in contacting and engaging visiting consultants and mentors; develop a pro forma and fiscal needs; conduct faculty and staff reviews and assessments; represent the program externally with community contacts; conduct community meetings; and recruit experiential mentors.

Networking and public speaking were critical components of success, and I tried at every turn to enhance the image of the University and its new graduate school while championing and befriending the elite business faculty and its staff—a group that looked with extreme doubt that the Welch MBAL (the graduate program was originally titled Master of Business and Leadership) vision had merit. I also had good reason to believe those veteran faculty folks at the undergraduate school of business wondered why in the world Welch had chosen me— a guy without academic credentials—to do such heavy lifting. It was in the midst of all this that Cheryl and I conducted program assessment and needs analysis before the move to the Equities House—all this was to be done within eight months.

Marty Becker & Team

IN ACADEME I IMMEDIATELY WENT ABOUT PUTTING together an infrastructure of student mentors from the Charleston business community and created a Board of Advisors of the best and brightest business people to guide the school. My go-to-guy was Marty Becker, president and chief executive officer of Alterra Capital Holdings Ltd., and later chairman of the board of directors of QBE Insurance Group, a top 20 global general insurer with assets of nearly $50 billion. Marty was highly respected by business people nationally and internationally. It was a momentous day for the school when he agreed to chair the board. With his imprimatur, I could attract the best to our quest. Marty came through—he attracted board members of standing from around the state.

Finding board talent was easy compared to recruiting students—a most unusual task. All year long we recruited but could not count on a *student in the seat* until the tuition dollars were in hand, causing me to say we could not assume we had an enrollee until we had seen the whites of his or her eyes.

My marketing experience came in handy: I wrote copy and we advertised for students—the oil that would propel our machine:

During my time at UC Ed Welch made it clear that Henry Harmon was a major benefactor of UC, but my personal relationship with Harmon was not to impact the school's agenda. Henry Harmon was much appreciated, but Ed made it clear Harmon did not, in any way, run any part of UC.

Welch also emphasized that I was free to pursue my agenda as long as he knew what it was and approved said moves. In other words, Ed ruled with an iron hand. I bristled a few times but appreciated fully that Ed Welch was the life and breadth of UC (along with his wife Janet, a dynamo in her own right), and I respected the fact that he was a world-class salesman and visionary. Ed got things done that traditionally could not be done, and he could raise money in a truly impressive way.

I was fortunate to work with Ed and with Charlie Stebbins, the Provost, who had the most difficult job at UC. Charlie was the problem catcher, the guy to whom Ed threw the foul balls and prickly faculty questions and jabs. I learned that dealing with faculty was a job no one would want and one that few humans could carry off successfully—Stebbins being the exception. I also learned to respect the faculty—throughout my tenure as Dean, I constantly preached that Charleston and West Virginia did not fully appreciate the enormous intellectual capacity at the University of Charleston.

CHAPTER 141

Graduate School Infrastructure

PHASE TWO OF THE UNIVERSITY OF CHARLESTON'S AMBITIOUS MBAL plan was to be completed between August 2008 and August 2009. I had my work cut out for me in that I expected a quality curriculum in the classroom and experiential programs with well-structured student time outside the classroom. I expected a clear understanding by students of what expectations were and that we would be true to the PBL approach.

I stressed to faculty and staff that I insisted on a team approach with mutual respect among staff and faculty as well as excellent communication and backup procedures for unexpected absences; faculty members were also to project respect for undergraduate faculty members, especially business school faculty who, for the most part, did not like the idea of a grad school in which they were not vested. They were to do this both internally and externally.

I laid out rules for expenses and how they were to be cleared and documented for budget purposes. I explained that disputes and differences were to be discussed candidly with the Dean, and that class times and faculty hours were to be posted and emailed to students.

I realized that academe work hours were often different than those to which CRA staffers adhered, and I emphasized that faculty were required to have a minimum of two hours' office time on regularly scheduled work days in addition to class time, registering comings and goings with the receptionist.

I asked that the faculty join me in identifying outside image-building opportunities and events that would give the school added appeal. I also placed on the platter implementation of a scholar's program and development of a mentor's program by October 1 of that year. A comprehensive marketing plan was to be completed by December 1, 2008, and visiting consultants were to be identified and on board by that time.

I broke the work out into committees under the headings of Curriculum, Faculty, Experiential, EMBA & EMFA, Scholars, and Building and Administrative.

I scheduled regular meetings with Provost Stebbins, who tracked our progress and gave advice. I updated Stebbins on March 8, 2008, that marketing advertising was being prepared for placement for faculty and staff positions and our faculty search committee had been formed. I reported to Charlie that our admission application was online and we had one applicant thus far. Charlie just smiled and I thought—uh, oh.

Steve Walker, CEO of Walker Machinery, agreed to join our advisory board, and Rex Repass, CEO of Repass Partners, a national public opinion research firm based in Cincinnati, offered to volunteer his services to explore how a research curriculum could be utilized in PBL—we were on our way. But, we needed faculty.

CHAPTER 142

The Faculty Search

MY ADS FOR FACULTY AT THE UNIVERSITY OF CHARLESTON
GRADUATE SCHOOL OF BUSINESS, THANK goodness, brought
lots of response. I did not know at the time that there was a
cadre of educators out there in the world of higher education
that were itinerate in nature—just like those traveling disc
jockeys that inspired the song WOLD.

I said in our ads that the University of Charleston was seeking a full-time professor for its Graduate School of Business. I
related that ours was an innovative program that would offer
traditional undergraduate students the opportunity to enter
graduate school upon the successful completion of their sophomore year and to complete their MBAL over the next three
academic years.

The curriculum, I said, would use problem-based learning to
align teaching and learning with real-world business problems
and solutions. I enthused that students would be expected to
find relevant information, construct meaning, and propose
solutions to problem situations.

Here I injected a phrase that probably had prospective faculty scratching their heads: "Faculty who excel in linking theory to practice from the functional areas of business, entrepreneurship, global business operations, and the University's liberal learning outcomes are encouraged to apply."

I explained that applicants would be required to maintain and promote strong experiential cooperative learning that featured a traditional MBA core with specialization in leadership, entrepreneurship, international commerce and communication skills—and I hoped that explained it all.

I finished with a flourish—"Applicants should demonstrate leadership in developing student academic excellence, strong advocacy of leadership elements of the program, and form and build relationships with business constituents *outside the University*."

Applicants were to have earned a PhD in business management or a related field and/or have experience in leading business operations, finance, or investments along with teaching and research experience at the undergraduate or graduate level. Finally, I asked for demonstrated skills in international and/or entrepreneurial leadership, strong mentoring skills, and experience as a facilitator of problem-based learning. Obviously, I wanted it all. I was looking for extraordinary faculty.

CHAPTER 143

Ed Welch's Vision

THE INNOVATIVE PLUNGE TO EVEN think about a Graduate School of Business at the University of Charleston required faith that Ed Welch's vision would actually succeed. It was an extraordinary amount of work and I think we did it well—up and running in eight months, attracting not thirty, but twelve students that first year—a sufficient number to get our feet wet and give those twelve kids extraordinary attention. We also brought in good faculty members (not with *all* the credentials I had hoped for, but darn near) and created foreign programs in Italy and Shanghai. We did it by projecting success—we worked with the media and achieved great coverage, boasting we had attracted superior faculty and would place our students in excellent jobs.

President Welch's vision for the school was augmented by his wife, Dr. Janet Welch. She delighted in decorating our quarters as she had done on the main campus years before. It was reminiscent of when Ed Welch first arrived at the University of Charleston to take over a failing institution—his diminutive wife walked through Ed's domain and made notes. This small but determined lady, called by some the *Divine Mrs. Welch*, strode into Riggleman Hall's Geary ballroom and was dismayed with the drab appearance and pedestrian use of what she knew could be grand space.

Within a few short years she transformed it (and many other campus venues, including the President's home) to a regal art center that hosted the most important campus events and many of Charleston's special, elegant affairs. She did the same for the graduate business school, embedding art and framed pictures of the main UC campus to draw the two venues together.

In May, 2017, Ed announced he was retiring after three decades of leading the University of Charleston. He and Janet said they had decided to join the Class of 2018 and graduate from UC at the end of the academic year

A book needs to be written to chronicle the team of Welch; they are two of the most important figures in Charleston's history as they transformed UC into a driving center of successful economic and intellectual outreach.

CHAPTER 144

Cheryl Fout & George Hohmann

TRANSITIONING FROM THE WORLD OF business to that of academe felt comfortable enough to me in the early stages; the graduate school was indeed a "startup" and I had credentials to corral both the interests of business leaders and of the media. All this could not have happened without the skill and drive of my assistant Cheryl Fout, whom I respected and admired as the consummate professional and a dear friend. Cheryl—about five feet and weighing 100 pounds soaking wet—was simply the engine that brought everything together. She was cowed by no one and loved by all (except those she deemed to be guilty of not pulling their weight or who were simply incompetent).

Cheryl moved to the UC main campus and the second floor of the School of Pharmacy to assist me in executing our plan. In both my business and in the UC initiative I had strong women helping me—and I would not have succeeded in either endeavor if they had not been there.

Cheryl knew my work habits and knew the business men and women I needed to convince the public and potential students that the UC Graduate School of Business made sense and would be a success— and could be created from whole cloth.

The first strategic move of Ryan & Fout was to visit selected businesses to obtain their "buy-in" to an experiential leadership graduate degree that would see much of our curriculum outside the classroom and in the offices and factories of established manufacturing, warehousing, retailing and professional firms. We received enthusiastic support throughout the Kanawha Valley and we began to develop the full curriculum for the school, a curriculum built around experiential classrooms where our students would spend a considerable amount of time in their second year, learning in *real time* in the offices and factories of the businesses that were partnering with us.

Charleston Daily Mail Business Editor George Hohmann was a strong advocate of our school but he confessed he needed more information to really understand our arcane approach to a master's degree. He queried me as to our curriculum and I realized if the cerebral George Hohmann was scratching his head, others must be totally confused by our approach.

I prepared a memo for George that said our program was unique in that it offered a 2+3 and 3+2 curriculum. The 2+3 agenda was open to all sophomores at the University of Charleston at the end of their sophomore year and to sophomores from any other college or university who have a minimum of one year of business education.

Further, I told him, the first semester of the first year of the graduate program—the 2+3 curriculum had two tracks.

Track one would embrace those sophomores who had two years as business majors. They would participate in the first semester of the first year in a "variable experiential" program that would be designed to integrate those students into a more advanced problem based learning curriculum.

Hoping I still had George's attention, I went on: Track two of the 2+3 program would consist of non-business majors who would spend their first semester in traditional core business studies to bring them up-to-speed in business management, marketing and communications, finance & investment and accounting. Those students, I said, also would receive intensive tutoring and a strong one-on-one executive mentoring program.

I explained that the 3+2 program would encompass juniors, seniors and individuals who had just received a baccalaureate degree. Each of these students would be required to have a business learning background. The 3+2 would be open to all University of Charleston junior and senior business majors, and to juniors, seniors, or degree holders from other colleges and universities who had at least three years of business education.

George absorbed it all and, with the base of information provided, wrote many in-depth stories about the school, eloquently explaining in terms laymen could easily understand the depth and width of an extraordinary experiential approach to an MBAL.

CHAPTER 145

A World Of Difference

WHAT I DID *NOT* CONVEY to George Hohmann of the *Charleston Daily Mail* was that academe was surely different from the hard-driving world of advertising and public relations. I realized that in spades one morning when I arrived at 8:45 for a 9:00 meeting with Bernie Wehrle, CEO of McJunkin-Redman Corporation (later MBC Global). Four faculty members and I were to outline our vision and curriculum for Bernie and key executives with the hope that the company would become part of our experiential effort. The clock ticked. It was 8:59. Bernie's assistant came down the long hall.

"Mr. Ryan, Bernie will see you now," she smiled, greeting me.

I smiled back, and explained that my colleagues must have encountered some delay, and we started walking down that long hall. I heard arrivals behind me and saw my folks sauntering into the building. Bernie's assistant and I stopped and waited for the group to catch up with us. I felt relieved.

Bernie's assistant and I then began to stride purposefully toward his office for the very important meeting that was so critical to our startup. We turned the corner at the end of the hall and continued our rapid move down yet another corridor. I glanced over my shoulder and realized my colleagues were nowhere to be seen.

Not until we had reached the door of Bernie's suite of offices did the group re-appear, turning the corner we had passed seemingly hours before, coming into sight, moving at a leisurely pace, laughing at comments that were being made. What a relaxed group!

I realized then and there that academic folks are wired differently than I. I was intent on the goal, ready to sell, practicing in my mind my approach, intense, wired for the conversation, delighted to be there. My co-workers were highly intelligent, wonderfully didactic, and immensely likable. But they knew little about and cared absolutely nothing for—*the sale*. To them, this seemed to be just another meeting in another academic day. My assessment is not meant to denigrate—these were exceptional educators.

But, we sure had been wired in different factories.

CHAPTER 146

The Genius Of Ed Welch

My UC boss, Ed Welch, was *double wired*. He was an educator, for sure, but Ed was a great salesman *and* an astute business person. He sold every day of his life, opening the pocketbooks of every affluent person with whom he came in contact. UC would not be where it is today—an elite example of what a private, small university can be in providing extraordinary education—without Ed Welch. Ed and I differed on some things, but in the arena of vision and sales, we were simpatico.

Governing a small staff of educators was a challenge. I enlisted many of the tenets I had subscribed to in managing a business, and some did not work. I counseled one young staff member that she should listen more and talk less in meetings and she burst into tears. I had also hired a "show-horse" Ph.D., who was incredibly intelligent, but he wanted to dazzle and impress all those with whom he came in contact. In teaching and guiding young people he was more in love with himself than his students. I remain grateful to him, however, for accepting the challenge of a startup.

I continued to woo the media and I was happy that we were able to convince the reporting world that we were doing a very good thing for the Kanawha Valley and its economy by creating the UC Graduate School of Business. We were successful and I know of no negative news story or criticism from the community about our operation during the time I was at the helm.

The graduate school was not accredited but Ed explained to me that was not a problem— because UC was. I accepted the thinking and told those who questioned our non-accreditation as a grad school that we would seek accreditation at a later date. I sought and hired Ph.Ds. and enlisted support from adjunct professors and we opened our doors. It wasn't perfect, but the downtown space for the school was spectacular and helped recruit kids that had graduated from WVU, Marshall and other West Virginia schools.

We also were able to reel in grads from other universities. Most notably for me was a student I recruited while on a fly-fishing trip to Blackberry Farm in Tennessee. The young fellow, who served as our fishing guide, had just graduated from the University of Tennessee and mentioned to me he planned to attend grad school—he just didn't know *which* grad school. I eagerly offered UC as a prospect, gave him my card, and sent him materials referencing our program. I could hardly believe it when he accepted. I am proud to say he was a standout student and was gainfully employed in an excellent job upon graduation. I also am proud that the school has had an outstanding success record in placing its graduates.

At the university I had a certain number of vacation days. The thing that most pushed me to leave the position after 1½ years was a university memo that I had exceeded my vacation allotment by a half-day and would be docked a certain amount of my pay to make it up. Academe had not singled me out—it was just the way the school operated. I understood that, but I bristled at being treated solely as an employee and not as an executive. The stern admonition made me feel as though I was not appreciated as a captain braving the storm—I was a deckhand who had to punch a clock. My reaction was not hubris—it was the thinking possessed by any entrepreneur—a person who cannot abide a perception that his or her work is of the norm.

The UC experience had been a great time with incredible people and one I would always treasure, but it was time for me to leave.

CHAPTER 147

Hilton Head Island

IT WAS 2009 AND I told Dr. Ed Welch it was time to find a true educator to continue the University of Charleston MBAL program. We found the right guy in Bart Morrison, whom I had recruited and hired as one of our Ph.Ds.

Morrison was an exceptional individual who cared for people and knew how to run the operation—he also was stellar in the classroom. He remained at the helm for two years and was recruited back to Assumption College in Massachusetts from whence he had come. He was the right guy in the right place at the right time, and I felt the school was secure as I departed.

With that accomplishment behind us, Becky and I decided to spend more time at a vacation home we had purchased in 2009 on Hilton Head Island, South Carolina. We quickly found we wanted to return to the island each time we motored back to Charleston, and in 2010 made the big break—selling our home in Charleston and moving to Sea Pines Plantation on Hilton Head.

Making a move such as ours was traumatic; we left behind in Charleston a lifetime of friends, favorite haunts and events, neighborhoods, business contacts, awareness by others of who we were and what we had contributed to our community.

Once we were ensconced in Sea Pines, we set about to learn as much as we could about the paradise that Charles Fraser created. I decided to run for the Community Services Associates (CSA) Board and served three terms; the last year as chairman of the board (the title was later changed to "president"). I also ran and was elected to a concurrent three-year term on the Association of Sea Pines Plantation Property Owner's (ASPPPO) Board.

The man who preceded me as CSA Chairman was a lean figure with snow-white hair by the name of Bob Mang. Mang was nationally renowned in merchandising and management in the retail world. He was retired, but he never lost the ability to command—and he was a demanding disciplinarian.

Bob saw flaws in the CSA organization and took steps to correct them. He turned to me to continue corrections he had put in place and I fully understood the challenges that lay ahead. I learned more in three years of board service than I would have in ten years as a resident without such involvement. The work was large at times, and I had several weeks where I put in more than thirty hours of volunteerism.

Much of that was because the paid executive who ran the multi-million dollar operation had been recruited away, leaving the board to run the place. The board also was attempting to resolve a large lawsuit that had been filed against CSA (brought before I was on the board). The lawsuit was settled without damage to property owners and we resolved a number of issues with residents, one of which was property owner opposition to multi-million dollar improvements to Sea Pine Resort holdings.

There were some cantankerous property owners, to be sure. I asked long-time CSA staffer Jeanne Pearse if "plantation angst" was a new development or had it always been present. Jeanne, without whom the history of CSA would be incomplete, affirmed that it had certainly been a factor during her twenty-plus years with the organization, and quoted Charles Fraser as having said that disgruntled residents represented "the well-to-do with little to do."

My vice-chairman was a fellow by the name of Rob Marsac who had also served as chairman of the ASSPPO board. Rob, with snow-white hair that challenged Bob Mang's, was a retired litigator from Detroit—I wasn't getting in the boat of leadership at CSA without him. I told the board that I would not accept the chairmanship unless Rob was voted vice-president. The board agreed and Rob and I went forth to face the many issues that were the stock and trade of such service.

Rob was fearless and just a terrific individual who became a great friend. He loved the water and my wife and I, and at times our grandkids, were privileged to join him and his wife as he boated out of the South Carolina Yacht Club at Windmill Harbor on Hilton Head.

There were others with whom I served who enriched my life on island. One was Karl Becker, a retired attorney who contributed countless hours of counseling—he was the one true expert on the covenants that Charles Fraser had written that governed Sea Pines Plantation. He was quiet, modest, and highly intellectual.

CSA was like a town hall and I served in a capacity similar to a mayor during the time we recruited a new executive. The CSA men and women were first class and exceptional people with whom to work.

I love great quotes and wrote down two board member comments that I will always treasure. Mark Griffith, who succeeded me as CSA president, assessed a long-awaited decision regarding traffic issues, by saying, *"You don't know—until you know."* How could one argue with that? Another board member, David Borghesi, said, when discussing insurance coverage: *"Insurance is cheap—coverage is expensive."* It was a wonderfully expressive comment, full of wisdom, as anyone who has ever filed an insurance claim knows.

Board service behind me, I turned to writing, not on a full time, but *almost* full time basis. I wrote and published *Dead Men's Clubs*, a novel about a frustrated golfer, and *The Pullman Hilton*, a Christmas mystery based in my hometown of Keyser. I found I loved writing novels, and then began a third book, *My Life With Charles Fraser,* an oral history gleaned from Hilton Head Island residents who knew or worked with the oneiric Sea Pines founder Charles Fraser. It was an exciting endeavor that broadened even more our knowledge of a very special place.

This book, *Alacrity*, is my fourth effort as an author, and my latest book is the story of the 2008 disappearance of Elizabeth and John Calvert, business owners on Hilton Head Island, and the subsequent death of their accountant, Dennis Gerwing.

CHAPTER 148

Retrospect

I LOOK BACK ON MY life, and I thank the good Lord for the experiences I have had and the people I have encountered. Charles Ryan Associates, I am proud to say, is an extraordinary achievement built by phenomenal people. My expertise and good fortune was the ability to create a culture that caused the men and women who came to CRA—hundreds of them— to want to be associated with me. Building a business is daunting—building one whose stock in trade is intellectual capital is even more so. Long days of grinding it out were made happy days by a camaraderie that existed in spades within the walls of our agency. We were indeed, the chosen few.

I was equally lucky that a special lady from Charleston thought enough of me to marry me. Becky and I spent memorable years on Abney Circle in South Hills in one of the great homes in Charleston. Holidays, birthdays, and every event special to families were celebrated there.

My daughter Shandon (named for Shandon Church in County Cork, Ireland) Tweedy was born in 1966. She was a joy from the beginning and the apple of my eye. She is the principal at

Horace Mann Middle School in Charleston. She is thought to be the first female principal in the school's history. She graduated from the University of Charleston with a teaching degree and, while working 60-hour weeks, earned her master's degree from Marshall University. Son-in-law Steve is an accounting graduate from West Virginia University and CFO for Diamond Electric Corporation, a Japanese firm with operations in West Virginia. He also is an entrepreneur, having purchased a car wash in South Charleston that is the second "wash" he has operated. He loves the business.

Shan and Steve celebrated two great kids, Ryan and Lauren. At this writing Ryan is 18 and a senior at George Washington High School. Lauren, 22, is a 2017 magna cum laude graduate of the University of Alabama who, upon graduation, applied for an internship at Georgetown Law with more than 500 other students and was one of eight accepted.

My daughter Amy was born in 1970. She lives in Penn Yan, New York, where she is engaged in the arts. She graduated from the elite Simmons College in Boston with superior grades. She is smart and funny. She and I share a love of English comedy and the *Saturday Night Live* approach to humor. She started her writing career early—I treasure the nine pages of the small legal pad that she took from my desk when she was eight years old to write *Sally the Salamanter—Book by Amy Ryan*.

Salamander was spelled several different ways and punctuation was still to come. Never mind, at eight, she was precocious. Her mother, her sister Shandon, and I were all included in her little story. It brings tears to my eyes as I hold the pages in my hands and read what she wrote.

> *"I first saw Sally in the mud. I picked her up but I got scard and threw her by acxadent. Then I got brave and picked her up. I put her in a old pan that I foud in the creack. I came up the stairs vry slow so I would not spill the water. My Dad shouted "Amy" time for "dinner" or something like that. "I said" Look what I found "Dad," I said. First "I said" so and so and now I kow it's a tatpole. I went in to eat my Dinner. I told me mom and my sister. She said it's a salamander Amy. I went to speak to my mom. And she came down to take a look. She said it's a salamander "Amy." I said it is? She said "yes" look at it Amy. "Everything" a salamander? I said. But I said it like this solomanter. No Amy sal-a-monder shan said. Then I said it. I went in to get a bowl. I put her in the bowl. I took her in. I fed her some bread. Sally. I loved her and I still do."*

Becky's only child, Jennifer, was born October 8, 1976. Jennifer and her husband Chad Porter live in Charlotte with their two children, Lily, 14 and Blake, 11. Jennifer, a graduate of the University of Charleston Carleton Varney School of Design, operates her own design business in the Ballantyne area of Charlotte. Chad, a graduate of the West Virginia University College of Law, is an attorney with his own practice. Blake has all the natural moves of an athlete and excels in basketball and Lily is the quintessential young lady—sweet as can be.

We have been so fortunate in that Shandon and Jennifer and their families are close. Jennifer and Shandon call each other "sister" and our four grandchildren regard one another as cousins. Becky and I consider them all *our* grandkids. Our mixed family grows sweeter each year as the grandkids mature. We are so very, very proud of them.

In 2016 Becky and I decided to relocate to Charlotte to be near Jennifer and Chad and closer to Shan and Steve and both sets of grandkids. In retirement, Becky and I are proud parents, grandparents and partners that give unconditional support one to the other. The magic that was there twenty-three years ago remains intact, and I thank the good Lord that He brought Becky and me together. I love her with all my heart.

I keep by my desk a note she wrote to me when presenting me with a birthday gift of a case of Silver Oak wine. It reads, in her beautiful handwriting, "As good wine gets better with age, so do you, my love. I love you—Becky."

ACKNOWLEDGEMENTS

ALACRITY IS A COMPENDIUM OF my personal recollections but, I am tremendously appreciative of the help I have received in researching and writing this autobiography. My wife Becky, lifelong friend Jack Canfield, and my daughter Shandon provided editing assistance. West Virginia friends Bill Phillips, Dan Page, Denny Vaughan, the late Hike Heiskell, Jim Haught, and the late Pete Thaw supplied details and fact-checking on many of the political stories contained herein.

I am, as always, indebted to my business partner, Harry Peck, for his dedication and contributions to my success. Without Harry, there would be no CRA—he was the man I could confide in, a man I could trust like no other. He was and is benevolent, but with ferocious strength of character, integrity, intellect and insight. Harry and I were Mr. Inside and Mr. Outside, complementing one another and creating a formidable team. Whatever thanks I have given him in this book is not enough.

I am proud of CRA's current owners, Caryn Durham and Susan Lavenski, who picked up where Harry and I left off–continuing to do sensational work, taking CRA to even greater heights. I am deeply honored that they continue to call their company "Charles Ryan Associates".

WSAZ-TV's Emil Varney made this book so much more meaningful with his historic pictures from the 1960s. Emil, WSAZ's Bill Kelley and I covered hundreds of stories together and Bill and Emil tutored me, a young reporter who was getting his feet wet in TV, in the nuances of *news with pictures*. They were pioneers who made WSAZ-TV a news leader. The station, to this day, owes a great deal to Emil and Bill, as do I.

My thanks to Bill Bissett, president of the Huntington Chamber of Commerce, and Matt Sheppard, vice president of Chesapeake Energy, who provided remembrances of their days at the agency.

My WCHS-TV co-anchor of the 70s, Roy Brassfield, assisted me in recollections of the Kanawha County textbook demonstrations and the black lung wars that led to major demonstrations in the state's capital.

I owe a very special nod to my sister Hellice Zitkewicz and niece Joyce Simmons for their family genealogy search and the history of my father's first family.

Jack Canfield wrote the foreword to this recollection and he shows in his remarks that he knows me well. Ours has been a true friendship that began in our hometown and continued through the years as our paths as journalists and entrepreneurs intertwined. Thanks, Jack, for a special relationship.

To all the men and women of Charles Ryan Associates, I give my thanks and appreciation for your skill, tenacity, and professionalism. I am forever indebted to you for giving me the gift of working with you for 33 years.

Founding and building an agency is a challenge. It requires extraordinary work ethic, total belief in your product and a love of the game.

I am a blessed individual who has had a richly rewarding career and life, filled with warm remembrances of working and playing with incredible people in a special state where Mountaineers are always free to dream and create.

> *"No matter how many places ya' been, ya'*
> *ain't seen nothin' like West Virginia."*

> —HAROLD LAMBERT

INDEX

Made in the USA
Lexington, KY
17 February 2018